KU-254-217

Sir John and Lady Laing after the consecration of Coventry Cathedral 1962

Laing

Laing

The Biography of
Sir John W. Laing, C.B.E. (1879–1978)

by

ROY COAD

HODDER AND STOUGHTON
LONDON SYDNEY AUCKLAND TORONTO

920.
C 36061.
14. 3. 79.

British Library Cataloguing in Publication Data

Coad, Frederick Roy
   Laing.
   1. Laing, *Sir* John William
   2. Construction industry – Great
   Britain – Biography
   338.7'62'40924   HD9715.G72

   ISBN 0 340 23985 9

*Copyright © 1979 by Roy Coad. First printed 1979. All rights reserved. No part of this
publication may be reproduced or transmitted in any form or by any means, electrical or
mechanical, including photocopy, recording, or any information storage or retrieval
system, without permission in writing from the publisher. Photoset and printed in Great
Britain for Hodder and Stoughton Limited, Mill Road, Dunton Green, Sevenoaks, Kent,
by Lowe and Brydone Printers Limited, Thetford, Norfolk.*

To the late
WILLIAM STANLEY GRAHAM

formerly City Treasurer and Freeman
of the City of Carlisle
and
elder of the congregation at Hebron Hall
in affectionate memory

AND TO HIS FELLOW CUMBRIANS

They have taken with them to the grave
their powers, their labours, and their
errors; but they have left us their
adoration.

JOHN RUSKIN
The Seven Lamps of Architecture

Foreword

THE SUBJECT OF this biography, Sir John Laing, was a remarkable man. In his lifetime he succeeded in transforming a small Carlisle business into a large multi-national corporation, which is now a household name. What is not nearly so well known is that at the same time he also succeeded in giving away much of his wealth to a variety of Christian causes, not only in this country, but also overseas. The temptation facing anyone writing the biography of such a worthwhile person as this is to be uncritical. Yet in this highly informative and well-researched account of his life Roy Coad avoids that temptation and writes with a genuine feeling for Sir John while keeping a sufficient distance to retain objectivity.

Apart from being an interesting biography in its own right this book is, in my judgement, a significant contribution to the contemporary debate on capitalism and Christian social ethics. The outstanding feature of Sir John Laing's life was his total Christian commitment, and what is particularly interesting about the book is the way it brings out the relationship between his faith and business life. He was convinced that by running a construction company which provided employment and new homes to a great many people he was performing a public service. It also emerges that for him, private enterprise was not only superior to state council housing as a way of satisfying the nation's housing requirements, but an important check on the growth of government and hence a means of maintaining the healthy individualism of the British people. In addition, his method of doing business was infused by a generosity of spirit. At a time of personal and business crisis as a young man he resolved that 'he would make God a participating partner in his business'. As a consequence he renounced the ruthlessness with which he had been brought up and eschewed especially the Victorian practice of buying in the cheapest market and selling in the dearest. In the building industry he was a pioneer in introducing various schemes to improve employee welfare. At the same time, he drew up a personal financial plan which entailed giving away a substantial part of his income in his early life and transferring a large part of the equity of the company to a charitable trust in

7

later life. His personal lifestyle was simple and modest, remark-ably so by comparison with others of comparable achievements. Yet he also kept his business affairs in a proper perspective. Although interesting they were part, nevertheless, of a temporal order. As a man who knew the reality of the spiritual world he never forgot that 'he looked for a city whose builder and maker is God'.

Being a Christian, therefore, transformed Sir John Laing's view of business; and I am convinced that any Christian with respon-sibilities in the business world will find this book an inspiration as well as a challenge. But at the same time and for the same reasons it is a powerful rebuke to those theologians of our time who seem unable to conceive of modern corporations as other than sinful structures. In terms of the contemporary trend of evangelical social ethics, it is a timely reminder of the dangers of using sociological pigeon-holes and of an over-concern with the affairs of the *civitas terrena*.

Brian Griffiths
Professor of Banking and International Finance,
The City University, London

Author's Preface

THERE MUST ALWAYS be something impertinent about biography, an intrusion upon the uniqueness of another individual. The danger of misrepresentation is increased when a man of achievement has embodied in written form as little of his own personality and thinking as did Sir John Laing; at best the portrait is mediated at second hand, through the reminiscences of those who knew him (partial, as all reminiscence of another must be), and then through the comprehension of the author.

Yet, I suspect, the life of Sir John Laing will interest many different students of their fellow men. Its first and obvious appeal will be to those who are attracted by the profound and vital religious faith that dominated him, and scarcely less interested will be those in the churches (and especially in the evangelical churches) who are looking afresh at the relationship of religious faith to the economic and social order. Others may be interested to debate whether the story illuminates or modifies those accepted ideas on religion and economic life that have derived from Weber, Tawney and their followers. John Laing may indeed have been a Crusoe ('the isolated economic man who carries on missionary activities on the side') against Bunyan's Pilgrim – or was he? Do his actions lend credence to Dowden's comment that 'a good conscience simply became one of the means of enjoying a comfortable bourgeois life'?* I suspect that readers of this biography will form their own judgments.

Sir John grew up in a tough and ruthless industry. I have tried to illustrate the early conditions by including some incidents from the early days as they were told to me. They might seem harsh, but I believe that they are necessary to the account if it is to be honest, and if we are to be able to trace the full extent of the influence of John Laing's faith upon his development. Read with this understanding, they enhance both the vitality of his faith and the extent of his achievement.

There have been those who have shared a religious background similar to that of John Laing, and who have ended by harshly rejecting their upbringing. I am glad to have been able to

*Max Weber, *The Protestant Ethic and the Spirit of Capitalism*, 1976 edn., p. 176.

undertake this corrective study, for there are many works depicting the negative reaction. The two contrasting attitudes seem to me to throw into relief the diminishing and the enlarging aspects of belief: so much depends upon the ability of the individual to penetrate beyond the diminishing effect of the sectarian mentality to the enlarging effect of a true relationship with, and experience of, God.

Others might consider the influence of the successful businessman, for good or ill, on the lives of others. How many men and their families have enjoyed fulfilled and happier lives because of the opportunities created by men like Sir John—even as others have been dominated and exploited by men less humane or scrupulous? It is ironic to realise that some of his most constructive and generous acts, the formation of his charitable trusts and his employee shareholdings, are precisely the actions which the administration of modern taxation has tended to regard with suspicious jealousy. One day some social commentator will look more closely at the odd irony that high taxation—so often regarded as an instrument of the redistribution of wealth—has in fact an inbuilt vested interest against its dispersion.

I would like at this point to quote an impressive tribute to Sir John by Mr. Peter Cousins, made during the course of a kind and generous assessment of this manuscript. 'I'm not sure' he writes 'that readers will realise the immense impression of peaceful happiness, simplicity and contentment that JWL radiated.'

Acknowledgments are set out in the details of sources at the back of this volume, but I should like again to thank Sir Kirby and Sir Maurice Laing for their kindness and courtesy during the course of the work on the biography, and also to thank Ken Jerrard for his unfailing interest and encouragement. This book should really be his—but its contents are my own sole responsibility, though the gathering of the information would have been impossible without his help. My wife, too, has helped with the gathering of much of the information, and we both have extremely happy memories of the many Cumbrians who received us and talked to us so willingly and helpfully—two southerners who appreciated the kindly welcome of the north. For my wife's patience in a form of grass widowhood – and that through a time of some domestic difficulty—I am more than grateful. To Miss Beryl Read who so excellently typed the manuscript in its atrocious handwriting, what can I say but 'thank you'?

Contents

Illustrations

Laing

CHAPTER 1

Cumbrian Inheritance

SOME TEN MILES south of the historic border city of
Carlisle, where the land begins to rise towards the great hills
of the English Lake District, lie the country parishes of
Sebergham and Castle Sowerby. The prospect of the land is all
northward. On a clear day, the distant horizon is bounded by the
arc of the hills of Dumfries and the Scottish Border country: the
bulk of Criffel across the silver line of the Solway to the north-
west, and northward the low flat top of Tundergarth, by Carlyle's
village of Ecclefechan. The hills continue eastward, until they
merge into the long southward march of the English Pennines,
with Cross Fell prominent in the east.

Behind, and southward, the bulky massif of Blencathra and
Skiddaw looms so close that, if you happen to see them as the
weather brightens after rain, is seems that only an after-breakfast
stroll is needed to reach their summits. From the heights of
Skiddaw, the river Caldew flows by the two villages, and on
across the plain to Carlisle.

Cumbria is a country set apart from the rest of Britain by the
hills. For centuries, it was hotly disputed by English and Scots
quarrelling over a plain that, long before, had already been
bisected by the Roman Wall. Reaching from the far east coast of
England, the Wall terminated on the west coast not far from
modern Carlisle, the fortress of Luguvallium. Yet a major
influence on the Cumbrian people came not from English, Scots
or Romans, but from the Scandinavian Vikings who raided and
settled the flat coastline, leaving their traces in local place names
and dialect, and in physical characteristics still to be seen among
the children of West Cumbria.

It is a country with its own deeply-rooted culture; Carlisle's
ancient grammar school is mentioned by Bede, and traces its
foundation back to 686 and to St. Cuthbert of Lindisfarne, though
it was later re-founded by Henry VIII. The Scottish side of the
Border, for its part, can boast of names like those of the saintly
Samuel Rutherford; Edward Irving, the fascinating preacher

from Annan; Thomas Carlyle himself; and Thomas Telford the great engineer—the last two, respectively, a stonemason's son and a stonemason's apprentice.

There were two other young stonemasons who, about the year 1800, came south to the upper Caldew valley seeking their fortunes. David Laing and his younger brother James were sons of a mason, another James Laing, who might well have been born as early as 1730. The elder James was evidently a freelance craftsman, moving from hamlet to hamlet in the Borderlands north of Carlisle, as he found work among the scattered farms, a life which must have been similar to that pictured a century later by Thomas Hardy in *Jude the Obscure*. James Laing's two sons, the last of six children, had been born in 1777 and 1781; the name they carried was an old Scottish name, in its Lowland form associated with Dumfries, the county from which James came.

At Sowerby, a local farmer, John Simpson of Macy Bank, is said to have engaged the two young men to help with the harvest. David was clearly a useful man and a courageous one; there is an old story that, during the harvest, one of the farmer's cows was found to be rabid and was shut in a loose box to die. David volunteered to open the door and kill it with his mason's maule as it emerged. He succeeded.

The two parishes seem remote today. Castle Sowerby has long lost its castle (if indeed it ever had one), and its little church of St. Kentigern, dating back to the twelfth century and probably built on still earlier Roman foundations, broods out the last years of its millennium in fields on the edge of the moorland. At one time a possession of the Scottish Crown, its township has long since disappeared, a victim of the Border feuding. Neighbouring Sebergham edges a steep and green little valley cut by the Caldew as it enters the pastures of the lowlands: it was here that a twelfth-century hermit, William Wastell, is said to have made a clearing in the Inglewood Forest and to have built a little chapel, receiving a grant of land from King John and later bequeathing it to the Prior of Carlisle for the spiritual needs of Sebergham's inhabitants. The mediaeval Pipe Rolls of Cumberland have references a little later to land there owned by one Galfridus de Sebergeham.

Today, Sebergham consists of a few houses that one passes unnoticed on the road from Penrith to Wigton; it is affected as little by the transport to the east pounding the great traffic arteries between Scotland and England as it is by the crowding holiday-makers in the Lake towns on the other side of Skiddaw.

But David Laing, in the early nineteenth century, found a prosperous little community. Agriculture was thriving, and there was much building work among the farms in the district. There was some local industry, also. Coal lies beneath the ground, and attempts (later aborted by water) were being made to mine it, and there have, at some time, been mills operating by the river. (Mr. J. P. Templeton, the local historian, has traced the remains of no fewer than eight mills near the village of Caldbeck, a little upstream from Sebergham.) David Laing chose to settle, and on Christmas Day 1809 he married Jane Mason, the daughter of a local farmer, at Castle Sowerby church. He is known to have undertaken building work widely in the district, and to have prospered sufficiently to be living by 1838 at the Old Parsonage, Churchtown, Sebergham, a large and comfortable house, and to have had a considerable family of dependants resident with him.

David and Jane Laing had nine children: five daughters were followed in 1817 by the first son, named James for his grandfather and uncle. Three other sons followed, two dying in their teens.

The third James Laing followed in his father's footsteps, becoming a mason and builder. He married a girl six years his senior, Ann Graham of Sowerby Mill, where she had lived with her uncle, Thomas Pearson the local miller. As a girl, Ann had been accustomed to go up to Carlisle with the cart laden with sacks of oatmeal from the mill, her only food a packet of raisins: it is said that, years later, James's son Thomas annoyed the then miller, William Pearson, by bringing back a sack of the new-fangled flour from Carr's mills in Carlisle. 'He was quite sure that we would not thrive on it at all,' remembered Thomas's daughter Sarah. 'He was a kindly old man. I used to love to watch him drying and making flour and oatmeal.'

Ann proved to be a strong character. After three sons, John, David and Thomas, had been born, she is said to have persuaded her husband to buy a long strip of land, costing some £20 and fronting the roadway through Sebergham, and there to build three houses, including one for their own occupation. She herself is said to have helped gather stones for the buildings from the river Caldew, at the foot of the hill on whose brow the houses were to stand. It is to the first of these houses, bearing a date-plaque 'JAL [James and Ann Laing] 1848' that the great Laing organisation today looks back as its foundation. The house stands today (though much altered).

Like his father before him, James Laing prospered, and was soon the main builder in the immediate neighbourhood, carrying out work for farmers and tradesmen and for the great local land-owners such as the Duke of Devonshire and the Earl of Lonsdale, as well as in local churches and public buildings. Skilled men in those days were paid 3s. 6d. (17½p) a day, labourers 2s. 6d. (12½p) and apprentices about 1s. (5p), but trade with local farmers was often by barter.

The family had its eye on greater things. In 1856, a little jobbing work had been undertaken in Carlisle itself. James and Ann now had five children – their eldest son, John, had been born in 1842, David in 1843, Thomas in 1846, Margaret in 1849, and William, the last child, in 1850. All the sons seem to have engaged actively in business, and it was natural that their ambitions should extend to the city that was the centre of local activity. Carlisle was growing steadily, the population increasing from 22,000 in 1841 to 36,000 in 1881, in the wake of the opening of the railways and also as a result of an increase in cotton spinning. (This trade had led to the building of one of the city's landmarks in 1835–6, the 305 ft. high Dixon's chimney in Shaddongate, which still stands, minus its corbel top, nearly a century after the demise of the firm that built it; the trade itself was to collapse disastrously after the American Civil War.) There was work to be had, and accordingly James and Ann moved to Carlisle about the year 1867, their sons John and David moving with them, and William following, possibly a little later.

In Carlisle, James's eldest son John soon took over direction of the business. On 8 November, 1878, the Carlisle Health Committee approved plans for an office, store-room and stable for John Laing in premises in Newcastle Street, under the shadow of Dixon's chimney. The buildings were to fill a space between two rows of workmen's cottages, opening directly on to one side of the street, and faced board-school buildings on the opposite side. The plans show that the total frontage was less than forty feet, the depth about seventy feet: into that area were packed store-rooms on two floors, a single-room office, and a passage leading to an open yard with stables. Walls were of solid fourteen-inch brickwork.* The cottages on either side were shown as belonging, respectively, to J. Laing and to D. and J. Laing. John Laing, now thirty-six, had married four years before (an event of which more is to be recounted later), and it was in the cottage in Newcastle Street that his son, John William Laing,

---

*The yard and buildings have since been replaced by houses to complete the terrace.

20

future head of a world-wide enterprise, was born on 24 September, 1879.

In 1884, the *History and Directory of East Cumberland* recorded John and William Laing as builders and brickmakers at 21 Newcastle Street, and David Laing as a coal-merchant at the Caledonian Goods Yard and 3 Paternoster Row. Thomas Laing was still living at Caldew Terrace, Sebergham, in the parish of Castle Sowerby, and is described as a mason and builder.

John William Laing did not arrive in this world at an auspicious moment. The boom of earlier years that may have attracted his grandparents and parents to Carlisle broke just about the time of his birth. Yet under his father the business had established a sturdy reputation, and within a year before his son's birth he had engaged two hands who were destined to play a large part in shaping young John's skills and outlook: these were John Rigg and Bob Franklin, both craftsman masons, skilled men of the highest quality and then the élite of the trade.

Slowly, the business progressed. Houses and other buildings in Carlisle, including a hotel, were built by the partnership of John senior and his brother William, and it is of interest that, during this period, their brother Thomas carried out considerable alterations to the church at Sebergham, raising the roof and executing some first-class carved work on the ceiling inside.

In 1889, a contract of major importance, both for the business and for John Laing the younger, was secured. This was for extensive building work at Sedbergh School in Yorkshire.* John senior and his whole family moved to Sedbergh while the works were in progress, and the boy was sent to the local school, where a remarkable schoolmaster made a lasting impression on him. John Laing carried with him for the rest of his life both the lessons in living that his schoolmaster taught him, and happy memories of the years in Yorkshire, of his enjoyment of its countryside, and of his first 'maintenance contract'–papering the whole of the inside of his parents' house for a reward of one shilling a room.

While the John Laing family were at Sedbergh, the building by the firm of houses in Carlisle continued, the occupancy certificates being issued in the joint names of J. and W. Laing. After the completion of the Sedbergh contract, the Laings returned to Carlisle, but to a much larger home in St. James's Road. Soon after this, it would seem, John senior and William

---

*Sedbergh was transferred to the new county of Cumbria in the reorganisation of local government under the Local Government Act, 1972.

parted, to carry on business separately: although they were engaged in substantial joint housing developments, from 1892 the occupancy certificates for the completed houses (which were often built for renting as a private investment) were thereafter issued in their separate names. Certainly the brother William disappears from the story from this time, though continuing to carry on building work on his own account. David, as we have seen, had already set up on his own account as a coal-merchant, and was to become a prominent local citizen and councillor, and, from 1899 until his death, a director, and later deputy chairman, of the society which became the Cumberland Building Society. Thomas, at Sebergham, later took up farming.

The return to Carlisle brought the boy John Laing to a further stage of his development. Just before his thirteenth birthday, on 16 September, 1892, he entered Carlisle Grammar School. It was during the short headmastership of the Revd Samuel Maitland Crosthwaite, who had previously been assistant master of the King's School, Canterbury, and headmaster of Queen Elizabeth's Grammar School, Faversham. Crosthwaite was a strong man who had taken up his appointment in 1890, but sadly died in office (of a cerebral haemorrhage) on 27 December, 1894, having doubled the number of boys in the school during that short period. The school itself offered a full curriculum of both classical and modern studies. Again, John Laing responded to strong leadership and the opportunities afforded him. Entering Form 1, he was not only promoted within a short period, but also ended his first year with the Form 2 (classics) prize. He was able also to develop a taste for active recreation that remained for the rest of his life; a chief love soon became walking and climbing in the magnificent hills of the Lake District. At home, the budding entrepreneur was encouraged by his mother's practical kindliness; enterprise was duly rewarded, and he was paid full market price for vegetables supplied to the family from his efforts in the garden. Surplus supplies could also be sold in the market, while the local auctioneer could always be relied on to find a buyer for step-ladders or other marketable products of the carpentry skills which John was developing.

The achievement of the form prize had the opposite effect to what his headmaster might have expected. John Laing was restless and practical; his father's business was beginning to grow quickly, and the boy's heart was in the excitement and practical challenge and the companionship of hard work that the business represented. Blessed with a quick and intensely active mind, he was a doer rather than a dreamer, and the prospect of further academic attainment seemed actually to have repelled him. To his first biographer he explained, characteristically, that he feared that he 'could never repeat this feat' of the prize, and must leave before the next prize day. His father was now in his fifties, and there must have seemed little enough time for John to develop the skills of leadership and practical management he would need. Accordingly, he persuaded his parents that he should leave school in order to join the developing business, although his grandmother, Ann, still a formidable character at eighty-two, did her best to persuade him of the merits of a professional life. According to the Grammar School Memorial Register, he left school at Christmas 1893, a little into his fifteenth year. His debt to it was real, and his loyalty remained strong, despite his short association with it; from later generations of its scholars have come much of the backbone, as well as directors and many executives, of the world-wide Laing organisation.

The choice was certainly no casual act of boredom. On returning from Sedbergh to Carlisle, the elder John had received one of the plum contracts of the year—the building of the extensive Ashley Road Schools in Carlisle. Extensive private housing developments in Carlisle were in hand, for the city was growing again and these were boom years for house building.[1] The business now had fifty regular employees, some splendid craftsmen among them, and the still tiny offices where father John and his eldest daughter organised all the tenders and administration had moved from the Newcastle Street premises and were now in Denton Street.

John Laing set himself a deliberately hard schooling in the trade. He later recalled his father's insistence: 'My father believed in his son having three years' practical training, so as to get a knowledge of humanity, of the British weather, and of the difficulties of actually doing work and overcoming these difficulties.'[2] The emphasis on the weather marks the builder of hard experience, for a farmer is scarcely more at its mercy than the builder. To the farmer, the weather is sometimes foe, sometimes ally; but he works with it, and in the end its processes bring his work to fruition, but to the builder (and particularly to the builder of those days in the north-west of England), the weather was almost invariably an adversary; the summer sun was able to threaten parts of his work almost as dangerously as the rains and storms of winter, and he himself was vulnerable to every discomfort the elements could inflict. In the last resort, everything a builder does is an act of defiance of the elements, and in the long run it will succumb to them, if man does not destroy it first.

John Laing learned from those days a deep understanding and respect, which he never lost, for the man on the job. When the first edition of the company's journal *Team Spirit* appeared over fifty years later, he wrote on its opening page, 'What I am always against is people who are in an office, nicely warmed and dry, trying to tell the man who is up to the ears in mud, and drenched to the skin on a wet day, how he should do his job.'

The men from whom he learned his trade were tough, skilled and proud. Bob Franklin, the master mason, was as concerned with the quality of his work a hundred feet from the ground, where only birds could see it, as with that on the facing-stones by the main entrance to a public building. 'If I were to get slovenly over my work at one hundred feet, I might get into a slovenly way altogether.' [3] Under the tuition of men like Bob, and the dry humour of John Rigg, John Laing was taught the skills of masonry and bricklaying. 'Now, John, I should not like you to catch cold,' said Rigg on one occasion, when he suspected the boss's son of putting a little less effort into his work than he wished;[4] and John Laing added, 'When I was working as a brick-layer under Rigg, I remember there were three speeds for working. One day I found myself working at a very leisurely rate, so I stepped up my speed and almost doubled the output and found it so much more enjoyable.' [5]

Rigg was a great reader and a keen fisherman, who once held the year's record for a salmon taken in the River Eden. John Laing developed a deep respect for him and Rigg's name became legendary in the enterprise. Generations of later trainees at Carlisle, including several men who reached the very top of the organisation, trained under him: Charles Craft, later a director of the Company and president of the Institute of Building, remembers him vividly, with his bowler hat and 'dickie', in charge of large contracts there as late as the early thirties.

John Laing set himself deliberately to match the best. There are stories of him setting himself in competition with any likely lad among his fellow apprentices and workmen, challenging them to special feats. On one occasion, he went without food for twenty-four hours 'to see what it was like'. 'I knew that many poor people had to do this by force, but I wanted to do it for fun. When I was approaching twenty-three hours without food, Rigg, who was a very thoughtful man, said to me, "John go home—there is something wrong with you today, and just tell your mother what I have said." He thought I was ill, but I sauntered on the way home so as to complete the twenty-four hours.'[6]

On another occasion, he challenged a particularly quick worker among the apprentices; spurring each other on, they each laid two thousand bricks in unpointed nine-inch brickwork in nine hours – double a good day's norm. It was a happy rivalry, to which his employees responded with spirit. John Crowther remembers from his pupil days, nearly thirty years later:[7]

> In the yards, they kept the stables with the horses and carts, and they had a pile of scaffold poles – fir ones, not iron ones. There was a chap there called Tommy Weightman, a very stocky chap, and he was lifting them up and putting them on a trailer lorry. A lot of the old men would call Mr. Laing 'John', and this chap turned round to him and said, 'You couldn't lift one of these, John, could you?' Mr. Laing said, 'Oh, I think so', and he just bent down and picked one up and put it on his shoulder. Tommy Weightman stood there with his mouth open.

Those days of apprenticeship left permanent habits with John Laing. One of the later leading site-agents recounts how he would often measure a man against a bricklayer—'that man is a two bricklayers' man'—and another retired executive remembers his disturbance when an arbitrator at the time of the Second World War set what he considered a completely inadequate standard for bricklayers—below their union's own figure—for measuring 'payment by results' contracts.* John Laing remained proud of his skills and his trade: he never forgot that he was a master mason and bricklayer, trained by practical experience in a hard school.

But, of course, he was very much more. He may have left the grammar school by deliberate choice, and have apprenticed himself to a tough trade in tough conditions and long hours, but he did not intend his education to stop there. Carlisle, as we have seen, was the centre of a district with a long cultural tradition (even the hamlet of Sebergham had had a circulating library and

---

*The wartime standards were reduced to take account of the absence of skilled workers in the Forces, so that much current work was in the hands of elderly or unskilled men.

reading-room in its school as long before as 1858), and the city had boasted a Mechanics' Institute since 1824, Working Men's Reading Rooms since 1851, and a Public Subscription Library since 1768. John Laing made full use of these facilities; building and engineering works and journals, other technical literature, law, history, and (among more general works) the works of John Ruskin in particular, were all systematically studied and absorbed. He was fascinated by technical problems in construction and by the related financial processes, and had an enquiring, innovative mind. He completed his apprenticeship early in 1897, at the age of seventeen, when his father was already fifty-four, and the firm quickly showed his impact. John Laing junior was not going to be content with house or even hotel and school building: he had his eyes on civil engineering. An indication of the new adventurousness came when, on 14 June, 1898, a first contract was signed with the City of Carlisle for the erection of its central electric lighting station, said to be the first electricity power station in the north-west of England. It was John William Laing's first supervisory contract, and he was not quite nineteen.

John Laing stood at the threshold of great things. But there was another influence on him, as real and profound as any of the hereditary influences we have considered. That influence requires a chapter to itself.

CHAPTER 2

The Brethren of Carlisle

ON 4 JUNE, 1874, John Laing the elder married Sarah Wood, and sealed one of the wisest choices of his life. If he had been looking for a wife of the strength and character of his mother, Ann of Sowerby, he found her in this dignified daughter of a Cumbrian farming family. Her parents, Thomas and Ann Wood, lived at Welton, the first village from Sebergham on the road to Carlisle, in a big farm that stood back from the green. They had had a large family, Sarah being one of a family of five girls and five boys.

They were a deeply religious family, who had been influenced by the evangelical revival in Britain in the years following 1859. One of the journals of the vigorous evangelistic movement that sprang up in the wake of the revival, the *British Evangelist*, had reached their home, and led eventually to the religious conversion of the family, to association with the revivalists, and to the establishment of a meeting-place in the village: two of the family later became missionaries. The elder John Laing himself had experienced a similar conversion about the age of twenty-five, through the personal influence of a policeman friend named Lamb. Such a mutual faith became a most powerful influence, cementing the marriage of John and Sarah.

At about the time that the John Laings set up home in Carlisle, an independent congregation associated with the Brethren was forming there: it was with this congregation that the newly-married couple felt closest affinity, and in August 1874 when the records of the congregation began, they were already members. John William Laing, who was born five years later on 24 September, 1879, was their third son, two boys born in the previous four years having died in infancy. Another son, born in 1883, also died within a year, but three daughters, Annie, Isobel and Sarah (Sadie) survived. The simple piety of the Brethren meeting and the strong social cohesion of its fellowship were to leave a deep imprint on what was plainly a most happy family, and notably on John William Laing himself. So important was this influence on his personality and his thinking that it is impossible to understand his later development without a digression into the background and atmosphere of the community.

The Brethren movement traced its beginning to a moment in Dublin in 1829, when a few individuals had met 'for communion in the Name of the Lord with all, whomsoever they might be, who loved Him in sincerity', but it was essentially a coalescence of a number of different tendencies arising in the aftermath of the eighteenth-century evangelical awakening. Within a few years, the movement had brought together in a loose fellowship congregations formed in many different towns and villages of Britain, notably in Plymouth (whence the nickname Plymouth Brethren), Bristol and London, and had established links with a similar and slightly earlier movement in Switzerland and, a little later, with indigenous movements in Italy (where, unlike Britain, where political action was frowned upon, it was at first very much involved with radical politics under Teodorico Pietrocola Rossetti and Bonaventura Mazzarella), and elsewhere on the Continent. Its leaders in Britain were mainly dissident Anglicans, often clergy or ordinands, but with some dissenting ministers and laymen, and a leavening of former members of the Society of Friends who had parted from the Society in the wake of the Beaconite controversy in the 1830s. This latter dispute had centred on members in Kendal, and from their numbers had sprung one of the first Brethren congregations in the north-west of England, in Kendal itself: it is of interest that a main element in the Carlisle leadership also looked back to the Kendal Society of Friends.

The Brethren sought a simple, untrammelled fellowship of believing Christians, in which they hoped to avoid the strong divisions then apparent between the Christian denominations. They refused a regularly appointed ministry, on the grounds that the churches should draw on the gifts of all their members, and in doctrine they were essentially evangelical with a strong millenarian tendency; on baptism they held varying opinions. In life-style they were frugal and abstemious, many of them advocating a rigid separation from 'worldly' activities. Conflicting doctrinal tendencies soon caused tensions, however, and in 1848 they had divided into two distinct groups whose destinies were to be very different: an authoritarian 'exclusive' group, which was dubbed 'the Exclusive Brethren', and a loosely defined group with no denominational organisation or discipline, which included the powerful Bristol church under the philanthropist George Müller and most of the ex-Quaker element, and which was firmly baptist in doctrine and congregational in polity. This group was dubbed 'Open' Brethren in contrast to the other; the name 'Christian Brethren' had already been used before the division, and it persisted, but the movement tended to disclaim any name for itself.

The evangelical revival of the 1860s gave an emphatic impetus to the Brethren movement, many of the ardent evangelists of the day finding its loose organisation, its evangelistic ardour, and its simple untrammelled form of worship to be ideally suited to their own free spirits; very many new congregations accrued to the movement, particularly in Scotland and in Northern Ireland, where there had been few meetings before.

The Carlisle congregation itself seems to have been a product of this new consciousness. A prime influence in its formation is said to have been the preaching of the Revd William Reid, who became minister of the Warwick Road Presbyterian church in 1867, but who shared many Brethren views and is said later to have associated himself with them. (David Laing, the brother of the elder John, became and remained an elder of this Presbyterian church; neither he nor the other brothers joined John and his wife in their Brethrenism.)

The most remarkable members of this new congregation were Jonathan Dodgson Carr, the founder of Carr's Biscuits, and his three sons, Henry, Thomas William and James. When the minutes of the congregation started in August 1874, all four Carrs, with their wives and a sister, were members; Thomas William Carr was indeed the first secretary. J. D. Carr was an outstanding man. A member of the Society of Friends, he had left Kendal at the age of twenty-five and had walked to Carlisle, where he established himself as a baker in 1831, building himself a flour mill after three years. He received the Royal Warrant from Queen Victoria for his biscuits in 1841. He was a pioneer, and largely the originator of mechanisation in biscuit production, and his factory in Carlisle boasts of being the birthplace of the biscuit industry (though both Crawfords and Meredith & Drew were founded a little earlier). He had been prominent in the movement for Repeal of the Corn Laws and was a founder and vice-president of the then Cumberland Co-operative Land and Benefit Building Society (the society of which David Laing was later deputy chairman), which was launched on 16 April, 1850, at a great meeting of a thousand persons in the Athenaeum, Carlisle.

Of J. D. Carr, many stories are told. On one occasion, having been given in Carlisle market two more sacks of grain than he had bought, he is said to have asked the local police to trace the seller. They failed, and he later visited the police station with a sum of money. 'It's the money I got for the flour I milled from the two extra bags. Do what thou likes with it, but it isn't mine.' He was said to have been able to carry three sacks of flour—seven and a half hundredweight—one on his back and one under each arm, the length of his mill and back. But above all, he was a concerned and careful employer, providing welfare facilities and working conditions well in advance of the time, insisting on quaintly paternalistic conditions of apprenticeship that carefully regulated the moral state of the lads concerned, and taking a close interest in housing conditions and matters of general social welfare. When he left the Quakers is not known: he and his sons are said to have been members of William Reid's church before joining the Brethren. (It is interesting that his brother John was one of the founders of Peek Frean & Company, another famous biscuit manufacturer, one of whose other owners, Huntingdon Stone of Greenwich, was also a leading member of the Brethren and a generous benefactor of their missions.)

J. D. Carr himself died in 1884, five years after the birth of John William Laing, but his three sons remained active leaders of the Brethren congregation until their deaths at the turn of the century, and therefore, throughout Laing's boyhood and adolescence. Henry Carr, who succeeded his father as chairman of the company, was active in encouraging evangelisation in the district for miles around, while his younger brother, James, was a noted open-air preacher, visiting the local villages and also race meetings, fairs and any other suitable public attractions.

John Laing senior, and his wife were loyal members of this congregation. John Laing is recorded as a 'doorkeeper' (apparently an office of the eldership) in its early days, and was from time to time appointed to visit recalcitrant members. The congregation was growing quickly, and the atmosphere in which John William Laing's own Christian convictions were forged was one of intense spiritual awareness, of a cohesiveness of social life in which the church fellowship was dominant (and, indeed, it watched over its members' activities with an almost oppressive concern), and above all of uninhibited, aggressive evangelism. The more ardent spirits were expected to—and did—announce their convictions and concern for the souls of others from every public vantage point they could seize.

The main weekly service of the Brethren was the communion or 'breaking of bread'. A table in the meeting-place would be furnished with a loaf and a flagon of wine and, one by one, different male members of the congregation would lead it in a prayer of devotion, announce a hymn which would be sung by the congregation without instrumental accompaniment, or read (with or without comment) from the Bible. At the climax of the service, the loaf of bread would be broken, and passed on a plate from hand to hand round the whole congregation, each taking a morsel; after which the wine would be poured into large glasses which would also circulate, each person taking a sip. It was a simple imitation of the Last Supper as described in the New Testament. The tone of proceedings was sharing and intensely reverential, and a sense of the presence of Christ would be earnestly invoked. On the occasions when the different contributions harmonised, the atmosphere could reach an intensity of worship that could make a lasting impression on the participant.

These were days long before the universal impact of the media. Life in a small isolated city such as Carlisle would centre on local concerns and local activity, and a closely-knit and caring community like the Brethren congregation would decisively shape its members' social life and personal interests. They would meet several times on a Sunday and again during the week for mutual Bible study, prayer and, above all, for evangelistic activity in the district. There were a number of educated men and able preachers in the congregation, which flourished under a vigorous leadership, although its insistence on encouraging the abilities of all its members, and the habit of deferring to each other in many activities, could also lead to quaintnesses. Years later, John Laing himself described his boyhood days in the church:[1]

My experiences . . . go back . . . to when the meetings were held in the County Hall, where Henry Carr and Thomas William Carr frequently took part in the morning services. From there, the assembly moved to the Gospel Hall in Scotch Street, where Mr. Moss had a draper's shop. The entrance to the building was very narrow, and the actual hall about 45 feet long by 24 feet wide. The only window in the hall was at the far end, where almost the whole of the wall was window. The elders of the meeting at that time were Edwin Page, John Laing (senior), Robert Gall and Mr. Wilson, who was manager of the North British Railway Locomotive Shed. His job was quite responsible, as the greatest industry in Carlisle at that time was the Railway.

The younger generation were inspired by a certain brother who had many good ideas, but was terrible for preaching about hell. I remember him saying that hell was 10,000 feet below the surface of the earth and that people who went to hell would not only suffer from the intense heat, but also from a tremendous compression . . . I mention this to show how the world, including the assemblies, have changed, although, even as quite a young boy, I did not agree with this particular brother in these matters.

Mr. Gall was the best Bible teacher in the group, and Mr. Cauker and his wife were almost as good. Mr. Cauker and Mr. Gall were employed by the Carr brothers as evangelists, and I received much help when in the Sunday School, through Mr. Gall's teaching.

The Brethren are often depicted as fundamentalists and excessive literalists in their attitude to the Bible, but this is to misunderstand them, and to reduce a real spiritual vitality to mere mechanistic terms. In more recent years, they have had their proper share of academic biblical scholars, and their attitude is generally conservative, but informed; in those earlier days, when life was often more isolated and shaped by simple activities, their personal devotional reading and study of the Bible were major cultural influences, even if they were not often balanced by other influences. The very simplicity of their way of worship, and their rejection of the traditional forms by which church procedures are normally shaped, threw them back more strongly on to the Bible and the general evangelical tradition from which they interpreted it. These were their main channels of continuity with the historic life of the Church, and (except for later deterioration among the extremists or 'exclusives') preserved them within the boundaries of Christian orthodoxy. In their open communion services, in particular, readings from the Bible often functioned as a sort of substitute for the liturgy they rejected, so that the Scriptures were absorbed deeply into their devotional attitudes.

It was little wonder, therefore, that John Laing, steeped from earliest childhood in such an environment, grew up (in the words of a later writer) to be 'a deeply religious man and what he

James Laing (1817–1882)

Ann Laing (1811–1902)

John (senior) (1842–1924)
and Sarah Laing (1844–1924)

John Laing and his sisters

James Laing's account book, 1848

Detail from John Laing's
early cost book (p. 39)

calls "a tremendous believer in God"'.[2] The evangelistic teaching of the Brethren, particularly in those districts which were the product of later nineteenth-century revivalism, emphasised the necessity for personal faith and commitment to Christ, and John Laing himself always looked back to such a childhood conversion at the age of seven as the root of his Christian experience, despite later struggles.

Family life was happy and united. His mother was a strong character, puritan in outlook, marked by personal calmness and charity. John Laing senior was athletic and a sportsman and fond of outdoor activities; more reserved than his wife, at times he seemed dour. He was a hard worker, a stickler for quality, and a grave and gentle man. Mark Ferris, an old foreman, spoke of picking up a stone as a young man to throw at a bird. He felt a hand laid on his arm, and there was old John Laing. 'Has that bird ever harmed you?' he asked, and the boy dropped the stone.[3] As parents, John and his wife were on the old side; John Laing senior had been thirty-seven when his son was born, and Sarah thirty-five, but there were the three sisters and many cousins and friends to provide youthful companionship. Both parents brought to Carlisle their love of the country in which their childhood had been spent, and there were frequent family outings in the horse-drawn cart, and visits to the farms of relatives and of Sarah's parents. The Thomas Woods would hold religious services in their barn at Hutton Roof, and would at times have visits from noted evangelists of the day, like the celebrated Gipsy Smith, who would sometimes visit them when up for the big fair at Appleby in Westmorland.

Wallace Haughan, a Carlisle man who spent his life with the Laing organisation and later became a director and head of its Canadian operations, writes of John Laing in those days:

Cumberland was where he spent his youth, and he had lots of nostalgic feelings for it and lots of interesting stories about his youth . . . On one of these journeys, we were driving through Flimby on the Solway Firth, and the only thing it had in its favour was the sea, although even this was blocked from the average person because of the railway line running along the sea front and the slag heaps. In any case, he talked about his mother and said what a wonderful woman she was and how she was always determined that her family should have a month's holiday at the seaside every year in good times and in bad times, and one must not forget that most small contractors in those days, probably around 1890, very often had bad times. However, in that particular year he mentioned, they must have had a very rough time and they thought they would not have a holiday. In the end, Mrs. Laing finished up by renting a small cottage in Flimby.

Many stories survive of climbing and walking expeditions in the Lake hills, the girls in ankle-length skirts–and hauled up by ropes when this garb made it necessary! John Laing became a skilled rock climber, and the old postmaster of Ambleside remembered him well. 'He was a fine fit lad,' he said to Nigel Redfern, a later Carlisle regional director of the Laing organisation. Some years later, John Laing took the opportunity of climbing-holidays in Switzerland. His sister, Sadie, described how he had been the first of a season's climbers to reach the summit of Mont Blanc:

> You had visited a guide and asked if he would take you up; he replied that there must be two guides. You said you had only enough money to pay for one, so could not go if there were two. He said he would take you. On the way up, you met others coming down who had been advised to go no further, the gale was so severe. However, the guide was still willing and so your ambition was realised.

She remembered, too, a family outing to Pillar Rock in the Lake District. Two of the sisters, Isobel and Sadie herself, were with John, together with Jack Mewton, fiancé of the third sister Annie, and Isobel's own Will Cowan.

> Will hated rock climbing so when you got as far as a vantage point to see us all hurtling to our deaths, his worry was lest he saw Isobel killed. Jack was leading–as we got towards the top, the more difficult part, there was Will praying that we might go no further. It was our intention to go on, of course. When Jack's trouser seat got caught in a jagged rock causing a large three-cornered tear, no one even had a safety-pin; it put paid to any further ascent. So Will's prayer was answered.

Two close friends of those early days, David Beattie and a cousin, Thomas William Wood, later became John's strong supporters and helpers, as he and the new generation took over affairs in the Brethren congregation after the death of the Carr brothers.

34

Thomas William Wood farmed in those days at Highberries, Scaleby, and later moved nearer Carlisle to Tower Farm, Rickerby, on the eastern outskirts of the city. John Laing spent many hours in his cousin's company, both as a boy and as a man: he was alert to understand farming ways, and particularly enjoyed leisure times in the fields. On one occasion, the two young men went out shooting rabbits. 'J.W.', as his cousin called him, shot at a rabbit and, as it seemed wounded, threw down the gun and ran after it. There was a sudden explosion and he found that half the gun barrel had been blown off!

David Beattie first met John Laing in 1898. It was the rather unnerving question, 'David, if you die tonight, where will you go?', suddenly shot at him by the young John Laing, that in his own words, 'eventually led, not only to my conversion, but to our lifelong friendship'. Apprenticed with the Laings, he later developed a monumental mason's business in partnership with John Laing, taking it over himself during the First World War and developing it into a substantial undertaking: this was only the first of several successful businesses other than his own in whose launching John Laing shared. David Beattie later described him as 'a man of uncanny foresight and penetration, and gave one the impression that he was able to see what was on the opposite side of a stone wall, without having to climb up to look over the top'. Beattie himself, an interesting man, later developed an interest in hymnology, and was also a careful collector of the histories of Brethren congregations, a subject on which he gathered and preserved much valuable information. He published books on both subjects.

John Laing did not allow his own intellectual curiosity to be hemmed in by the limited boundaries within which some of his friends and contemporaries were content to wander. We have already touched on his programme of reading. His interest in Ruskin obviously left a deep impression on him, and traces of Ruskin's thought are surely to be found in his own later ideas, both on housing conditions and on employee relationships. That the young John Laing ever met the aged Ruskin at Coniston is unlikely, but had the older man survived a few years beyond 1900, we can be sure that John Laing would not have missed the opportunity—he never passed up such chances in later life!

Other works which demanded his attention might have been regarded by some of his Brethren contemporaries as more dangerous, but a young man who could write of his delight in climbing 'there is tremendous joy in facing and overcoming the

35

really difficult climb with no one to see the struggle. Just to face the most difficult one can accomplish and overcome, gives real pleasure',[4] was not going to avoid an intellectual challenge. So he tackled head-on the most serious contemporary dispute between religion and science: the still-flourishing debate that had grown out of Darwin's *Origin of Species* of 1859. He read what he could—Darwin, Huxley, Wallace and their opponents. The result was a period of intense intellectual and spiritual struggle that he often recalled in later life. On the one hand, it seemed, were ranged the very real personal spiritual experiences that he had himself enjoyed: they could not be denied. Yet, intimately bound up with them, if not their chief generator, were the words of the Bible, and those words, it seemed, were contradicted by the evidence and argument ranged on the other side.

Even today, there are those who believe themselves to face a similar distressing choice, and sometimes the help they receive from those who should know better is as potentially disastrous. 'These thoughts are wicked. You must put them from you.' So wrote a 'well-known Christian teacher', to whom John Laing wrote. Hundreds have been turned from the faith by as little. Happily John Laing always recognised cant when he saw it. He went back to his Bible, and read again and again the simple portrait of the person of Christ in the Gospels, letting it sink deep into his consciousness as he wrestled with doubt.

'*The Origin of Species* no longer worried me,' he later wrote.[5] 'The Bible account of the creation in Genesis 1 begins in simple dignity, "In the beginning, God created the heaven and the earth." The six days of creation, I realised, were geological days and became to me a source of inspiration and a tremendous aid to worship.'

It might not seem an earth-shaking realisation to most of us today. Effectively, he was interpreting the opening chapters of Genesis as a poetical and summary statement of basic truths, which in no way impinged on the validity of scientific fact or theory. No doubt there are many today who would argue that he was hopelessly wrong: but then, our ingenuity often tangles snares for our own feet, and few are blessed with the simple ability to go directly and naïvely to the heart of a problem; John Laing's later life showed him to possess this ability to the border of genius.

Later he was to find his thought confirmed by James Jeans's *The Mysterious Universe*. 'He always afterwards showed traces of Darwinism in his thinking,' said one close friend of his from later evangelical life, almost ruefully. Perhaps John Laing had found, in his simplicity, the key that allowed him to rejoice for the rest of his life in both his faith and the tangible world he saw around him.

'Nearly two thousand years have passed,' he wrote when finishing his account of his early intellectual struggle. 'Great changes have taken place in the world of education, but Christ's doctrines are as perfect and as forceful today as when they were first spoken. One single verse of Christ's teaching surpasses all the laws of England – "Whatsoever ye would that men should do to you, do ye even so to them."' [6]

CHAPTER 3

Crisis

WHEN, ON 14 JUNE, 1898, the first contract was signed with the city of Carlisle for the erection of its central electric lighting station, the business of John Laing (soon to become John Laing & Son) was clearly pointed in a new direction. The younger John Laing was not yet nineteen, but it is plain that his influence with his fifty-six-year-old father was already strong, and it is said that this was his first supervisory contract. (He had indeed been largely responsible for the building of the Institute at Castle Carrock while still in his apprenticeship.)

The power station contract must have been a daunting enough responsibility for a lad barely out of his apprenticeship, but John Laing never considered youth a bar to responsibility; well into the 1930s, men were being placed by him in charge of responsible works at extremely young ages. The results were the proof, and by this test the power station contract must have been successful for, after its opening on 11 May, 1899, it was followed by a second contract at the power station in 1900, and by substantial further works there in later years. Indeed, from that date the Laing organisation has been responsible for a very high proportion of major public and private works in the city of Carlisle.

The contract was not the firm's first venture away from straight building into civil engineering, for John Laing senior had signed a contract with the city corporation for improvements to the screening chamber at its sewage works four years before. But, by any standards, it marked the coming of age of a local building firm(though it antedated that of John William Laing himself).His successes were not accidental. The younger John Laing had realised that the secrets of success in contracting were to be found in accurate estimating for tenders, backed up by a rigorous control of performance. Costs of materials at that time presented little problem, but the costing and control of labour productivity was almost unknown. In those days, mechanical equipment was almost non-existent; the key to success, therefore, lay in knowing precisely what work it was reasonable to expect a man to finish in what time; how much he was to be paid for that time; and then to persuade him to do it! It was on these basic principles that John Laing was to develop and refine a system of controls that would ultimately take his business to the top of the industry.

It would not have been called by that name then, but in essence what John Laing set up was a system of work study. His father had strong (and natural) doubts 'whether the men would stand for it', but his son's remarkable powers of persuasion and conviction were already highly developed and, by taking the older men like John Rigg into his confidence, he was able to win their willing co-operation. A large and strongly-bound ledger still survives in which many of the early exercises and notes were recorded. It gives a fascinating insight into working-procedures on building sites at the beginning of the century. Many of the main operations have each their own section of the book, and in each section there are recorded in different hands information on costs and times from many sources, together with details of actual experiences on trial work, careful drawings of work (particularly in the stone-carving section), a note of what was done and how long it took, and detailed over-all costings of certain house-building schemes.

Some of the entries are rich in technical detail: 'Kit senior worked a specimen quoin rock on both faces well scutched on beds with 13" chiselled margin down both sides of external angle in 25 minutes (note some time will have to added [sic] to this for waste time).' This is followed by a drawing, and then a similar exercise for another job. A few notes refer to time taken by J. W. Laing himself, in similar precise detail.

Details recorded of working-class housing in Carlisle show that terrace cottages were being built in 1900 for between £150 and £175 each, and let at five to six shillings (25p–30p) a week: the cost had altered little in thirty years, and was in general terms to remain reasonably constant until the First World War. This price would have corresponded to about £750 to £900 in 1948;* as the

*The indices on which comparisons through this book are based are:

(a) For construction work, contract prices and turnover figures, the 'Index of the cost of new construction' as given in Tables 4 and 6 (New Building Work) of *Price Index Numbers for Current Cost Accounting* (HMSO, 1976).

(b) For all other figures, the 'Index of Prices of Consumer Goods and Services' (as compiled from the Cost of Living Index, consumers' expenditure deflator and general index of retail prices) used by the Institute of Chartered Accountants for its published tables in its *Working Guide* to Inflation Accounting and subsequently the Retail Price Index.

Company put the average price of a municipal house in 1948 at £1,250,[1] the figures are a graphic illustration of improved housing standards over the first half of this century.

The book contains costings also for a stone-planing machine, apparently the firm's only piece of mechanical equipment until a coal-fired steam crane was used at Barrow Docks in 1906. The stone-planing machine remained in use years later, for John Hindmoor remembered it in use when he joined in 1920:

> Wilson with machine when watched all time by J.W.L. (but not assisted in any way) except by Dan for 10 minutes took 1¼ hours to dress a 4' 0" length of 11" × 6" double splayed coping in Woodburn, cost say 1½ hours at 1s. 6d. = 2s. 3d. Mason 1 hr. jointing 9d. Total cost per foot run exclusive of polishing 9d.

The 1s. 6d. per hour rate used appears to cost in the machine itself as well as the labour.

Horses, too, came in for their share of work study. Godfrey Harrison records that original estimates showed that, if a horse were fed on good hay and oats, he could draw a load of 35 cwt., and would die at the age of ten; but it was later found that if horses were not so heavily loaded, were fed less oats, but put out to grass on summer nights, their life expectation increased to seventeen years—an indication that apparently inhuman costing systems could at times lead to humane conclusions.[2] Indeed, John Laing himself soon reached very firm conclusions on human working hours: experience taught him that a fifty-hour total week (short for those days) was the productive maximum for manual work, sixty hours producing no greater output and, after a short period, showing reduced output. Long travelling-time would further reduce capacity, although he found, when studying his own working capacity, that the variety inherent in supervisory would could increase it and permit him to work considerably longer.[3] (But then he himself was one of those unusual men, so often men of great achievement, who are able to manage on four or five hours' sleep a night.) These conclusions later led him to oppose official suggestions for seven-day wartime working.

There was, of course, one obvious snag with these careful work-study observations: they depended on a very variable factor: the quality of the worker observed. For this reason, names were carefully recorded. In 1905, a contract was secured that was close to John Laing's heart: the building of the tower of the parish church of St. Martin at Brampton, a little town seven miles east of Carlisle. The work had been estimated to cost £1,700 in 1884—equivalent in building terms to £45,000 today—and Laing's tender was for £1,644. It was not his first experience of church building, for the chancel (and later the nave) of Kirkbride Church had been restored during his apprenticeship, and work had also recently been completed at Bewcastle in the Border country. Brampton's ancient twelfth-century church had been built some distance outside the town and had long fallen into disuse; services were held for about a century in what had been the chapel of a local almshouse foundation, until it was decided to build a new church, which was consecrated in 1878, the tower having been left unfinished. The church, in the traditional Early English style, had been designed by the pre-Raphaelite architect Philip Webb, with stained glass by Morris and Burne-Jones. John Laing found working to the plans of such an artist as Webb (then still alive but in retirement), supervised by George Jack, Webb's former chief assistant, a stimulating experience, but a later comment indicates the slow trial and error by which he was developing his work-study and costing methods:[4]

> As there was one type of stone repeated several times, before we made up the tender, I got one of our masons to dress a stone like that and see how long it took him. I told him that he must not work extra hard because I was going to base a tender on it, but he must have been either more skilful than the average, or he had worked more industriously, because I lost £100 on that job.

A key factor in the development of the system was the arrival, in 1903, of William Sirey. Sirey, also a member of the Brethren congregation, took over the tendering work and together with John Laing developed it into an instrument of great precision; from the time he joined until his early death in 1941 he was a close friend of John Laing and a vital factor in the progress of the business. In 1903 the firm also secured another man who was to be one of the most important members of the team around which the expansion before and after the move to London was built, G. G. Lowry.

Working conditions in the industry were primitive and hard, and in some parts of the country atrocious. An old north-country man wrote in the Company journal in 1949:[5]

41

It is the year 1899 and the labour basis on contracts is 9d. [less than 4p] per hour for tradesmen and 6d. [2½p] for labourers, and apprentices begin at 4s. [20p] per week. All start work at 6 a.m. and finish at 5.30 p.m. Meal hours are 8 a.m.–8.30 a.m. and 12 noon to 1.00 p.m. No mid-morning or mid-afternoon teas, no buses, no walking time, but it is a case of be on the job at starting time no matter how you get there. No coddling, make your own tea at meal hours, sit on a plank to eat, and work hard or you may lose your job for there are hundreds out of work . . . bacon and cheese were only 6d. [2½p] per pound and eggs twenty for a shilling [5p] and plenty of them . . .

I lost my father when I was only seventeen and I was then the eldest of three at home and the only one working. My mother was crippled and it needed all her ingenuity to keep going on my 15s. [75p] a week.

I attended technical school four nights a week although the fee was difficult to find. In other spare time I made furniture to sell, but even at that for a long period I had to work without a lunch, for there was nothing to pay for it.

When George Lowry joined in 1903, the working hours in the Laing business had been reduced by an hour a day to fifty a week (five days of nine hours and five hours on Saturdays), and wages were 8½d. per hour for tradesmen and 5d. per hour for labourers, with an extra farthing an hour for hod-carriers who climbed ladders. There was no pay in those days for time laid off for weather. All transport was by horse and cart, and concrete was hand-mixed on sixteen-by-eight-foot platforms of one-inch timber, two being put together to form a sixteen-foot-square platform. Concrete would be hoisted by jenny wheel, and stonework by block and tackle, or, on larger contracts, by a hand crane. As we have seen, a coal-fired steam crane was brought into use in 1906 at the Barrow contract.

The Brampton church contract was, by this time, a small one for the organisation. Several very substantial buildings had been put up: schools, warehouses, public buildings, and an extremely large contract at Garlands Hospital (the Cumberland and West-morland Mental Hospital) in Carlisle, for which the tender was between thirty and forty thousand pounds (equivalent in 1977 terms to nearly a million-pound contract); this contract alone employed 200 men for two years. This expansion meant watching finances closely, for the extent to which a contractor can expand on his own working capital depends entirely on the speed with which he can get his money in, and on his success in keeping down his administrative overheads. Applications and certificates at the hospital were checked and paid monthly, and John Laing himself meticulously checked off the County Architect's bills of quantities in three weeks – on top of all his other responsibilities.

H. E. Ayris, who joined a leading local architect's practice at about this time, well remembered his own contacts with the firm:[6]

> John Laing and Son were good to me, explaining the ways of the Border builder. . . . With the younger John, a man approaching my own age, I was 'at the opening of the ways' for I had come to an office full of possibilities for an architect. And young John was with me in being a trier and a student of the good work of others. We noted and conferred together on labour and materials and encouraged the good. . . . His office organisation was helpful because of accurate and up-to-date costing, which enabled him to tender well. From labourers to foremen he had the best of operatives, bound to the firm because the standard of the work was high and resulted in appreciation from many quarters for years.

To handle the increasing volume of work, the firm had, in 1904, built itself new offices and a yard in Milbourne Street, Carlisle, but by any standards it was not being extravagant; those who remember the offices describe them as 'a small wooden building'. An 'out office' was also registered at the corner of Linton and Oswald Streets, apparently in connection with extensive housing being built and let nearby; this was possibly the firm's first branch office. Later a joinery works was opened in Shaddongate nearby.

The area of work was also expanding, and during the first decade of the century there are references to work in Durham, Gateshead and Glasgow. Mr. W. R. Burnett, then aged ninety-four, remembered in 1952 how the firm had built his school for him at Seascale in 1903:[7]

> Mr. John Laing himself spent a good deal of time in Seascale in lodgings so that he could be at hand. The workmen, of whom there were about 20, lodged at the Home Farm, about half a mile from the site. One point my uncle remembers vividly is the fact that the foreman, Mr. Rigg, always wore a bowler hat whatever the weather conditions or the work in hand.

43

Mr. Burnett remembered also how a carter had backed his horse too close to a shaft dug for the foundations, so that it fell in and was killed; the school had a tradition that its ghost haunted the buildings. Casualties among horses on those old building sites were scarcely less uncommon than among the workmen.

It was two contracts away from Carlisle during this decade that marked a turning-point in John Laing's own experience and in the development of the business. He was seeking wider horizons and sterner challenges, and civil engineering work, with its severe demands on skill and knowledge, attracted him enormously. Those who remember the early days say that his father gave him his head, but his mother, strong character though she was, grew increasingly nervous over his ambitions. He was about to test himself severely.

The first of these contracts was for the construction of a reservoir complex in the Lake District hills north of Skiddaw, within a few miles of the old family home where his father had grown up.

The river Ellen rises on the northern slopes of Skiddaw and feeds the little lake of Overwater, a tarn of about fifty acres, and the northernmost outlier of the English Lakes. From Overwater, the stream passes through a narrow, curving valley in the hills, before reaching the remote village of Uldale and eventually passing across the plain to the coast at Maryport. On 2 July, 1901, the royal assent had been granted to a Bill empowering the ratepayers (in fact the Joint Water Board) of Aspatria and Silloth to dam the valley above Uldale and to construct what today is known as the Chapel House Reservoir, to supply their respective towns.

John Laing tendered for this contract and won it. By the later standards of his Company, it was small, but for him at that time it was a testing venture. It involved extensive banking work to Overwater itself in order to enable it to function as a reservoir; the construction of the dam across the valley below the lake to form the additional Chapel House reservoir; cutting a by-pass channel beside the dam and the lower lake; and extensive related works. All was done by muscle power alone, and the logistics, for a small concern, were formidable. Some two hundred navvies, the toughest and roughest of the trade, had to be housed, fed and kept supplied for months in remote moorland some ten miles from the nearest railhead; the only transport was by horse and cart over rough hill tracks. All the equipment had to be transported by the same means.

John Laing, now in his mid-twenties, was in complete charge, and was joined on the site by his friend, David Beattie. The early months of the contract ran into very rough weather, and double shifts had to be worked during the summer months to keep the work to schedule; John Laing himself (who had not costed a site agent into the tender) supervised both shifts, working at the height of the season from 2 a.m. to 11 p.m. His ability to manage on an hour or two of sleep must have been tested to the full. But most important to his future development was the long experience of living and working directly alongside the band of hard-drinking, roaming men who constituted the navvy force of the day, of learning to know them as men, and to understand the often bitter stories behind their lives. Some of these men became familiar acquaintances on the firm's successive contracts; others became regular employees. It was not until the progress and completion of the contract was secured that Laing was able to break off for a little less strenuous 'rest cure' (as he later described it), a climbing holiday in Switzerland, while his father for a time relieved him on the job.

One associated feature of the Uldale contract did not then directly affect John Laing & Son as the contractors, but it held out a warning of an area of potential trouble that was to bring the firm close to disaster on its next venture into civil engineering. That was the capacity for dissatisfaction (and resort to litigation) of some of the landowners of the day. In a later booklet recounting the story of their works, the Water Board complained that 'unexpected difficulties were met with, and what at first looked like a comparatively inexpensive scheme soon, through costly arbitration proceedings, developed into a scheme costing nearly £60,000.' The contractors were not concerned in these 'difficulties'. The doughty Miss Gough, owner of both nearby Whitefield House (today known as Overwater Hall and occupied as a very pleasant country hotel) and of the Whitefield Estate on which the works took place, fought the Board for her compensation through long arbitration proceedings before three arbitrators and up to the Court of Appeal. (In justice to Miss Gough, the sudden arrival of a camp of two hundred hard-fisted, rough-living navvies on her remote doorstep must have seemed the end of her world!) If only £40,000 of the Water Board figure related to the actual construction work, the scheme would have been equivalent, at 1977 building prices, to a contract worth a million pounds.

John Laing always remembered the Uldale contract with

pleasure and excitement, and referred to it frequently in later years. The challenge of the work itself, the primitive and rough working conditions, the control and companionship of the tough labour force all left an indelible impression on him, but not least he had enjoyed the outdoor life in the close presence of his familiar Lakeland hills, with the peak of Skiddaw itself on constant watch over the little valley where the men worked.

The Uldale contract seems to have been followed immediately by the mental hospital work already described: a contract of similar size in money terms, but very much less demanding as a project. But John Laing, the experience of Uldale satisfactorily behind him, soon eagerly took the chance of another civil-engineering scheme. The contract was considerably smaller than that for Uldale–little over £10,000 (or a quarter of a million at 1977 building costs). It was for the construction of new surface-water outfall sewers by the docks at the industrial town of Barrow in Furness, south of the Lake District mountains and some seventy-five miles by the coast route from Carlisle. After Uldale, the risks and demands of this work must have seemed small, but among the careers which John Laing was said to have studied with close interest was that of Weetman Pearson, later Lord Cowdray, the great engineer who had tunnelled beneath both the Thames and New York's Hudson River. Was he unaware of Pearson's nearly disastrous experiences as a very young man, when he had met running sand while sewering Southport in Lancashire?

The Barrow contract was won by John Laing & Son, and was signed by his father and John Laing himself on 6 September, 1906, William Sirey witnessing it. The stipulations laid down in the specification were onerous. They had been prepared by Mr. Walker Smith, borough engineer and surveyor (later to be city engineer of Edinburgh, Director of Housing, Ministry of Works, 1919–25, and Sir Jonah Walker Smith, M.P.), and provided that 'the Contractor shall be held responsible for all accidents arising from the inclemency of the weather, land springs, floods, tides or other cause whatsoever, and be chargeable with all risks attending the execution of the work and for all damages and accidents consequential or otherwise . . . by or in consequence of carrying on the works.'

The Corporation was indemnified fully against all actions or proceedings, extending to all costs, and the contractor made liable for all damage and inconvenience to any adjoining premises or business. Specific indemnities were also given to two landowners whose land was to be crossed by the sewers: the Furness Railway Company (whose lines were crossed by the works) and the local importers and traders, Burnip MacDougall & Company. The original contract price had been increased, and was agreed at £11,660.

Trial borings had been taken by the Corporation, and the results made available to the tenderers: they showed sound dry clay. The tenders had been based on these borings, but John Laing learned from an official of the Corporation that he would find running sand in one place. From the start things began to go wrong. The weather turned exceptionally bad during the winter months, and on one occasion the workings (which started at the sea wall) were swamped by a freak tide, well above any experienced for the previous forty years. But the most serious difficulty arose from an altered line of the sewer, agreed by the Corporation at the request of the local landowners themselves. The new line took the excavations close to the landowners' own buildings, and just at this point John Laing encountered the full difficulty of running sand, and a high water table. To aggravate the situation, Walker Smith's correspondence tended to be aggressive and unhelpful—perhaps made more so by pugnacious letters he was himself receiving from the landowners.

On 27 February, 1907, John Laing & Son wrote to the Borough Engineer, drawing his attention 'to the waterlogged state of the ground we are, and have been encountering . . . which was represented to us as being dry, by your trial holes.' They went on, 'We expect it is also a disappointment to you, seeing it has turned out so different to the test given,' and suggested that this, and difficulties caused by the amended line of the sewer, entitled them to compensation. Walker Smith, who was at the same time receiving cross letters from the landowners, replied antagonistically to Laing's letters. Laing then pointed out that, if the sewer had not been diverted, they would have been working at the position of one of the dry boreholes; he also claimed that, when they had drawn Smith's attention in advance to probable difficulties, the latter had dismissed them. Smith's response, on 13 March, 1907, was hostile, and contained the odd statement that the borehole in question had not even been on the original line of the sewer.

Throughout 1907 the dispute continued. The landowners' buildings had undoubtedly been damaged by the works, but it was disclosed that the cellars of their buildings had always been unusable because of standing water. The structural damage to their buildings was remedied by John Laing & Son, but they persisted in further claims on the Corporation for dislocation of their business and for compensation under several heads. Walker Smith passed the claims to Laings under the terms of the contract, and they, now acting under legal advice, rejected them as unfounded.

John Laing was beset on two fronts. On the one hand, he had a serious grievance against the Corporation. The problems with the running sand had involved him in a great deal of extra cost, not least in the remedial work necessary on the adjoining buildings, and it was likely that the contract would run him into a serious loss. But Walker Smith stood on the conditions, and was unyielding as to a variation in the contract price. The official's statement had shown that the existence of running sand was known locally, and John Laing's consequent suspicion of ill faith in the siting of the boreholes had not been allayed by Walker Smith's odd reply of 13 March. Meanwhile, there hung over them the threatened action from the landowners, and also the possibility of substantial damages if the claim were to be upheld in the Courts.

There is no doubt that John Laing was intensely worried. A few years later, his concern could have taken trouble of this nature in its stride, as part of the normal hazards of construction work. But the firm was still small and he was just twenty-eight; he had deliberately expanded the activities of the family business into new and dangerous areas, and his father was now sixty-five. The fear of bankruptcy for the family must have been as real as it could ever have been in the days (not long before) when work had been hard to find, but this time it was largely by John's own act.

During the course of the contract he had himself been ill with a poisoned leg, possibly his only illness throughout his long working life. It had not kept him from his work, and his employees remembered him being lifted down into the excavations by hoist to inspect the workings. He had also decided, very reluctantly, that his responsibilities compelled him to avoid the risks inherent in his more dangerous rock-climbing expeditions, but he took up another diversion which proved little less hazardous. A correspondent writes that, during the Barrow contract

The young John lived as a paying guest in the home of my paternal grandfather, one Thomas Robinson, and John was of like age to my then unmarried uncle, Fred Robinson, and the two formed a friendship which proved to be lifelong. My uncle . . . owned a small sailing boat on the Walney Channel. On one occasion, John requested that, since Fred was employed on Saturday afternoons, perhaps he would lend John his boat for the afternoon. Enquiry showed that he had no experience of sailing but with easy confidence he assured Fred that he would be all right, if Fred would just give him instructions as to how to handle a sailing boat. So off he went to the Walney Channel, found the boat and set out. It so happened that the wind freshened to a near gale (those were the days before weather forecasts) and evening came but John did not return. Night fell and the Robinson household were consumed with anxiety. Sunday morning came and still no sign of John. The Robinson family were casting about as to the best way of communicating the sad news to Carlisle, for this was in a pre-telephone era, when, at about 3.00 p.m., tired but sound in wind and limb, John arrived. He had taken the boat out of the northern end of Walney Channel into the Irish Sea intending to circumnavigate Walney Island. When the westerly gale blew up, he had sense enough to stand out to sea to avoid being blown ashore on the west coast of the Island until the gale moderated next morning. He then managed to make the south end of Walney Island and re-entered the Channel, where he had beached the boat safely at Rampside, from where he had walked the five miles or so back to Barrow.

The experience was no deterrent: he took shares with friends in a sailing boat and, whenever he could, went Saturday sailing. On another occasion, he was grounded at low tide with William Sirey, and the two found themselves stranded until well past midnight, when the high tide refloated them.

The sewers were eventually completed on 19 June, 1908, nearly a year after the original schedule, and reinstatement work was to continue until 8 October. On 24 June, the landowners Burnip & MacDougall issued a writ in the High Court against the Corporation of Barrow in Furness, John Laing & Son being joined as third parties. On 29 December, Walker Smith, still hostile to Laings, opined in a letter to the Town Clerk that 'it is quite clear that the stiffest fight will be not between Messrs. Burnip & MacDougall and the Corporation but between the Corporation and Messrs. Laing.' In May 1909, writing as the 'late Borough Engineer and Surveyor', he informed the Town Clerk that he had certified Laing's total amount at £11,760 (a figure allowing just £100 of extras), from which he then deducted a penalty of £1,700 for late completion. John Laing & Son, he said, had not agreed, and were claiming £3,512 more. He might have added that, in the event of dispute, the matter must go to arbitration. The arbitrator under the contract was—Walker Smith himself!

John Laing was in deep trouble, and his personal worry was not lessened by the distress of his parents, and of his mother in particular. Visiting friends in Barrow, she had confided that 'it would have been much cheaper to have closed down the business and taken the family to live in Switzerland for a year, than to let John loose in civil engineering'. What John Laing himself was to make of his adversity, the aftermath would show. Half a century later, he was visiting Barrow again, and took Fred Robinson out in his car for the afternoon. At a point near Furness Abbey he stopped the car, and walked away alone. When he returned, he told Fred that he had been back to the spot where, at the height of his troubles, he had sought God and vowed that, if He would show him the way through his troubles, he would make Him a participating partner in his business. 'The Lord has kept His part of the contract,' he added, 'and I wanted to assure myself that I had kept mine.'

There were just four hopeful factors. The first was that Walker Smith was no longer borough engineer; earlier that year he had left to become city engineer of Edinburgh. The second and third were two excellent friends: in Tom Strong of Carlisle Laing had a personal friend and lawyer of first-class ability and reputation, who was firmly loyal to his client, while his bank manager, Joseph Wills of the Clydesdale Bank, Carlisle, had implicit confidence in him, supporting the firm without question through its crises. The fourth factor would be proved in the event: his own personal integrity.

The lawsuit went at its own pace. Preliminary hearings on the question of third party directions were settled on appeal by a judge in chambers in March 1909, and John Laing & Son were firmly joined in the action. In the meantime, Tom Strong took over personal negotiations with the Town Clerk of Barrow and his committee (which included the mayor). Internal correspondence indicates that earlier relationships between Walker Smith and the Town Clerk had not been entirely harmonious and with Smith no longer on the scene, the negotiations were amicable. Eventually, on 9 August, Strong accepted the town clerk's offer of a further £2,000, making a total bill of £13,760 18s. 0d.

with no penalty deduction, and stipulating that Laings would take over all responsibility for the litigation, with the support of the Council, and would indemnify the Council against any damages awarded over and above the £250 the Council had already paid into court. The Council paid its own costs.

The first part of the troubles was over, and John Laing later said that the settlement enabled the firm to come out of the contract with neither loss nor profit: he himself had worked throughout its two-year term for nothing. But the legal action was still be be heard.

Eventually, in October 1909, the action was heard before the Official Referee of the Barrow in Furness District Registry of the High Court. It lasted seven days, and according to John Laing's own recollection recorded by Godfrey Harrison, the plaintiffs brought twenty-six witnesses to Laing's six. (Counsel, it may be noted, was paid between seven and twelve guineas a day.) On 28 October, the Town Clerk could report to the Mayor and his Committee, 'I beg to inform you that the trial of this Action before the Official Referee was concluded today. The Referee was of opinion that the sum of £250 paid into Court by the Defendants with their Defence on 15 January, 1909, was ample to meet the Plaintiff's claims and awarded them that amount only.'

The plaintiffs lodged an appeal, but withdrew it, and on 28 February, 1910, John Laing & Son finally received the last of the monies payable to them.

John Laing had been moved to the core. He never forgot Barrow, and looked on the contract there as a turning-point in his life. Nor did he forget his vow by Furness Abbey.

In relief at the settlement with the Corporation, and while still awaiting the outcome of the litigation, he had drafted a 'programme for his life', which he later summarised in his own words: 'First, the centre of my life was to be God – God as seen in Jesus Christ; secondly I was going to enjoy life, and help others to enjoy it.' The paper on which this programme was drafted was carefully and confidentially preserved by him well into his old age, as a constant personal reminder. He drew up also a 'financial plan', which has survived:

Following a period of solemn prayer and dedication when in Barrow, I drew upon a sheet of Furness Abbey Hotel notepaper during September 1909 showing how I proposed to dispose of my income. That says:—
If income £400 p.a. give £50, live on £150, save £200

51

If income £1,000 p.a. give £200, live on £300, save £500
If income £3,000 p.a. give £1,000, live on £500, save £1,500
If income £4,000 p.a. give £1,500, live on £500, save £2,000.

To this he added the proviso that, once the savings brought in interest of £500 per annum, he would live on £500, give away half of the remainder of his income and save the rest. He was, in modern terms, setting himself a maximum standard of living approximating to that of middle to upper management.

He was following closely the example of his parents, who had made a principle of giving away a substantial part of their income, and, in following their example, his resolution undoubtedly included an acknowledgment of how nearly the family had come to financial disaster. Certainly he was to realise how deeply his father had suffered in spirit when, during the course of his summing-up, the Official Referee (as John Laing remembered it) referred to the evidence of the plaintiff's witnesses, and then to that of John Laing himself, adding 'whom I implicitly believe.' At that point his father burst into relieved tears.[8]

John Laing attributed to this crisis in his life the beginnings of several other changes in attitude. At the firm's centenary in 1948, he said, 'Upon succeeding in getting that contract completed, I determined to try to live my life in a less ruthless manner. I thought that I would try from that time onwards to enjoy life and to see if others could enjoy life too.' Even if some of the ruthlessness was still to be detected in later years, it was out of the years of Uldale and Barrow that there grew his practical concern for the working man and his conditions, which he gradually worked out in later life.

The experience also accelerated developments in his economic attitudes.[9] 'The ethics in business at that time,' he was to write much later 'were "Buy in the cheapest market and sell in the dearest". Honest but hard! This was contrary to the teaching of the Lord Jesus Who said, "Whatsoever ye would that men should do to you, do ye even so to them."' And, again:[10]

We were born in the Victorian period when it was thought that the best method of business was to buy in the cheapest market and to sell in the dearest market . . . To illustrate this, I had employed a first-class carter at the rate of eighteen shillings a week (in those days a first-class carter could earn twenty shillings . . .) and he seemed very contented with his eighteen shillings so I continued to pay him at that rate for a considerable period and then gave him a rise. This pricked my conscience somewhat and so I collected all the arrears and waited to give it to him in a lump sum. When I did this he just said to me that he would like the money to be used towards paying for the new Hebron Hall because he was now comfortably off, but that he could have done with the extra money earlier at a time when his children were at an expensive age. I have always regretted not paying him a fair wage . . . To be fair to my parents, they always taught me to be kind and helpful to employees, but in Victorian days people had different standards in the business world. The Carlisle motto was 'Be just and fear not' but the Lord Jesus wanted His followers to be not only just but merciful too.

It was an interesting reversion to the ethical ideas that R. H. Tawney showed to have been general in the days before the rise of modern industrial capitalism; John Laing would have approved of the New England puritan, quoted by Tawney, who denounced the 'notorious evil . . . whereby most men walked in all their commerce—to buy as cheap and sell as dear as they can'.[11] Whether John Laing succeeded in restoring to large-scale enterprise some of the ethical standards that Protestant individualism may have helped destroy is a question that our later story may need to examine.

He also took away from Barrow a prejudice against 'working in water' that lasted through several decades of his enterprise's later development, and senior staff members remember it as a matter of policy in the 1930s. A site agent who found himself coping with running sand in later years needed to watch his work with especial care! But even more marked was the careful financial prudence that characterised all his later dealings. The high proportion of 'savings' laid down in the 'financial programme' drawn up after Barrow was not, as his later actions proved, with an eye to the accumulation of personal wealth, but simply because he realised that, if his business was to be strong enough to survive the sort of set-back that he had experienced, its own capital reserves must be built up steadily and prudently. John Laing was never again to enter under-capitalised on a dangerously risky assignment. He was also to carry into his later business life an intense dislike of litigation, and would never have resort to the law where it could be avoided.

His personal friendships, and loyalties too, had been sealed. Mrs. Kimber, his bank manager's daughter, remembers her father telling her that John Laing had said to him, 'If I win, I will never leave the Clydesdale Bank.' Nor did he or his successors, as a glance at the annual report of the present day gigantic Laing organisation will show. To Tom Strong also he remained intensely loyal, and years later, when he was developing his vast housing and factory estates in the London suburbs, it was the Carlisle solicitor who handled the legal work. Most interesting, however, was the reaction of Jonah Walker Smith. After the settlement with the Corporation, John Laing recorded, he had returned to greet Laing with smiles, expressing satisfaction at the settlement. 'All through life after that, if ever Walker Smith was introducing me to anyone, he always introduced me as his dear friend.' John Laing could be forgiven for adding, 'I am glad I have never met another like him!'

CHAPTER 4

Consolidation:
The First World War

J OHN LAING HAD come of age with the birth of the new century. At the age of twenty-one, he had been appointed 'clerk' or secretary of the Brethren congregation, an office which placed on him the responsibility for affairs of the congregation and for the engagement of speakers (it may be assumed that the gentleman with Jules Verne notions of hell was not frequently on the list!). The death of the last of the Carr brothers, Henry, in 1904, called for a new and vigorous initiative. Despite John Laing's business commitments, it came.

They were the days of great Gospel missions, often led by American evangelists. Moody and Sankey were still fresh in the minds of many, and they were being followed at that time by Torrey and Alexander. It was to an evangelist named Maplesden, an Englishman who spent much time in America, that the Carlisle congregation of Brethren turned in 1905. John Laing was a prime mover in his Carlisle campaign. 'For five months the team met about 6.30 a.m. for prayer before going to work,' David Beattie later recalled, 'and again at 6.30 p.m., followed by a procession . . . through the main streets, headed by a very energetic young man using a large megaphone to announce the meetings.'[1] The young man was John Laing. The campaign revitalised the congregation; starting quietly, attendances grew until the organisers had to hire, first the Queen's Hall, and then the Albert Hall in Carlisle. John Laing recalled how the halls were filled night after night, with a space at the back crowded with standing listeners. 'Every evangelical church in Carlisle received new members,' from the converts, he said, while the Brethren congregation itself had afterwards to hire additional accommodation at the Queen's Hall for its regular services, as the hall in Scotch Street was no longer adequate.[2]

Those who remember the congregation at that time speak of the active part in it taken by John William Laing; indeed, to one member he 'almost seemed to be the meeting—you know what he was like, if he thought a thing was right it didn't matter what people said, it bounced back.' He was a frequent speaker at the regular open-air services, and many older local people who had no connection with the Brethren congregation, remember his preaching there. He was no very gifted speaker, and the church looked for its main teaching to other and senior members of the congregation, but John Laing had a particular flair for simple directness that was highly effective when he was in contact with the ordinary non-church-going men and women he knew so well from his workaday life. One relative who lived in his home as a girl remembers him as 'a marvellous story teller'.

It was an active and interesting church. John Laing's own parents were much involved in its affairs; his father, grave and courteous, was one of its elders, and his mother, kindly but rather severe and straitlaced, one of the leaders of a girls' Bible class. Members alive today still remember the group of older men who acted as Bible teachers to the congregation: all of them were hard-working laymen, who served their local community well.

With a working-class base in the membership, the leadership was sturdy provincial middle class: local traders and business-men (some founders of business houses still thriving today), prominent railway officials, farmers: solid citizens to a man. (Of their children, the next generation, one was to become deputy town clerk of Carlisle and later town clerk of Fleetwood, and another city treasurer of Carlisle). Of the older Laings, one old member exclaimed, 'Oh, they were a homely couple – you would have to go back to my generation to know what that word means.' (It was very different from its American connotation!) 'They were the élite of the assembly, but everybody knew that. He was a quaint old man and she was a nice woman: they were well, well mated.' An elderly business neighbour, not connected with their church life but (with his father) supplier to the Laing business for eighty years, confirmed this view: 'A family I have always greatly admired, the Laings. I have known them for years . . . a grand family, hardworking, no side about them, never lost their heads. The sons are just the same.'

Life in those few years, before the First Great War brought the technological age noisily into the world, seems incredibly far removed from today: arduous, and yet with a humanity in its dimensions that we have long lost. An older member of the Brethren meeting remembers how her father had worked for the Laings as a carter when John was still little more than a lad:

When we all had the fever, old Mrs. Laing used to cook the

dinner and send John Willie* down to our house with it. I was the only one who didn't take the fever, and he handed the dinner in . . . Old Mrs. Laing used to have our Bible Class as well. You daren't have your hair waved and you daren't have a flower in your hat. She used to say, 'When we have our tea, if our children have butter, they don't have jam!!' There was Annie and Sadie and Isobel his sisters. They were nice. Isobel was the sweetest woman you ever could have met; she married Mr. Cowan of Glasgow – he made chocolates . . . Once when they were very poor, my father took them for their holidays in a furniture van, I think to Silloth. My father was a carter and was in among the horses. He used to work for Laings, but there came a time when they had no work in Carlisle.

Town and country were very close in a compact provincial capital like Carlisle, with its regular markets and meetings. Life had its own pace – it is said that a boatload of Irish geese arriving at Silloth would be walked the twenty miles to Carlisle Cross, and after being bought by a farmer would then be walked home by his men. Yet, if the pace of life was different, its efficiency was not to be sneered at: Mrs. Armstrong, the daughter of Thomas William Wood, remembers her farmer father telling her that on one occasion he was due to meet John Laing at Wigton one winter's day in order to cycle to Caldbeck. For some reason he was delayed; what to do about his cousin waiting (with less than placidity, for John Laing was always a stickler for punctuality) in the square at Wigton? He sent a telegram, reading 'Laing, standing at Wigton fountain, late but coming.' It reached Laing, and preserved their friendship!

During that first decade, John Laing became friendly with a Brethren family from Stockton-on-Tees. William Harland, the father, was a chartered accountant, but his parents and those of his wife had been boat captains and owners from Whitby. The three youngest children of a family of ten, Henry Chapman (born 1881), Walter (born 1883) and Beatrice (born 24 July, 1885) became close friends of John Laing, who was later to speak appreciatively of the influence of William Harland on his own character and behaviour in the difficult and changing days after Barrow. Henry, a chartered surveyor, and Walter, his father's successor

*The old Carlisle custom is to use both Christian names, and John Laing was invariably called 'John Willie' by the older generation there: a usage he disliked intensely. It also served to distinguish him from his father.

57

as a chartered accountant, were to be lifelong colleagues. During those early years, they became close companions, joining John Laing in his expeditions to the fells. Henry Harland was later to recall the outings:[3]

> You remember, John, the occasion . . . ? Walter, you and I were having a well-earned holiday at Seathwaite. We had walked from Keswick and had made Seathwaite Farm our headquarters for three days' walking. We certainly walked, didn't we? And didn't it rain in torrents part of the time? Nothing daunted we did some ordinary climbing up Scafell Pike and you would do a bit of rock climbing. In no time you had scrambled across on to the pinnacle and standing on the rocky crag you urged Walter and me to follow . . . 'Come on, Henry, it's as easy as going to bed.' I didn't find it quite like that, but I followed you, and I too was on top of the world with you. Do you remember the bathe we had before the tremendous supper after being up the Pike? You knew a bathing spot, a deep pool in a swiftly flowing mountain stream, and there we were, perfectly nude and perfectly happy–far from the madding crowds. Those were the days when friendships were made which only time can sever.

As the friendship grew, John visited Stockton, too, and Henry had another characteristic reminiscence of his exuberant and extrovert friend:[4]

> Do you remember a walk we had, just the two of us? It was Saturday night in the market-place at Stockton-on-Tees. Time, nine o'clock–great crowds jostling and sellers of goods shouting their wares. Suddenly you said, 'What a grand place for an open-air meeting. Let's have one, Henry.' We stopped in our stride. I took your hat . . . and just a brief prayer to ask for God's help and you were telling the great crowd what the Lord Jesus meant to you. Literally hundreds of eager faces looked at the two young men standing there alone–yet not alone, for the Lord was with us. How the folk listened to your message of God's love in sending His only Son to die for sinners. On the Monday following, a man came in to my office in West Hartlepool and said, 'I saw you and your friend in Stockton market on Saturday night and listened and I want to tell you how I admire your pluck and stand for God.'

But it was Beatrice who was the greatest attraction. At the time of his Barrow anxieties, John Laing and Beatrice Harland were engaged. In later life John Laing recounted with amusement the story of how, in his enthusiasm, he had told Beatrice that he would like to buy her a very fine ring to show how much he loved her, but would she not think it good if he bought a less fine ring and gave the rest of the money 'to the Lord'. 'No,' said Beatrice, 'I would not!'

They were married on 29 September, 1910, a Mr. R. G. MacInnes performing the ceremony at the Brethren meeting hall. John had shared with her the life programme that he had drawn up after Barrow, and she was whole-heartedly with him in shaping the careful and unostentatious life-style they later developed. The marriage, a deeply happy one, lasted until her death in 1972. Beatrice Laing was a natural complement to her husband, by temperament unassuming and retiring, yet a strong character. In the words of an old friend, 'She was a very fine woman, who took a great deal of the strain off him at home.' Many years later Sir John Laing wrote with gratitude of how he could, at the end of the day, 'step aside into a home where there is perfect trust, confidence and peace of mind, and where there is a partnership in which the wife is wise, kind, cheerful and patient.'[5] Unobtrusively, she was able as the years went by to share his problems, and in particular to take an active part in many of their philanthropic activities, her concern being always practical and thoughtful.

On marriage, John and Beatrice Laing moved into a house at 42 St. James' Road, Carlisle, within easy walking distance of the offices in Milbourne Street. His uncle William was still living at No. 64, and through most of his childhood his parents had lived at No. 4, before, a few years earlier, building themselves a house on a ridge of high ground on the north bank of the Eden at Etterby Scaur. The house at 42 St. James' Road provided a convenient base from which to extend the young couple's church activities. 'We used to go every Friday night to St. James' Road,' an elderly member recalled. 'All the young people were invited . . . he was really good with young people.' There were also regular large tea-parties for the children, on holiday occasions, in large hired halls in Carlisle, and occasional special ventures like a 'tramps' breakfast'.

John's church commitments were extending. The Christian Brethren, shaped as they had been by the evangelical revivalism of the last half of the nineteenth century, had always regarded

59

evangelistic activity as a cardinal obligation of their church life. Countrywide, a majority of their congregations had been formed or strongly influenced by members of that extraordinary band of freelance evangelists, from all social classes, that had characterised that period of popular evangelicalism. In the first decades of this century the tradition was still strong, even if declining. Campaigns in the villages of the countryside, by groups of men out on bicycles for a Saturday or Sunday from the towns, were to survive until after the Second World War (and motorised groups are still to be found), while full-time evangelists with tent and caravan were to be seen (and, indeed still are to be seen) in many parts of the United Kingdom and in the English-speaking countries overseas. Sometimes, where local feeling was friendly, the village hall would be hired; the evangelists were not normally sectarian in spirit, but were ready to co-operate with any friendly local church, chapel or clergy.

The Carlisle Brethren had regularly formed such groups, and in 1912 it was decided to sponsor a full-time evangelist with tent and 'Bible carriage' (a horse-drawn caravan like a gipsy van, with texts painted prominently on all sides). A Mr. Browning and his wife were engaged and several 'pitches' arranged during the first season, in villages in mid-Cumberland. John William Laing is recorded as one of those who preached in the tent during the season, and he and a Mr. Winter of Penrith acted for some years as honorary treasurers of the fund which was set up to finance the work.

The work soon established itself, and it continues (in modernised form) to this day—as indeed does similar activity by Brethren in most counties. Very different in character from the spectacular 'crusades' of the more publicised evangelists, the work is painstaking and laboured, and the men who give their lives to it receive little publicity, and live devotedly on a pittance. They are careful and informed workmen at their calling. John Laing continued his interest, and (at times) his active participation, in work of this nature for the rest of his life: his influence is very apparent in the early reports of the Cumberland and Westmorland Gospel Tent Work, not least in securing for their pages articles from the pens of some of the most prominent national leaders of Brethren.

In business life, the early married years were not easy. The building industry generally had entered a period of depression, and its unemployment reached in 1909 the highest point since 1881. Carlisle suffered, like other places, and there was little work to be had. The firm seemed for a year or two to do little more than keep its head above water. John Laing's father, sixty-eight in 1910, was by now in semi-retirement, for the Corporation Contracts Register records that a contract for a further extension to the Electricity Works taken out that year was in the sole name of 'John William Laing, trading as John Laing and Son'. The additional work there was to be a mainstay of the business for several years. During 1910 considerably less than £8,000 was paid into the bank, and that would have included the final £1,800 from the Barrow settlement; activity was indeed greatly reduced from the years of Uldale and the Garlands Hospital, when there had also been much other work in the district. (£8,000 then would be equivalent to building work of rather more than £200,000 in 1977.)

The old buildings in Newcastle Street were at this time occupied by David Laing, now a local councillor, in connection with his coal-merchant's business. He stabled horses there, and regularly did carting for his nephew's firm. In 1910, and until the date of his marriage, John Laing had drawn a wage of two pounds per week, and some of this he had paid back into the business!

Yet the future working team was retained and added to. Another man who started his life with the business about this time was James Kelso, a bricklayer who, with his inseparable friend George McKnight, was to become one of the stalwart 'characters' of the John Laing tradition, of whom many stories are told. Forty years later, after his retirement, he recalled his early experiences for the Company journal: 'We worked hard in those days. We started at 6.30 a.m. and did not knock off until 5.30 p.m. And we had no tea breaks.' He remembered how John Laing kept the same hours, and how he was respected by the men for his hard work. 'At 6.30 on most mornings, he would be found on one of the firm's contracts seeing that everything was in order. He visited the sites on a bicycle, for motor cars were rarely seen in Carlisle in Edwardian times.'[6] James Kelso himself was soon to learn that John Laing's supervision of his work was no formality: he was found one day kicking a football about a site, and was promptly transferred to Scotland and kept working very hard on a contract there!

This contract may well have been a housing contract for the Kirkconnel and Sanquhar collieries, where in 1910 the firm had its only substantial work (apart from that at the Electricity Works and a regular maintenance contract for the War Department in

Carlisle). Like that other work, it was to last until well into the First World War, and to help the business through its difficult years. John Laing was also building a few houses in Glasgow with his brother-in-law William Cowan; the return rail fare from Carlisle to Glasgow was ten shillings (50p) and lodgings could be had for a shilling or two a night.

As the Kelso anecdote shows, John Laing's close supervision of the work and the men for which he was responsible was already becoming legendary; yet a tough discipline (for those years, and many still to come, were the times of 'hire and fire') was becoming balanced by a genuine human concern. Sixty years later he recalled how, 'having found a job for some of those unemployed men . . . I hurried off to tell the men I had found a job for them – I found them all in the pub.' [7] He had been brought up in a strong teetotal tradition, and, although as a young man he had not been a complete abstainer, he had soon become aware of, and intensely sensitive to, the immense drink problem among the labourers of his day, in their often bitter working and living conditions, and he himself became teetotal in personal practice. At Uldale, he had seen how the navvies would go off every weekend to spend their earnings in the inns of the district. In this at least they were well catered for: in Carlisle there was said to have been a pub at every other door in Rickergate. Clarence Payne, who joined the firm in 1914, described the conditions:

I remember the labourers in those days. They used to like their drink, and they were able to get a sub every week. They put in a day or two's work and could come to the office and get half a crown or five shillings to go and get some booze to keep them on for the week. One of the very best stonemasons that we had was a very fine fellow when he was sober, but when he went off on the booze you wouldn't know when you were going to get him back. He was such a good craftsman that John William would almost give him anything, but at the same time he used to say, 'Now, you won't be long before you're back,' and I have seen him go out – Sir John himself – hunting him to try to get him back.

This mason was by no means the only employee for whom John Laing would hunt in this way. It is said that one of his most senior and respected employees was similarly subject to alcoholic episodes; on one occasion he was found in a bad state outside Carlisle, and as John Laing was bringing him back he begged that without 'just one more pint' he could not last. John Laing, insisting 'one and one only', took the man into a pub, gave him his drink, and then brought him home to dry out.

This extreme social problem (for he was very conscious of the consequences of alcoholism for the families and living standards of the men) was a major factor in setting John Laing's thinking in the direction of the welfare and savings schemes that he was later to develop. More immediately, it would have been a leading motive behind the support his firm gave as builders to the State Management Scheme of supervision of the licensed trade in Carlisle during and immediately after the First World War.

The family owned a considerable number of cottages and small houses in Carlisle that they had built, for the most part, around the turn of the century, and the business organised the rent collection for many of these. About this time the rent collector (a cousin of John Laing) informed the tenants that rents were to be increased. There was some protest, and one lady agreed to be spokeswoman for her neighbours. John Laing came to see her himself, and eventually persuaded her of the reasons for the increase. Her daughter recounts how, towards the end of the discussion, she and her sister came into the room; turning, John Laing exclaimed, 'Oh, what lovely girls!' and added that he had a brother-in-law, a confectioner, in Glasgow: he would send some candies for the children. A fine box duly arrived, and he had won a permanent friend out of a family that could have been antagonists. It was by little acts of this nature that John Laing, hard-headed businessman in other respects though he could be, was beginning to establish his characteristic reputation. One local author wrote:[8]

> The Cumbrian has a genius for rugged individuality, independence of spirit, inspired bloody-mindedness in short, which may have a desperately disconcerting effect upon the natives of lesser counties. If he decides that he wishes to pursue a different course from yours, or perhaps that he wants to be rid of you altogether, he will either go about it with a directness which can be pulverising, or alternatively employ a delicacy of touch which makes swansdown seem a harsh substance.

The extract may read like a guidebook puff, but by those standards, as by every other, John Laing was a true Cumbrian, and moreover with a winning, happy temperament and a disarming smile that was throughout his life to disarm tougher opposition than any he had yet met.

Meanwhile, trade had been slowly improving. Turnover in 1911 was £9,000 and in 1912 £11,000 (at 1977 costs equivalent to about £225,000 and £275,000) and, in addition to the running contracts already mentioned, the firm, though still slack, was working on extensions at the Garlands Hospital and on a number of country houses, quality work* much in the Laing tradition. There was even a small export of some timber prefabricated sections to Iceland, for a church (in fact a two-storey mission premises in Isafjördhur) designed by an Icelandic architect, to which we shall refer in more detail in the next chapter.

Stanley Laing, grandson of John Laing's uncle Thomas, started work with the firm in 1912, and remembers how a year or so previously the equipment brought back from the Barrow contract had been stacked in a field near his parents' home.

They were pretty quiet then, but looking for jobs out of Carlisle. They just had a small wooden office and yard in Milbourne Street. John Laing was always going round the sites on a bicycle; his father had a bicycle with a little auto wheel like an autocycle. Many a time he left his bike and did not know where he had left it . . . It was a 6.30 start in those days, with half an hour for breakfast at eight o'clock. Fourpence an hour for labourers and sixpence for bricklayers,* and if it was a wet day you lost your pay; no half time. Labourers had their own shovels to buy and hod carriers their own hods. We worked to five–ten and a half hours a day and about one pound a week money.

There was of course also a mid-day meal break.

The records show that by 1912 John Laing himself was travelling indefatigably around the scattered worksites– Glasgow, Egremont, Eskmeals near Barrow, Aspatria, Sellafield, Whitehaven. He would take his bicycle on the train with him. A neighbour remembers how he always had a green bicycle (coloured bicycles being uncommon) and often wore a green suit.

In 1911 John Laing and his wife had in fact bought their first car, the licence the following January costing six guineas, and the

*This recollection may be unrepresentative. The Government *Statistical Abstract for the United Kingdom 1913 and 1923-1936* (HMSO 1938) gives average hourly rates for thirty-nine large towns in 1913 as 9.9 pence for bricklayers and 6.6 pence for labourers (Table 137 p. 156). See also page 42.

John and Beatrice Laing at the time
of their marriage, 1910

John Laing in uniform,
First World War

John and Beatrice Laing *c.* 1920

The first house at Sebergham built by James and Ann Laing, 1848 (p. 19)

Easiform local authority house at British Empire Exhibition, 1924–5 (p. 76)

insurance ten. It was a little Ford, and apparently not too reliable. Lady Laing spoke half a century later of how, on a trip to Bamburgh, their 'tin Lizzie' at first refused to go and then raced up and down hill at an alarming rate. A little later, as they descended Kirkstone Pass into Ambleside, the brakes refused to work. It was perhaps understandable that John Laing seems to have continued to use his bicycle for business purposes! The little Ford was to have an extended history. John Hindmoor, who remembered getting sixpence as a boy for cleaning it, later remembered it converted to business use after the First World War: a box was built on the back, turning it into a small lorry carrying up to ten hundredweight, or several men. On one occasion, driving in from a country contract, Hindmoor was alarmed, after a long straight run, to find no response from the steering. He stopped at once. So many workmen had jumped into the back that the front wheels were clear of the ground!

In 1913 came the beginning of a breakthrough, with two major additional contracts: one with Vickers on the gun range at Barrow, and another for the construction of a new main post office in Carlisle itself. This latter was worth £20,000 (equivalent to a 1977 half-million-pound contract) and lasted for two years. Turnover of the business in 1913 was £18,000, and in 1914 £29,000, a very substantial increase indeed on the 'quiet' period before. In 1914, for the first time since Barrow, there was a strong positive cash flow.

Clarence Payne joined as a boy of eighteen in 1914 and remained for less than a year before joining the Forces.

The old man was in retirement when I was there and John William was carrying on the business in this little hut and yard . . . they were just branching out . . . beginning to get quite nice jobs . . . they had started to build the G.P.O. and I remember the masons in the yard there carving away the fluted columns that you see at the Post Office in Warwick Road. They did them in about four-foot lengths and they were put together . . . John William Laing . . . expected you to work hard, because he worked hard himself and long. He burned the midnight oil quite a good bit—he was a hard worker, there is no doubt about it, and he expected every ounce out of you . . . When I went to work for him there were four of us, that was the sum total of the office staff . . . William Sirey was managing clerk, he did a lot of the costing. He was very quiet, nice, a very decent fellow, and a very hard worker.

Then, in August 1914, came the outbreak of the First World War. Immediately the pace of life changed, and the first major impact on Laings (in addition to further work at Barrow for Vickers and the War Department) was the start of a considerable programme for the construction of prefabricated timber army huts. This work was set up in a field site in the Dalston Road, Carlisle, and is said, when at its peak, to have seen a trainload of the huts leave Carlisle every day. It lasted through most of the war, and hutting was sent throughout the country. The cash receipts in 1915 were slightly below those of 1914, but by 1916 the new work was having its effect, and expansion was under way – and fast. Local army camps were also built, but one of the largest developments took place just across the Scottish Border at Gretna.

Lloyd George had taken over as Minister of Munitions in June 1915, in the wake of the 'munitions scandal' of the spring. One of his first acts was to have an enormous factory complex built on the north shore of the Solway Firth, starting from the Border at Gretna. The site was chosen as being reasonably clear of the risk of any attack that was within the capacity of contemporary aircraft. (There is a vivid reminder of the war in an entry in the Laing cash book for April 1916 for 'Zeppelin insurance', but the premium of £1 15s. 6d. indicates the degree of risk assessed in the north-west.) The over-all supervision of the work, which involved not only the factories but also a complete new town for up to twenty thousand workers, was entrusted to Lord Cowdray's firm of S. Pearson & Son under the personal supervision of his brother Edward (later Sir Edward Pearson), and the work itself was divided among numerous construction firms. To John Laing & Son fell a substantial share of the work on the new township. Some of the first entries in their records relate to hospital and medical facilities at Gretna in 1916, an indication of the careful planning of priorities that went into the scheme. The factory went into production in the autumn of 1916 while the town was being developed. Shops and a church followed in 1917.

Gretna brought new personal contacts with men of material standing, who were of first importance to John Laing. Lord Cowdray, as a young man, had (like John Laing) built his early control of his business on a meticulous noting of costs, quantities and labour, and under Edward Pearson John Laing would have been able to compare and test his own system with the practice of others, under the direct guidance of a master of the method. His personal contact with Raymond Unwin, chief town-planning expert of the Local Government Board and the architect

66

responsible for the Gretna township, was to be a lasting one, and was to influence his own thinking on housing standards and estate planning, and to lead to many of the features he was later to incorporate into his housing developments in the London area in the 1930s, when (as Sir Raymond) Unwin was one of the most important figures in the attempt to humanise and control the great surge of the private builders into the London countryside.

The Brethren had a strong pacifist tradition that went back to their founders a century before, but it was by no means universal, and indeed they had included a number of military men and officers among their members. Despite the early Quaker influence, the pacifist tradition was not strong at Carlisle, and John Laing was not touched by it. Although he was approaching thirty-eight, the Carlisle Grammar School Memorial Register records that he was commissioned second lieutenant in the Cumberland Motor Volunteer Corps, a Territorial Army unit, in 1917: the venture could hardly have been expected to last long, in view of the national importance of the work in which his firm was by then engaged and of his own vital part in it, and as leader of a 'red badge' firm he was promptly discharged.

One unexpected result of the Gretna factory complex was to bring a further increase in the firm's workload. The arrival in an essentially country area of a vast, partly expatriate, workforce, often footloose, with money to burn and time to kill, was liable to produce problems under any conditions, and with Carlisle's inviting superfluity of licensed premises a few miles away drunkenness and its resultant disorder became an open scandal. To control the situation, the authorities took action that in peacetime, at that date, would have been impossible, and in 1916 the licensed trade throughout the Carlisle area was taken under public control under the authority of the Defence of the Realm Act (Liquor Regulations) of 1915. The Control Board, later the State Management Scheme, was to last for about half a century; numerous public houses in the district were closed; many others were altered radically, and local breweries were remodelled; a series of new state-managed inns was built. John Laing would have seen the scheme as a practical solution to a human problem that had concerned him for years, and the firm was extensively involved in the building of the new inns and the other work in connection with them. The work was of high priority, and 1917 saw a further large increase in the firm's workforce, which now numbered three to four thousand men.

The successful absorption of this sudden expansion, with an

extremely small administrative and supervisory team, was no mean achievement, and must have owed everything to the careful system of controls that John Laing with William Sirey and his chief managers had developed in the years before the war. The war years had brought to the business further members of the key management team on which later growth was to be built: T. Wardle, who joined in 1915; J. Lambert (1916) and W. M. Johnson (later to be a director of the parent company) in 1917. The war years had also seen the birth of John Laing's two sons: William Kirby in 1916 and John Maurice in 1918.

In 1918 came the beginning of national contracting on a major scale, with the securing of the contract for the construction of Crail Aerodrome in Fife, Scotland. The importance of the contract to the firm may be gathered from the fact that William Sirey was spared from Carlisle to act as agent. It employed three hundred tradesmen and a total workforce several times as large, and George Lowry remembered no less than a hundred horse-drawn vehicles used for hauling materials. The wartime urgency was indicated by a working week of over sixty hours, although even under those conditions the firm was not working on Sundays. Labour-recruiting posters advertised rates of 1s. 2¾d., plus bonuses worth another 3½d. per hour, for tradesmen, and of 10d. plus 3d. for labourers (approximately 7½p and 5½p respectively); by June 1918 the basic rates had been increased by a penny-farthing (½p) an hour, so that wages grossed over five pounds a week for tradesmen, often with subsistence payments in addition (£5 in 1918 was equivalent in spending power to £40 in 1977). The posters advertised a canteen on the site, with cooked food at one pound a week, and free lodging in huts, adding 'some small huts are provided where six or eight respectable companions may join and live together'. Lodgings in Crail (if preferred) could be had from twenty-eight to thirty shillings a week, and (the poster added) 'the place is a delightful seaside resort, dry and bracing'. These wages rates were typical: another old tradesman who started at Gretna in 1919 remembers being paid 1s. 6d. (7½p) an hour.

The Crail aerodrome work was followed by further Air Ministry contracts at Cramlington and Hylton in the north-eastern counties, both contracts involving the construction of vast hangars with enormous open spans, supported on timber trusses. The airfield contracts were a significant development, foreshadowing a long connection and long working experience with the Air Ministry, that was to be of great importance to

Laings as an undertaking and to the nation as a whole during the Second World War. John Laing built up through his work a relationship of great mutual respect with the successive heads of the Air Ministry. On one occasion he was discussing with General Biddulph, Director-General of the Ministry at the end of the First World War and after, the problems of one contract which was not going well. Biddulph felt that the Ministry's own resident engineer was at fault, and on John Laing's trying to defend the man replied, 'Don't say that, Laing; remember the old Chinese proverb that if a fish stinks it stinks at the head'–a lesson on the responsibility of leadership that John Laing took closely to heart. By a strange coincidence, too, the first Air Ministry contract had, like Gretna, brought him into the indirect influence of Lord Cowdray's leadership, for throughout 1917 and into 1918 Cowdray had been president of the Air Board (reconstituted as the Air Ministry on 3 January 1918).

But by now Laings were well launched as national contractors, and were undertaking work throughout the country. The one-time local Carlisle business, which less than ten years before had not achieved an annual turnover of £10,000, reached during 1920 a turnover of half a million pounds. By any standards it was an enormous transformation: a fifty-fold increase in money terms and, allowing for the First World War inflation in building costs, of fifteen times in terms of volume.

CHAPTER 5

Wider Horizons

'ONE DAY HE said to me, "You will see my name there; just 'Laing', not 'John Laing & Son'."' John Laing was standing with his cousin Stanley Laing on one of the building sites, and the builder's nameboard had caught his eye. 'He knew where he was going,' his cousin added. John Laing himself said at the end of his life, 'I wanted to be the top contractor in the country.'[1] For a youngish local builder in a small city in the remote north-west, it was a preposterous, not to say an impertinent, ambition. The country could number among its contractors men like Lord Cowdray, who had tamed mountains and defied oceans in distant continents. What motivated John Laing? Some men wish to succeed for personal enrichment, but he was to live modestly for his whole life, and to give away most of his gains. Others seek power, but outside his own business he was known for modesty and an unassuming presence. A clue to his psychology might perhaps be found in the urge that had driven him to mountain climbing as a young man: in his own words, 'just to face the most difficult one can accomplish and overcome.'[2] John Laing just had to succeed.

To men returning from the Forces, the contrast between the wooden hut they remembered in Milbourne Street and the smart new brick offices they now found in Dalston Road, on the site where the hutting works had been during the war, was startling; two young office staff, one being Clarence Payne, found no vacancies ('other people had stepped in, and we were unlucky'), but for craftsmen there was work and to spare.

The most significant growth followed immediately on the end of the war. During the war, the Carlisle post office, Vickers, Gretna, and the hutting work, had all set the firm on the road to expansion and had tested and consolidated its administration. Crail and the other airfields, and an Aberdeen War Department contract, took it a stage further towards national status as the war was ending. The business was poised for expansion or retrenchment, as John Laing might decide. He decided for expansion, and in a big way.

As he launched the business nationally, however, he did not forget his other interests. Within a period of a year, the business, his church and his home were moved to new premises (a characteristic combination in his thinking); the constitution of the firm was changed, and he began to give definite form to some of the ideas on training, workers' participation, and charitable giving, that he had been developing since the disastrous contract at Barrow. Meanwhile, he was looking for a location for the new headquarters of the national enterprise that was to be, and he was opening several branch offices. This year, which spanned 1919 and 1920, was to be a turning-point.

The business was installed in the new offices in Dalston Road, Carlisle, at the beginning of 1920 (premises which it has since steadily extended, and which are still the Carlisle Regional Headquarters); it was entirely in character that John Laing should have wished to see his church rehoused at the same time. Local churches tend to be conservative institutions, and to think long and hard over such radical changes. The Carlisle Brethren congregation had met in rented buildings for over half a century, and were now dividing their activities between two separate halls. In 1918 they had agreed, at John Laing's pressing, to buy two vacant shops in Botchergate, with a large empty building behind; one of the shops was therefore sold, and the other converted into an entrance hall, the hall itself being built in the reconstructed building at the back. The original hall adopted (possibly unconsciously) a feature which had been used in other meeting-places of Brethren in the distant days before their ubiquitous adoption of the 'gospel hall'; this was a lecture-hall-type floor, sloping down to a speaker's platform at the front. A large baptistery, a universal feature, was built into the floor, while the remodelled shop provided additional classroom space over the entrance. Hebron Hall, as the meeting-place was named, was opened with a month's evangelistic campaign. John Laing's firm had done the building work at cost. The local congregation had been kept regularly informed and consulted on developments, and the completed buildings were vested in trustees whose local representatives were John Laing, his cousin Thomas William Wood, David Beattie, and Walter Bell, an elder of the congregation who was a prominent local railway official. The premises were further extended (also by the Laing firm) some ten years later.

Settled in its new meeting-place, the congregation developed according to its own established traditions. One young visitor of those days recalls their close social links—'a tradition of inviting one another out to tea—always using the best china'. At one such tea-party in 1923 he remembers John Laing present with C. F. Hogg, a scholarly and gifted preacher who was a prominent leader of contemporary Brethren, and an exchange between them neatly illustrates the ambivalent attitude of Brethren teachers toward their own identity:

J. W. L. The word was not used in the sense in which a Plymouth Brother would understand it.
C. F. H. (eyebrows raised and eyes twinkling) And *who* are the Plymouth Brethren?
J. W. L. Well, I answer to it, anyway.*
C. F. H. I do not mind—so long as you don't include me.

The Brethren ideal of the Church had always deplored denominationalism, and the broader spirits among them refused to recognise their own or any other type of denominational Church as having any greater validity than any other; it is ironical that this refusal of a distinctive name ossified in some areas into a tradition blindly upheld by their more sectarian elements.

John Laing's rapidly expanding business involved his travelling throughout the country (often with only snatched sleep in the train), but his business activities in no way diminished his influence or his activity in his church life. For some time he headed a successful men's Bible class at Hebron Hall, and delighted to take the youths and young men on expeditions into his favourite Lake District fells, leading the way up the rocks with a boyish zest. A young relative who lived in his home remembered how the Laing and Beattie families would together take a picnic lunch on Sundays at Hebron Hall between the morning services and the afternoon activities, returning to their homes at the end of the afternoon to a Cumberland high tea before the evening service. She and her sister would be taken by John Laing at times when he went to preach in some of the village chapels, and she was impressed by the warmth of his welcome from the country folk.

An influential development among Christian Brethren at this time was the missionary study class movement. Their foreign

*In later life he strongly disliked the name, preferring 'Christian Brethren'.

missions work had always been a cardinal feature of their church life,* and during and after the First World War home support was encouraged by the formation of study classes in many of the churches, backed up by annual regional conferences. After the war John Laing and his friends started such a conference at Keswick, which ran for some years; at it he became friendly with many others of the more prominent and open-minded of the Brethren leaders: Arthur Rendle Short, later to be Professor of Surgery at Bristol and a prominent surgeon; George and Montague Goodman, London solicitors; and others. Another strong influence on his religious life at this time was Dr. Bishop of Wylam-on-Tyne, the country doctor 'dedicated to his work of medicine, and loved in his district', with 'a strong noble face . . . softened by the sudden amused smile', whom Anne Arnott describes in her book *The Brethren*.

In John Laing's life, Hebron Hall was as central as his business; his employees in Carlisle sometimes found themselves swept up into its activities, though themselves not associated with the congregation. One long-serving employee recounted how he was frequently pressed into service during his apprenticeship, perhaps to serve as door-boy at a wedding conducted by John Laing, or to distribute leaflets sometimes as far as twenty miles away. Somehow, if you worked for John Laing, you accepted such tasks in your leisure time and only years afterwards wondered how he had persuaded you. This man remembers how John Laing would order quantities of sausages from a Cumbrian firm he favoured, carefully dividing them out among local families he wished to help, the distribution nicely calculated according to the recipients' needs, and the apprentices again being called in to assist. 'When I started in 1921 you did every type of job—anything that was going, inside and outside.'

In 1920 John Laing also bought and moved to a larger residence, Fairholme on the Brampton Road in Carlisle. This was on the higher ground north of the river, in the residential suburb of Stanwix, favoured by many of Carlisle's more prominent

*Many Christian Brethren missionaries work independently, and are partly supported through a central office in Bath, which in 1976 listed 565 personnel from the U.K. on its prayer list. In addition, there is a substantial number associated with inter-denominational societies. This compares with a total U.K. Protestant missionary force of 5,862 in 1976. Of these, the personnel of the U.S.P.G. numbered 428, C.M.S. 358 and the Methodist Overseas Division 270 (*U.K. Protestant Missions Handbook*, Vol. 1, 1977, Evangelical Missionary Alliance, pp. 76, 78—adjusted for revised number of Brethren missionaries).

citizens, and it was a comfortable, roomy but unpretentious family home.

Behind part of the great expansion after the First World War there is a story which was to develop even more significantly after the Second. John Laing had foreseen the probable shortage of skilled bricklayers that would develop in the urgent post-war need for housing, and had for some years been giving thought to alternative means of housing construction: in the result he was to develop one of Britain's first major methods of system building, patented after the First World War under the name of Easiform (a name indicative of a flair for marketing publicity that was to make his name nationally known during the private-housing boom of the 1930s).

The use of concrete in actual house construction, as distinct from foundations, had never been extensive, although the material itself had been known since Roman times, and had given to Roman architecture a versatility, in features such as the dome, that earlier builders had not enjoyed. Concrete requires careful handling and understanding, if full advantage is to be gained from the qualities of low thermal conductivity and resistance to moisture penetration that it can afford, and if its serious potential disadvantages of cracking and chemical disintegration are to be avoided. For these practical, as well as aesthetic reasons, concrete has never displaced the versatile and simple brick in general house construction. Brickwork, however, has one serious disadvantage in times of labour shortage; it requires skilled men, who are scarce, to lay it. It can also be expensive, although the saving in cost often claimed for concrete can prove illusory.

John Laing, as we have already seen, had been involved in developing a prefabricated wooden building (later externally concrete-rendered on site), in the inhospitable climate of northern Iceland, as long before as 1912. It had been an interesting venture, in connection with some energetic Brethren missionary activity at Isafjördhur. The site of the mission building had been given by a trust that had been founded by C. A. Aitchison, member of a prominent Edinburgh bakery family, who had been a generous supporter of evangelistic work until his death in 1900; the cost of materials and other expenditure was met by Huntingdon Stone, while the labour and design work was donated by John Laing, working in collaboration with an Icelandic architect. The building was thus a unique collaboration between three successive generations of the great benefactors of

Brethren missionary work. From the outside it looked like a large, plain two-storey house, the ground floor providing an extensive meeting-hall, with living accommodation on the floor above. In 1917 it was taken over from the Brethren congregation by the Mission to Deep Sea Fishermen. The building had been made by John Laing in Carlisle and shipped to Iceland; today it remains in first-class order and is used as a community centre.

The venture was an indication of John Laing's interest in experimental building work; he went on to develop his own system of *in situ* concrete housing construction to such an extent that, when the war ended, he was well prepared for the housing emergency with the first version of the Easiform house. This early version had single-leaf walls in eight-inch 'no fines' clinker concrete; a contemporary manual suggests that four- to six-inch walls were in common use, and the extra inches would have been deliberately calculated.[3] The solid walls were, however, contrary to the tradition of cavity-wall construction that John Laing imbibed from his Cumbrian training, and he soon developed a cavity wall,* with an outer leaf of three-inch gravel concrete, lightly reinforced to prevent cracking, and an inner leaf of three-inch clinker concrete with good insulation properties.[4] Precision-made steel shuttering was later substituted for the original timber formwork.

Easiform was an immediate success. By using a standard system of 'climbing shuttering' that could be filled with concrete by unskilled workers, it was ideal for large-scale house construction; it gave employment where unskilled men were out of work; and it made little demand on scarce bricklayers. The houses themselves were of orthodox construction in their roofing and other features, and (when the external rendering was finished) were virtually indistinguishable from rendered brick houses.

John Laing had judged his market with precision. Extensive contracts for Easiform housing were in progress by 1920 in South Wales (at Pyle near Bridgend, and at Port Talbot, the latter in connection with the new steel works) and were quickly followed by similar contracts for local authorities at Hereford, at Wrexham

*This cavity wall in such concrete houses was an unusual feature, although commoner in houses built from concrete blocks or prefabricated slabs; as late as 1943, when the Burt Committee reported, it listed only one other example in an *in situ* concrete house intended for widespread production, although the architect Louis de Soissons had used it in a large private residence at Welwyn· Garden City in 1920.[5]

in North Wales, and (in 1924 and later) in Exeter, Gosport and London, and for the Great Western Railway Company at Plymouth. The City Surveyor of Hereford wrote to the Laing Company on 15 April, 1924, congratulating them on their 'organisation, to which is added the careful and personal supervision of your principals'. 'The works themselves,' he added, 'were carried out expeditiously, and every care was shown in the matter of detail, the workmanship being excellent and the materials were of first-class quality.' At Exeter the local press reported criticism by a local councillor, who objected to concrete construction; the City Architect repudiated the criticisms and a further contract was awarded. The Gosport Borough Engineer wrote to *The Times* to praise the new system, stressing the cavity walls and the roofs of tiles over felt; 122 houses, he reported, had cost £54,000 under the system.

This average cost of £443 a house (£428 for a non-parlour type) was an important feature in contemporary national terms. The Housing and Town Planning Act of 1919 had for the first time placed responsibility (as distinct from mere enabling powers) for supplying low-rent housing on the shoulders of local authorities, in an attempt to meet the desperate national shortage of homes in the lower income ranges (estimated at from 600,000 to 800,000 units), and obligatory standards of construction were imposed. As a result, building costs soared, and councils (underwritten by the Exchequer, without limit, until 1921) had been known to pay, in 1920 to 1922, over £1,000 each for tiny cottages. (The Ministry of Health reported a fall in the cost of a standard three-bedroom house without parlour from £930 in August 1920 to £436 in March 1922.)[6]

By 1924 the Laing Company could advertise that 'There are many dangers in any new form of construction, and these can only be provided against as the result of actual experience. Having now carried out a large number of concrete houses which have proved satisfactory in every way, we have patented our Easiform Construction.' The advertisement claimed that the houses were as warm, dry and substantial as brick houses, and that they did not necessitate a stereotyped design. Even *The Times of India* of 18 July, 1924 carried a description of the Easiform system developed by John Laing & Son of Carlisle, and the Company showed one of the houses in the Palace of Housing at the 1924–5 Wembley British Empire Exhibition. One of the largest Easiform estates of this period was at Eltham in south-east London, where the Borough of Woolwich had 862 houses built.

(The relative importance of this estate can be judged from the fact that Woolwich, the metropolitan borough which built more flats and cottages than any other between 1919 and 1938, built in total just under 4,500 dwellings during the whole of that twenty years.) As the labour situation improved and bricklayers became available, the system was less used by local authorities, but it was constantly refined and, twenty years later, in the post-Second World War housing drive, was to make an enormous contribution to national needs.

Although Easiform contributed significantly to the expansion of the business after the First World War, it was only a part of it. Other contracts (industrial and government, and for traditional brick local-authority housing) were in progress in 1919–20 in Cumberland, in several places in Scotland, and in Yorkshire, Lancashire and Northumberland. But the major developments at this time were in Wales, where much Easiform construction was under way, and branch offices were opened for a time in Cardiff and Wrexham, and by 1924 in Liverpool. The most important long-term event was the opening of an office in London in 1920. In charge of this office was John Laing's brother-in-law, Henry Chapman Harland, a surveyor who had been land agent to Viscount Furness, had served in the Royal Engineers during the war, and had subsequently been engaged on the construction of the Welland Ship Canal in the Canadian Great Lakes.

Turnover of the business reached half a million pounds in 1920, and although it fell back in money terms in the next three years, probably reflecting the substantial fall in building costs in that period, it approached three-quarters of a million pounds in 1924,* a figure which is equivalent to 1977 building work of almost ten million pounds. The growth in actual activity between 1920 and 1924 was probably considerably greater than these figures imply, because the index of building costs fell by more than a third during the period. John Laing had successfully broken through the first major traditional barrier to expansion.

The breakthrough was achieved by building an excellent site-management team on which he could rely implicitly. The very large Easiform contracts in South Wales were entrusted to George Lowry as contracts manager, with John Lambert as senior general foreman. Lambert was later in charge at Hereford, and devised many of the technical refinements of the Easiform

*Turnover figures take account of end-of-the-year work-in-progress variations.

system. These men, and others such as W. M. Johnson and T. Wardle who were already senior 'outside' men, were the foundation of the business for many years. J. M. Harper, later chief buyer and head of Contracts Department, joined in 1920. Two other men, who joined the business from Kilmarnock in Scotland immediately after the war and became key figures in the office administration, were John McKay, an old-fashioned painstaking accountant, who joined as a cashier at Crail, and Andrew Anderson, later to be secretary of the Company for over thirty years and eventually a director, who arrived in Carlisle in October 1919. Both were members of the Brethren congregation, and Anderson in particular was to be one of John Laing's closest confidants and supporters for half a century.

John Laing had been able to take a holiday in France and Belgium with David Beattie in 1919. The two friends had visited many of the World War battlefields, and Beattie's daughter recalls how 'my father said John Laing could get in anywhere—he himself just followed on. You just did not know where he would go next.' An insatiable curiosity for life, extended especially to anything connected with his own industry, combined in him with a formidable ability to charm or bluff his way into any place he wished to go.

The limited company, John Laing & Son Limited, had been incorporated on 21 December, 1920, and the first directors appointed after John Laing were William Sirey and John Hughes of Wrexham; Sirey was also the secretary. Through Hughes, the Company had expanded for a time into North Wales, opening the Wrexham, later to become the Liverpool, office. A notable contract (though not the largest) in North Wales at this time was at the little cathedral city of Bangor on the Menai Straits, where in 1923 to 1925 the Company built the new science block for the University College of North Wales, and an extension to the local hospital, as well as the city's impressive war memorial—work totalling some £120,000 (a million and a half pounds in 1977 terms). There had been trouble with water in the foundations at the science block, a reminder of old worries, but a problem that the contemporary business could take unconcernedly in its stride (a provision for a loss was made in the accounts for 1925).

The Liverpool experiment was not long-lasting, and when Hughes left after a few years the office there closed. Its opening had coincided with a period of considerable unrest in the building industry (over three million working days were lost in disputes in 1924), and John Laing had not taken kindly to the atmosphere he had encountered on Merseyside which was very different from the settled and familiar Carlisle relationship. Stanley Laing was in charge of some of the men there.

> I remember I had some fellows working for me and a load came in and I asked them to unload it and they said 'a penny an hour for doing it'. So I said, 'All right; you can have your penny an hour', and I stood with my watch in my hand and timed them and when they finished they got a halfpenny each and I said, 'You've had your penny an hour.' I had no trouble after that.

It was a different world from Carlisle, where the apprentices would give up their own time to run errands! Wallace Haughan (many years later head of Canadian operations and a director of the parent Company, and considered by John Laing as 'the best manager and business man I have ever known', with 'that wonderful ability of treating everybody as his equal and nobody as his superior') joined him in Carlisle in 1920. In 1922 Haughan was working on some small farm-steadings that the Company was building near Gretna Green for men returning from the war, and they were given paid time-off on Saturday mornings to compensate for the additional travelling time.

> I remember standing looking into what was then Robinson's shop window in English Street, Carlisle, one Saturday morning, when someone patted me on the back: it was Sir John, who asked me what I was doing looking in a shop window on a Saturday morning. I explained to him I was working at Gretna, and owing to the long daily hours we were given Saturday morning off. He looked at me with his famous grin and said, 'Oh, Wallace, this cannot be much fun for you, just slip up to the yard and help the masons to dress stone–I know you will enjoy that!'

Wallace Haughan was one of the few men who could quarrel with John Laing. He remembered how his employer would then say to him, 'Wallace, you can go; I never want to see you again.' 'But I would come back as though nothing had happened, and nothing more was said.'

Andrew Anderson had arrived in Carlisle in 1919, while the offices were still in Milbourne Street. He had been persuaded, a little unwillingly, to join the firm from his employment in

Scotland. 'My heart sank to my boots when I saw the office I was coming to; a ramshackle place in a builders' yard with a comparatively small office . . . the place was so congested that Mr. Laing had to use the room where Mr. Sirey was and which Mr. Wardle used.' But the new offices in Dalston Road were already under construction, and in a few months the staff had moved there, the surveyors and architects taking occupation first. The expansion took place with an incredibly small administrative staff; the industry at that time was intensely competitive, and the Company was tendering hard, its country-wide expansion being based partly on its unique product in Easiform, but (for other types of work) entirely on the precision of the tendering system that had been built up. At times all the staff would be called in to help the estimating department, and they would be in the office until one or two in the morning.

For the men on the sites, pressure was not so intense. An apprentice joiner who started in 1924 found a happy shop, but little overtime on a forty-four-hour week; yet jobs generally were difficult to find (there was fifteen per cent unemployment in the building industry), and Laings always had work. The joinery works was in Shaddongate near the Company's offices. 'There were houses in the front (they've all been knocked down since) and in the end house where our entrance was there was an old lady and she used to make our tea at dinner time. I would fetch it. We used to keep her in firewood the whole year round. Most of the men were regular employees.'

When another employee joined the office staff in 1920 he found a total administrative staff of about a dozen, with four surveyors (soon increased to eight); quite half of them were to spend their whole working lives with the Company, and to rise with it. By 1924 there were about thirty office staff. Even in Dalston Road the accommodation in the new building was spartan by modern standards. The office boys occupied a small room that served as the postal sorting-office, and John Laing himself had a separate office communicating with a larger one occupied by William Sirey and two others. In the large general office, all worked on big high desks and stools and there were glass panels on each side of the corridor. From these premises and with such a staff, incredibly, during the years to 1926, they tendered for and won the great countrywide Easiform contracts, in addition to a wide variety of other contracts. In Scotland they were still building at Grange-mouth and in north Dumfriesshire long after the more distant work at Crail and Aberdeen had finished; in England there were substantial traditional local authority and industrial housing schemes in the Cumberland coastal towns and in Penrith; at Penistone in Yorkshire and at Shrewsbury; at Darlington, for the North Eastern Railway Company; at Gosforth and Knaresborough; and in Tyneside. At Rossall School they built the memorial chapel, under Sir Robert Lorimer, the celebrated Scottish architect, and a new house for the headmaster. There was work for banks in several towns and for government and service departments at Hucknall in Nottinghamshire, at Newcastle-upon-Tyne, at Grantham and Wittering in Lincolnshire, all in addition to the full programmes of work in Wales and in the London area that were supervised from Liverpool and London. Over a period of seven years, John Laing won contracts from Plymouth to Aberdeen, from Anglesey to Brighton.

In Carlisle the Company went from strength to strength. A new brickworks was opened in 1921 at Blackwell to meet the post-war shortages. There was still work at the familiar Garlands Hospital and the electricity works, with extensions to the gas works and other public utilities. There was a full programme of local-authority housing, further work for the Central Board for the nationalised licensed trade, and private factories, churches and stores. The work in the Company's home area during this period was crowned by contracts awarded in 1924 and 1925 for the rebuilding of the St. Nicholas Bridge, a thousand-foot-long bridge with approaches, distinguished by its masonry, that spanned several different railway routes converging or crossing from different directions; the work had to be completed with the minimum disturbance to the heavy railway traffic through this important centre on one of the country's chief traffic arteries. The bridge was opened on 15 March, 1928.

The outstanding work of this period, however, was a series of successive contracts from 1923 to 1925 at the great army camp at Catterick in North Yorkshire. Totalling some £450,000 (in 1977 terms approaching six million pounds), this work alone represented in money terms more than the equivalent of the Company's whole average annual turnover in the four years from 1920 to 1923. With its own hospital and resident medical officer, two picture halls, and a recreation room, all provided for the contract employees, the contract's organisation was a remarkable feat for the still scanty administration, and it is hardly surprising that an employee who remembers the contract recalls that 'practically everybody in the firm was at Catterick'. W. M. Johnson was agent, with John Lambert general foreman. One man, then a trainee, remembers his own introduction to the job, typical of his employer's style:

> One Friday night he came to me and said, 'Oh, John, I want you to go to Catterick Camp.' We were just starting Catterick Camp in those days, covering in the old wooden offices with brickwork and building new sergeants' messes and so on . . . I said 'When?' and he said 'right away!' Next morning, Saturday, I turned up at the office, thinking to go to Catterick for Monday morning, and he came and said to me, 'Are you still here? I thought I told you to go to Catterick!' . . . I don't know whether he was joking or not.

The London connection was also expanding quickly during those years and had won some notable work: but that is a story for a later chapter.

What sort of man was John Laing in those days? He was in his forties, at his peak of vigour, and the summary of his church and business activities (for not a contract escaped his attention) is an eloquent witness to part of his character. But to understand him more fully and personally, we need to look at the broader background of his times, and at his reaction to them.

CHAPTER 6

Study of a Character

A T THE END of the First World War the construction industry was, in general, backward in technology and in its working conditions somewhere between poor and appalling. The Industrial Revolution had scarcely touched its methods. 'All concrete was mixed by hand,' writes Wallace Haughan; 'all materials were hoisted on a jenny-wheel, hand-operated crane, or carried by hod; all bricks were carted by horse and cart, and bricklayers' mortar was made in a roller pan, generally at a depot and carted by horse and cart to the various sites.'

Primitive concrete mixers had in fact first appeared as early as 1880, and excavators by 1900, but they were little used. The Laing business had bought a concrete mixer in 1913, and a steam-operated crane had been used for a time on the Barrow sewers, but these were isolated instances and it was not until the middle 1930s that mechanical plant began to come into general use.

Working conditions in the industry generally were atrocious. Very little provision was made to alleviate the harsh conditions when the weather turned sour, and feeding facilities on the sites were often confined to the brazier. There were no paid holidays, although in Carlisle there was an annual traditional unpaid holiday for race week, and apprentices were paid for their week's holiday. Employment could be terminated at one hour's notice for a labourer and two for a tradesman. If time was lost through rain or frost, pay was lost as well. The fifty-four-hour week (five days of ten hours, starting at six, and four hours on Saturday) was still common, although soon reduced to forty-four hours' basic time, with an extra two and a half hours in the summer. Wages in 1920 ranged from 1s. 1½d. to 1s. 6d. an hour, for labourers and tradesmen respectively, increasing by 1924 to 1s. 3d. to 1s. 8d. per hour. The increase was not a steady one, and national arbitration awards in 1923 actually reduced wages (the cost of living fell by thirty per cent from 1920 to 1923 and then levelled for a year or two, before continuing to decline more slowly). In some areas, such as public works in London, wages might be slightly higher than this, but in general a man would in 1924 take home for his basic forty-four-hour week (assuming no wet weather or other stoppages) about fifty-five shillings if he was a labourer and seventy-three shillings if he was a trades-man—equivalent in terms of the mid-1977 cost of living to a little over £25 and £33 respectively.[1]

The years to 1924 saw a good deal of unrest in the industry, with strikes and lock-outs. In 1924 this unrest culminated in the loss of over three million working days in disputes, with more than an eighth of the industry's workforce affected.[2] After that year, however, the contracting industry settled down to relative peace, despite the General Strike of 1926, until the Second World War, but unemployment was to rise from fifteen per cent in 1924 to over forty per cent (in public works contracting) in the mid-1930s.*[3]

All men are in measure trapped by the ethos and atmosphere within which they have to work, and John Laing was no exception. His was a 'hire and fire' industry of ruthless competition, where the weakest went to the wall. It was often so on the level of personal relationships: it was not for nothing that he had always cultivated physical fitness, nor that he had been a regular attender at boxing lessons in his youth, encouraged by his father, even if some of the local Brethren congregation were doubtful of the propriety of his recreations! Had not the chief Sunday sport of the navvies at Uldale (when their drink had worn off) been their impromptu fist-fights in the fields? Could their leader be a weakling? But what was true at the crude level was inexorably so at the economic. The ambient ruthlessness could not leave him unscathed, but, unlike many, he knew it (as his Barrow resolution had shown), and there were other and contrary influences at work on him.

If we stress the influence on John Laing of his religious environment, it is simply because religion was immensely upon him. He would not have liked that expression, but would have explained his faith in terms of a personal relationship with Christ, and it is precisely that understanding that is crucial. Life among the Brethren was lived in perpetual religious awareness: if some found it suffocating, those who successfully adjusted found that their actions and motives had a constant point of reference outside themselves and contemporary manners. This point of

*The building sector was less badly affected because of the extensive private housebuilding activity in the 1930s.

reference might vary, depending partly on the bias of the influences they encountered in their churches, and partly on their own character and comprehension. It might be legalistically founded in undue biblical literalism, or in the customs of their own sub-culture (there were many such individuals to be found), but in the best of them it was fixed by the constant direction of their worship towards the person of Christ, in their perception of the character of Jesus. They would not claim any achievement in reaching that standard, but the point of reference was there. It is just this feature that explains why John Laing in his later years would speak to his employees of 'a very valuable thing in my life—quite early in life I took the step of accepting the Lord Jesus as my Saviour and Master.'[4]

His mother's influence in this respect was paramount. She was an extremely strong character (one of her granddaughters described her as 'the chief influence on my childhood', although she lived a hundred miles away), and her strict religious fervour might well have been counter-productive, had it not been for the quiet balance of his father, a man who knew and understood the ordinary working man and his ways. Both parents practised a careful frugality, the result of necessity in their earlier married life, and this was passed on to their son. The father, too, passed on a care for high standards of workmanship and service; in his last years, when he was long retired, he would still visit sites regularly and (perfectionist that he was) sometimes order perfectly sound work to be taken down. When his judgment grew less sure, the foremen had to be instructed to listen with respect, but to use their discretion as to whether action was to be taken!

In his own family, John Laing enjoyed an ideal foundation for his strenuous life. Those years could not have been easy for his wife, but Beatrice Laing, a retiring but strong character, was a perfect foil for him, and provided him with a stable emotional and domestic background free of anxiety or strain. He learned to rely on her quiet wisdom. The two sons grew naturally into the environment of their father's business and way of life, and many of the older Carlisle employees have memories of them as small boys, perhaps escorting them back to their home after a visit to the offices and yard, Kirby quiet and reserved, Maurice full of questions as to *why* a chimney was being demolished in that particular way, *why* this, and *why* the other. One man saw a car travelling the Brampton Road draw to a painful halt outside Fairholme. Two pairs of eyes watched a driver delving beneath the bonnet. *'My* daddy would make that car go!' 'Oh, would he?' responded an irritated driver, 'and *what* would your daddy do?' 'He would put petrol in it!' Another remembers to this day the look of sheer happiness on John Laing's face as he pedalled a bicycle down the sea front at Silloth, the two boys precariously perched on the crossbar.

His church life, in one of the most informal of ecclesiastical structures, where every man was entitled to be heard and any man or woman could turn a hand to some job in the church, encouraged a strong sense of the importance and value of each individual, and of mutual inter-dependence. Protestant 'serious-ness' was there in earnest, but hierarchial authority was virtually absent. Woven by his religion into the emotional fabric of his life, like the sense of obligation to the higher 'reference point', this instinct of the importance of the individual could only have been reinforced by the long years of his sharing, as a young man, in the work and hardships of the men on the construction sites.

These considerations make it difficult to fit John Laing convincingly into the stereotype of the Protestant capitalist that has been popularly derived from the profound studies of Weber and Tawney. So much of Weber's *The Protestant Ethic and the Spirit of Capitalism* seems uncannily apposite, yet it breaks down utterly when Weber refers to the 'formalistic, hard, correct character' of 'the Puritan middle class'.[5] John Laing may have been one of those 'thinking, sober men', who 'believe that labour and industry is their duty towards God';[6] but, despite the ruthlessness which his trade bred, and which he could some-times show, one cannot see in him Weber's 'bourgeois business man', who, possessing 'the consciousness of standing in the fullness of God's grace and being visibly blessed by Him . . . as long as he remained within the bounds of formal correctness, as long as his moral conduct was spotless and the use to which he put his wealth was not objectionable, could follow his pecuniary interests as he would and feel that he was fulfilling a duty in doing so.'[7]

In many respects, Laing's was a reversion to what Tawney saw as the pre-capitalist social ethic. We can well imagine him joining with the Tudor divines to denounce the idea[8]

that the individual is absolute master of his own, and, within the limits set by positive law, may exploit it with a single eye to his pecuniary advantage, unrestrained by any obligation to postpone his own profit to the well-being of his neighbours, or to give account of his activities to a higher authority . . . in short, the theory of property which was later to be accepted by all civilised communities.

So far as technical matters were concerned, John Laing was from the first enquiring and innovative; but if this had been his only trait, he might have fulfilled Weber's stereotype. If he was at first slow in adopting mechanisation, it was (ironically) because of the earliest of his major innovations, his detailed work-study system. Before he adopted new machinery, it must justify itself in terms of his costing system, and he was also acutely conscious of the effect of mechanisation on employment.

The tendering and costing system that he developed became probably the finest of its time in the industry, and it was backed by a first-class control of labour productivity and the use of materials. Far ahead of most of the industry, he realised that the keys to sound contract financing were accuracy of estimating and labour productivity; he was not strong on materials costing, relying, as the business grew, on trustworthy buyers and a rigid system of stock control at the sites and yards. Like so many entrepreneurs, he did not fully understand the accounting function as such, but by the time when the business developed to such a size that this became vital, he had staff qualified and able to introduce this final integration of his system with over-all financial controls. In 1924 a pupil starting with the Company would find, in the words of one of the earliest articled pupils, that

> Costing was priority number one. Whatever you did, you did costing right from the start . . . you had to see what the bricklayers and joiners had done and measure up every day and take it to the office . . . Mr. Laing had his little book and he did not give us the standards; the figures went in to him and if they were not good enough he would come back and tell us . . . he used to do it himself then. In London things were bigger and it grew up from there.

Just how advanced were his ideas in this field may be gained from a comment in the *Works and Buildings* volume of the *U.K. Civil History of the Second World War*, published in 1952. In the section dealing with post-Second World War housing, this official history states: [9]

87

The great and varying changes in the prices of building materials, components and labour during the war led the Ministry of Works into a new and significant field of investigation, namely, costing systems applied to the process of house-building while the houses were in course of erection. This was a method so far unknown in Great Britain. The processes of traditional house-building were split up into a series of separate operations for which the expenditure in man hours, materials and money could be measured continuously.

But John Laing had been using the elements of such a system for forty years* (the Ministry scheme was in fact largely developed from his) and he had pioneered the use of quantity surveyors in the industry for this purpose.

During the First World War he had proved the effectiveness of his scheme in competition with other contractors, both at Gretna and Crail, and had gained absolute confidence in putting forward tenders based on his standards. It is said that one of his first tenders for a substantial contract in those days had so surprised the government department concerned that he had been warned that he would certainly lose money, and was given the opportunity to withdraw. He confidently refused, and carried out the work at a profit. The result and effectiveness of his confidence was made apparent by the expansion of the 1920s.

He said in 1948:[10]

> 'Our costing team has taken years to build up, from that start I made when I did it all myself. When we decide a man is fit to be a tenderer, we train him first on costing, then on management, then on bills of quantities as a quantity surveyor. Our tendering men serve about a ten years' articles† before they can become what we call tenderers. It's a hard, long, and difficult job.'

The technical ingenuity which developed the Easiform system of house building has already been fully described. Another development of the same period was a reinforced concrete suspended flooring method christened Ferrobrick. This led to several contracts in the 1920s. A further innovation of those years

*See pp. 107f. below.

†In fact, five years' articles and five years' subsequent training.

was also well ahead of general developments in the industry. A Ministry of Labour Committee on Apprenticeship and Training reported in 1926; at that time about three-quarters of the workers in the industry under twenty-one were trainees (chiefly in craft apprenticeships), but only twenty-nine per cent of these were under written indentures. Six years before that report, John Laing had already been considering placing beside the traditional craft apprenticeships a form of indentured training for contract management for grammar- and public-school entrants to the industry: the builder's pupil. He insisted on educational standards similar to those for entry to the business professions, and it was 1924 before the first official entrants to the scheme were enrolled; he had in the meantime taken on others in what amounted to a trial run of the scheme, ensuring that the pupils went through all the trades, and insisting on attendance at night school, carefully inspecting their reports. The early pupil already quoted succinctly described its early days. 'You were indentured as a builder's assistant—expected to do anything you were told.' The scheme was to be developed enormously over the years, and has remained an industry leader; later it was to incorporate training for professional qualifications, and a later director of the Company, John Gregg (who joined the Company in 1924, the year the scheme started) was an early member and president of the Institute of Quantity Surveyors.

A most interesting feature of the pupils' scheme was its effect on the development of the business; John Laing was building solidly for the future when he inaugurated it. Between 1924 and 1938 fifty-eight carefully selected pupils were enrolled. In 1953, thirty-five were still serving with the Company, virtually all in senior management positions: four of the fifty-eight (and one of the pre-entrants) reached the Board of Directors of the parent Company after the Second World War, and several others were directors of other group companies, or divisional directors. John Laing's own sons were to go through a similar, but accelerated, training. The scheme helped to pioneer the change from self-made industrial leadership to professionally-trained management.

John Laing and his Company were beginning to make their voice heard in the industry and had had trading contacts with other growing concerns, such as Mowlems and Trollope & Colls. He himself became a Fellow of the Institute of Builders in 1922. In the same year, John Hughes, writing as a director of John Laing & Son Limited, contributed an article to the *Builder* of 19 May, 1922 on 'The Housing Shortage, and Suggestions for its Solution'. The Government of the day had become alarmed at the expense to the exchequer of the unlimited subsidies to local councils under the Housing Act of 1919, and in June 1921 had limited the number of houses to be subsidised to little more than had by then been built.[11] At the same time subsidies to private housing under the Housing (Additional Powers) Act were suspended (both were restored, in a controlled form, in 1924 and 1923 respectively, and housing was to be a political shuttlecock for the next ten years). Hughes protested at 'the Government's decision to cry "Halt!" on the local authority housing schemes throughout the country, and also to withdraw the subsidy to private builders', and drew attention to the unemployment in the industry, which that February had reached 204,244 among navvies alone–22.5 per cent. He went on to argue the economics of local-authority housing, the cost of social services to the unemployed, and the human costs of housing shortage, and to put forward his own suggestions.

John Laing followed up this article by a letter to *The Times*, published under 'Points from Letters' in the issue of 13 February, 1924, under the heading 'Continuity in Building'. He stressed the importance to the stability of the industry of the proper planning of government works. After the experience of a further half century, we might well conclude that both pleas (and many like them since, from many sources) fell on deaf or disabled ears.

What of his personal relationships within his business? They were colourful days, spent among men who for a large part had seen the privations and inhumanities of the trenches or of the naval war; they had returned to a land promised to be 'fit for heroes', and many of them had encountered unemployment, poor housing and poverty. At a housing contract in Egremont, two V.C.s were among the workforce: W. M. Johnson was in charge there, and at the job was C. B. Hancock (twenty years later to be the commanding officer of the 'Laing Company' Royal Engineers in the Second World War), who in 1948 recalled one of the 'characters' on the site:[12]

I shall never forget Dan Chalmers, the 'Human Saw'. I can see him now, stripped to the waist, cutting rafters for roofs as hard as he could go all day long, and he always had two or three bottles of milk by him. He was out on his own all right, was Dan, for he was paid direct from Carlisle, unlike the rest of us, and we envied him his independent status.

There were scenes at nearby Whitehaven during the miners' strike a year or two later that could have been ugly. The redoubtable Joe Boothman was in charge of a contract at the Midland Bank, and a mob was tearing up cobblestones and hurling them through shop windows; he posted his men on the scaffolding, with every available missile to hand, and faced the crowd with dire warning of the consequences if any laid a finger on his work. Happily, there were no challengers.

The tendency of the costing and work-study systems, with their emphasis on target production and efficiency, could have been to reduce the operatives to no more than production units. It was here, and in the ruthlessness of the industry, that the crucial clash would occur with the other idealistic influences in John Laing's personality.

I must start by saying that when I look back over the fifty-seven years I have known Sir John [writes Wallace Haughan] and in the light of my own experience in the industry, I feel he was truly a Master Builder, and, even now, I feel it must be extremely difficult for anyone to realise the strength of this man's character, which very often gave the impression that he was a very hard man—and up to a point he was tough, but coupled with a fairness equally as strong.

The first thing to strike an employee was the extent of John Laing's knowledge of him. 'He knew everybody by name,' says one who knew him well at this time, 'all their pedigrees, their families and everything. When the firm grew bigger he had a list made out for him.' 'He knew everything about you,' says another. 'The only time I ever applied for a rise in my life, before I knew where I was he had all my money allocated out. "You're courting, aren't you? When I was your age I was courting and I used to put so much aside and give so much to my mother." He had it all worked out. Eventually he gave me about 7s. 6d. rise. He said to me, "Is your sister still teaching at such and such a school?"—my sister had only moved to that school about six months before!' And another: 'Sir John himself was a proper gentleman . . . there was an old labourer, he could neither read nor write. They called him John Wallis. He used to put the billy on the fire (there was no canteen in those days). Sir John would come—"is it cold, John, yet?" and would drink the tea with him.'

Yet he could be tough, and ruthless too. 'You had to be worth your salt to stay—there were many sackings in those days,' said an employee who joined in 1919; and an old bricklayer—'If he did not get good men, he would sack them. But you could not afford to be careless in those days.' One man, who spent his working life at the Blackwell brickworks, remembers how, after John Laing had moved to London, the men would at times arrive to find him at the works at 7.00 a.m.: he would have travelled up by the night train and walked out from Carlisle station. 'In those days, you always had to work for your money, or you'd had it.' There was a story, current in the firm when this man joined, of a man standing by a brazier just before starting-time at a Carlisle electric power station contract a few years before. It was a cold morning, and John Laing also arrived and stood by the brazier. The starting signal was given, but the man did not move. John Laing waited silently for a few minutes, then, 'What is your number?' The man told him. 'Then get your cards—you're fired.'

Yet, immediately after that story, the same worker went on to tell of another occasion when John Laing came on an employee winding one of the hand-operated cranes. 'You are not looking well—what is the trouble?' 'My wife has been in bed for some time and I have had to see to the children and do all the work before starting work at seven.' John Laing asked where he lived, and was absent for an hour or two. A little later he returned. 'You are needed at home; take two weeks off with pay.' When the man reached home, he found that John Laing had called, found things as he had been told, and had gone, leaving five pounds on the table. There were many stories of similar incidents. After Sir John Laing's death, another old Carlisle man wrote, 'He was visiting the building site on Dunmail Drive. He came to me and asked how many children I had. I told him. He said I must be having a hard time. He said when I finished work there would be a letter for me. To my great surprise there was ten pounds. He told me in the note he left to get something for the children. And believe me, ten pounds was a fortune in those days.' 'Wherever I went,' said another Carlisle man who joined a few years later, 'I met people who spoke of good things John Laing had done for them.' 'A very straight man,' said a site agent who had started work as a bricklayer-apprentice in 1924; 'he expected a full day's work, but if you did your full day there was nothing more said. He was a human man; and those who came up under him.'

To those who served well, John Laing was intensely loyal; the men knew this and respected his absolute integrity. He knew their limitations as men, and what could be expected of them.

'He expected commitment rather than loyalty,' was the comment of one man who had worked his way up the business to the top, 'but he gave loyalty in return.' 'You worked hard, because you knew you were appreciated,' said another. Occasionally, there were amusing incidents, which he would have savoured, such as the time when he found a new trainee at Carlisle whom he had not seen before, working enthusiastically. He went up to the boy. 'You're working very hard.' 'Yes,' came the reply, 'we've got to, John Willie's coming round!'

As the years went by, this loyalty expressed itself in many improvements in terms and conditions of employment. Payment for time lost by wet weather was introduced well ahead of the industry generally.* He later began working on different forms of bonus to reward efficient work. Traditional Christmas gifts or bonuses had been given in one form or other for many years, accompanied by a rule that no man was to be paid off, for any reason, in the week or two before Christmas; on one occasion when work was slack the apprentices even received an unheard of additional ten days' paid holiday. Surviving records show that productivity bonuses were being paid at some mid-1920s Easiform contracts; these bonuses were to be elaborated and improved as the years went by. Later came a savings scheme and the holiday-with-pay and pension scheme to be described in later chapters. If work was ever slack, Laing watched carefully from the earliest days for his regular workers. 'They always kept long-service men and found work for them,' a Carlisle manager reported, 'even if only clearing up and sweeping the yard. Anybody who had been in for a twelvemonth was almost sure to be kept on.' Such features, which might be taken for granted today, are the things which remain in the mind of old employees from the past—a clear enough indication of the different conditions normally to be expected in the industry at that time.

So John Laing built up a stable and loyal workforce. His basic rates of pay, particularly in the office, were rarely generous, but men appreciated the security and sense of personal concern that he gave them. 'You could call him a hard taskmaster in one way,' a retired Carlisle man added, 'and yet again he was a grand old chap.' An old retired Carlisle joiner could say at the end of his life, 'I am comfortably off, through John Laing. He helped with the buying of this house. He has helped his workers all his life

*The 1942 *Report on Training* (see p. 166) was still complaining of 'the special form of discontinuous employment known as "wet time"' (para. 14).

. . . it just felt like home to me, working for them,' and an old bricklayer added, 'I have no financial worries—they were a good firm.' An old ganger, Jimmy Veness, had worked for the firm in the period just after the First World War. John Hindmoor remembered him when he joined in 1920, a tough character sporting ear-rings, gipsy-style. He left the firm and lost contact, but years later John Laing in London heard through Thomas Wardle, his Carlisle manager, that he was seriously ill and destitute. Hindmoor remembered the telegram from John Laing: 'Relieve immediate distress and report—further instructions will follow.'

John Hindmoor remembered also the advice he was given by John McKay when he joined the office staff:

> There are two things I want to warn you about. First, if Mr. Laing asks you to do anything, don't say you can't do it; say you haven't done it before but will try. Second, at all costs don't tell him a lie. He can stand anyone, a thief, a rogue; but a liar, no. He says, 'I can weigh up everybody, but not a liar!' I remembered that all my days [he went on]. If ever I was challenged on a mistake, I admitted it and he would say, 'Well, I know you won't do it again.'

It is significant that John Laing was known on a number of occasions to have given employment to men who had served prison sentences, and help to rehabilitate them.

John Laing hated waste or carelessness of any sort. From later years there is a host of stories of his care for minutiae (a tradition still apparent today in the scrupulous neatness of the vast stores depot at Boreham Wood); nor could he abide waste of time or effort. Those who knew him well realised that this hatred derived from his own frugal upbringing and from an innate respect for the products of nature and of human labour. Stanley Graham, his Hebron Hall friend who became city treasurer of Carlisle, recounted a story of the 1920s, when John Laing was inspecting a housing estate in Carlisle. Down the road came a poorly-laden cart belonging to the chief rival builders in Carlisle. John Laing stopped it. 'My man, when you are drawing a load, make certain it *is* a load, and not half a load. The job will never pay if you carry just half a load!' The man's jaw dropped. 'But I don't work for you, guv'nor; I work for Bobby Bell!'

He was equally punctilious over personal obligations. Stanley Graham was travelling to Manchester one day, some years after this, and a gentleman boarded the train at Shap, where there was a big granite works. 'Excuse me,' he said to Stanley Graham, 'where are you from?' 'Carlisle.' 'That firm Laing's have got on, haven't they?–what do you think of them?' 'A lot. I know them very well.' 'I know a bit. John Laing once came to me' (the man was a director of the Shap Granite Company), 'and said, "I would like some information from you: I am tendering for a contract and I am quite sure you would know the geology of the land. I will pay you for it." I told him what I knew, but refused to take any payment–I told him I was not an engineer, and he could lose a lot of money. A fortnight later I got a letter from the leading tailor in Carlisle, saying that they had been instructed by John Laing to make me a suit; would I please call next time I was in Carlisle.'

But what of those Barrow resolutions? The years immediately following Barrow had been lean, and had been followed by the urgent business of the war years, but Laing had kept a careful reckoning of his self-assumed obligations to charitable giving. In one or two wartime years he fell short, but meticulously made up the shortfall in the following years. The business had prospered beyond his dreams, and he had at the same time methodically built up its financial strength by his careful 'saving'–not in personal assets, but by conserving resources inside the business.

The formation of the Company, on 21 December, 1920, gave him the opportunity to put into effect arrangements that took him far beyond the plans he had made in Barrow. For the first issue of shares, the business was valued at £41,209 (surely a modest figure) and ordinary shares to that value were issued to John Laing himself in payment; £5,000 in preference shares was subscribed in cash and allotted to charitable trustees. This was an interim arrangement only. The original articles of the Company had contemplated that employees would be shareholders, and had made provision for their retirement from membership under certain circumstances (this provision was amended in 1925 to provide that shares held by an employee leaving his employment with the Company should be bought back from him); and within six months over five thousand voting ordinary shares were issued to nine of the longer-serving employees. A year later John Laing's own ordinary shareholding had been reduced to 40,201, and employees held 8,451.

It was the beginning of a plan that was to be continuously extended over the years, and that is even today comparatively rare in industry–certainly in private entrepreneurial concerns of the nature and stage of development of John Laing's at that time. The great contractor, Lord Cowdray, in his rectorial address at Aberdeen University in the same year as that in which John Laing formed his Company had advocated the minimum wage, an output bonus on profits, and worker's participation in management, but had only hinted at workers' holdings of equity shares. John Laing was to put the output bonus into operation a few years later in his own business; management remained securely in his own hands, and the articles of his Company secured his personal control of the board of directors while he held at least five thousand shares: but workers' shareholdings were part of his thinking from the first. He held strongly to the view that employees who contributed to the business should share its fruits, and he continuously encouraged trusted employees of all grades to take shares, in later years often lending them the money to do so.

What of his directly charitable giving? With the expansion of his business, he had felt that even his Barrow dedication was insufficient. The five thousand preference shares given to charity when his Company was formed did not satisfy him, and in 1922 he transferred 15,000 of his ordinary shares in the Company to the Stewards' Company Limited, a Brethren charitable holding foundation: an astonishing gift of almost forty per cent of his own remaining capital interest in the business. The letter in which he embodied the terms of his gift stated that he wished the income to be applied for missionary work abroad and for evangelistic work in Britain and Ireland, for relief of the poor, and for relief of the sick.

When the gift was completed in 1922, John Laing was left with 23,201 out of 49,901 ordinary shares in the Company. Employees' shareholdings had further increased to 9,700, and members of his family held another 2,000.*

John Laing had with deliberate forethought passed over to others more than one half of the present and future value of his business, at the very moment when it was poised for an expansion that would take it to the top of its industry.

*John Laing instituted his employees' shareholdings in 1920, eight years before employees' shareholdings were advocated by the Liberal Industrial Inquiry (which numbered J. M. Keynes among its members) of 1928 in its report *Britain's Industrial Future*. The two British schemes quoted by that Report were those of the Brush Electric Company (of 1926, six years after the Laing arrangements) and the much older scheme of J. T. & J. Taylor of Batley. The Taylor scheme was less selective and tentative than the Laing scheme, but most of the Laing shares, unlike the Taylor shares, carried full voting rights.

St. Nicholas Bridge, Carlisle, 1928 (p. 81)

Middlesex County Hospital, Shenley, 1934 (p. 135)

Woodcroft Evangelical Church, Burnt Oak

The view from 'Fair Holme'

CHAPTER 7

Greater London

JOHN LAING STIPULATED three requirements for the new national
headquarters of his Company. It must be suitable for the
needs of his business: that meant space for its offices, depot
and works, with living accommodation for its staff near at hand
(he hated the commuter's daily ordeal) and good communications to the rest of the country. It must be near a district where he
could build an active church. Last, he must be able – and the lover
of the Cumbrian hills could not ask for less – to find a home
nearby, with a view across the open countryside that would be
some reminder of the broad horizons of his young manhood.

London was the obvious centre for any national business, and
it was in London that he felt that he could most easily find and
hold the men with the experience and breadth needed for the
growth that was still to come. (In the event, much of that growth
was to be built on men he brought with him from Carlisle, or
trained himself.) But London could not easily satisfy those three
requirements, and the choice required time and care.

A London office had been opened in 1920 under Henry
Chapman Harland at 3 and 4 Lincoln's Inn Fields. When the staff
increased, it moved after three years to Lincoln House, 296 High
Holborn. It was here that Frank Hockaday, later to be a director,
became in 1924 the first pupil to sign articles under the new
pupils' scheme (to be followed a few days later by two entrants at
Carlisle). George Lowry was there with Jim Donaldson from
Carlisle. Andrew Anderson had also come down from Carlisle a
month or two before. There were six or seven surveyors in the
London office by then and, although most of the estimating was
still being done at Carlisle, they were supervising a growing
number of contracts. The major London contract during this
period was the building of the pumping station at the new
Littleton reservoir of the Metropolitan Water Board on the
south-western outskirts of London. The construction of the
reservoir itself, at the time of building the largest artificial

97

reservoir in the world with a capacity of 6,750 million gallons,[1] was in the hands of Lord Cowdray's firm of S. Pearson & Son, virtually their last contract in this country before Cowdray closed down their contracting activities. Since Gretna, the paths of the growing Laing organisation had several times crossed that of the great Pearson team, and it is tempting to read a symbolic significance into this final contact: a handing on to the next generation.

The pumping station built by John Laing & Son Limited was no minor undertaking. The largest yet planned for London's water supply, it had four great centrifugal pumps, with an engine-house that pumped water through five-foot-diameter pipes over the forty-foot embankment; the boilers were fed automatically with 120 tons of coal a day from massive concrete bunkers. A special subway carried the ash wagons, which, when full, were raised to the surface by an electric hoist. The chimney was over 200 feet high.[2] The reservoir, with the pumping station, was opened by King George V in June 1925, and named for Queen Mary.

Other work in the London area during the first half of the decade included Air Ministry and other public authority contracts, and considerable contract housing, but the Company had not yet started its own private housing developments. John Laing had narrowed his choice for a site for the new headquarters for the business to two alternatives, Harrow and Mill Hill, both on the north-western outskirts of London; the decision was finally made in 1925 when he bought eighteen acres of the Copt Hall estate at Mill Hill. On 5 September 1925, the annual general meeting of the Company was held at Carlisle for the last time.

John Laing senior had died on 17 March, 1924. Not long before his death he had asked his son to read to him Joshua 23:14: 'And, behold, this day I am going the way of all the earth: and ye know in all your hearts and in all your souls, that not one thing hath failed of all the good things which the Lord your God spake concerning you; all are come to pass unto you, and not one thing hath failed thereof.' 'Son,' he said, 'I too have found that not one thing hath failed of all the good things. All are come to pass.' His wife did not long survive him; she died barely a month later, on 16 April. After his parents' deaths, John William Laing found that, of an income of £1,000 per annum, they had been giving away three-quarters.

A chapter was closing. The congregation at Hebron Hall was flourishing: there was sound leadership of John William Laing's own generation, and a succession of younger men to follow. In 1925 a subsidiary congregation in the village of Todhills, a short distance north of Carlisle, which had been established by the work of Henry Carr a generation before, was given its meeting-room by the Carr family and was able to build new premises, the Laing Company again doing the work at cost: the trust deed named the same four trustees, including John Laing, as had appeared on the Hebron Hall deed.

Later in 1925, work started on a new London home for John Laing and his family, near the chosen location for the new headquarters. He had found the site for which he was looking, on the west of the low hills that were to form the north-western boundary of London's continuously built-up area. It had the wide view on which he had set his heart. The new Fair Holme, named after his home in Carlisle, was a spacious family house, built to take the best advantage of the outlook across the open country towards Elstree in the west, a prospect which was to remain unspoiled for the remainder of his long life, and which was one of his chief joys. Year by year, he would have a fresh photograph of it taken for his personal Christmas cards, and when, many years later, he was paid compensation for the removal of development rights from certain land which he owned and which was over-looked by his home, it was characteristic that he should have immediately used the money for his charitable trusts, for he would never have thought of spoiling his beloved view.

Yet the pleasure of the situation had to be shared. After the house was completed a discreet notice appeared on his gatepost: 'The public may enter and use the seats around the side of the garage during daylight.'

At the same time, work progressed on the new headquarters for the Company in Bunns Lane, Mill Hill, on the southern slope of the same hills. In February 1926 they were ready for occupation, and the move from Carlisle was under way in July.

Most of the key men at Carlisle were given the opportunity to move to London. The company secretary who had taken over that position from the over-worked William Sirey—a Scot, W. R. Whitelaw—chose to return to Scotland, and Andrew Anderson succeeded him—to remain secretary for the next thirty-four years. During the next year or two, the leading managers, W. M. Johnson and J. Lambert, came south to join G. G. Lowry, leaving T. Wardle in charge at Carlisle. William Sirey and John McKay also moved to London in 1926, and with them other younger men destined to rise high in the Company, including J. Gregg and (in 1928) R. H. Woolliams.

One of the reasons for the purchase of such a substantial area of land was that John Laing wished to build houses for his staff near the offices. David Thompson, who had come with McKay from Carlisle, remembered the long hot summer of 1926 while he was in lodgings waiting for his house to be built. Bunns' Lane (now crossed by the urban section of the M1 motorway and the Watford Way bypass) was then a country lane; he remembered a byre for thirty cows and a piggery adjoining the new office building, on the site where today's vast complex stands. Occasionally, the pigs would break out and wander into the office, a rustic hazard to good order not experienced at Carlisle. 'Joslin's pigs are eating all the Lombardy poplars,' complained an early letter sent to John Laing, then still in Carlisle.

To Mill Hill, also, came most of the functions carried out at Lincoln House, and those of the central London staff who did not wish to take a daily trip to the north-western suburban outskirts left their employment after the move. One room only was retained at High Holborn, and for a few years it functioned as the central London enquiry office, after the large-scale private housing developments started. The move to Mill Hill had not yet taken place at the time of the General Strike in March 1926. John Laing was on a visit in London at the time, and he was distinctly irritated with those of the High Holborn staff who failed to arrive at the office on time, an incident which illustrated his passion for punctuality and his unfamiliarity with London commuting conditions, rather than his attitude to trade unionism.

In July 1926 John Laing was in his new home, and the head office of the Company was settled at Mill Hill. The annual general meeting on 17 July was held in Mill Hill. In his forty-seventh year, John Laing was embarking on a new life and a vast new business venture.

Once again that uncanny foresight, that had ensured that the Easiform house was ready just as the post-war demand arose, was in evidence. The site of the new headquarters, at what was to be the edge of London's continuous built-up area, and within a mile or two of the new Great North Road from Apex Corner and of the trunk roads to the Midlands, was inspired: but who was to know that forty years later the first great motorway in Britain, the M1 to the industrial areas of the Midlands and the north, would run within a mile of the Company's heart? John Laing's economic foresight was no less sure. He had tasted the effect of slump in his industry fifteen to twenty years before, and he now read off the portents from contemporary discontents. The 1930s were to gain the image of the wasted depression years, when unemployment reached its horrifying peak of nearly three million, twenty-three per cent of the insured workforce (in public-works contracting it was to reach fifty per cent). Misery nevertheless spread its poison unevenly. While South Wales and the industrial north suffered, the home counties and the Midlands relatively prospered. In London, with the growth of white-collar employment and the development of light industries, the great expansion into the surrounding countryside, which had already been under way before the First World War, was taking its second wind. In each year from 1929 to 1936, a quarter (and in most years many more) of all houses built in England and Wales by private enterprise would be built in Greater London, and that in years when private-enterprise housing was to climb from 113,000 per annum to an astounding 287,000.[3] In the north-west of London, the piercing of the Hampstead hills by the underground railway to Golders Green in 1907 had already led to extensive development in what had been the open country beyond the hills,[4] and the 1924 extension of the line to Edgware was the precursor of a further growth that would bring the continuous building-line to the edge of Highwood Hill and Stanmore Common.

At the time of the move to Mill Hill in 1926, the Company's chief works in hand included Easiform contracts at Plymouth, Exeter, Woolwich and Tottenham; at Carlisle the St. Nicholas Bridge, factory work for Carr & Company, and extensive local-authority housing; contract housing at Darlington, Greenford and Gosforth; major Air Ministry work in Lincolnshire; and the remaining work at Catterick. Further attractive contracts kept turnover for the next three years at an annual average of three-quarters of a million pounds (approaching ten million pounds in terms of 1977 construction costs). In real terms, the business had grown forty-fold in less than twenty years. In 1928, however, contract work showed signs of falling off. Three major contracts, at Gosport for the Air Ministry, the first hospital work at Shenley in Hertfordshire (of which more will be said later), and (a plum for this newcomer to London) the building of the new headquarters of the Federation of British Industry in Tothill Street, Westminster, were not sufficient to prove that activity in his industry would be able to sustain the Company at the levels for which John Laing was planning. Meanwhile unemployment in the industry was showing signs of an increase. A new policy decision was called for.

Laing had built his Company as well as he had built for his customers. Its financial resources had been steadily augmented through the years of expansion, and John Laing had created around him a proved team of management and workers that was an irreplaceable asset. If others could not provide sufficient work for his team, then he was in a position to provide it himself.

The business had undertaken no private-housing developments since his family had been building in Carlisle in the early years of the century, and then it had been for rent rather than for sale. John Laing's own preference was for the wider aspects of construction. It was irony indeed that what was essentially a diversion from the main route that he had chosen for his business should in the next decade, through his own marketing genius, make his name nationally known. The tide of speculative building that swept over the London countryside in the 1930s has become a popular cliché for unplanned philistinism.* How would this hard-headed idealist from the beautiful Cumbrian countryside react to this new conflict?

Before 1926 he had taken a first, somewhat tentative, step into the market for private housing in the London area, when he had started an estate at Imber Grove, Esher, at the beginning of the Surrey countryside to the south-west of London. This was an unrepresentative project that included larger, individually architect-designed houses for professional buyers, a class of development not entirely in accord with the ideas of John Laing. Inheriting the tradition of the Carlisle housing built by the earlier generation of his family and of his own Easiform system, he wanted houses that the 'ordinary man' could buy and enjoy.

This brought other considerations. If the development of such housing estates was to be commercially and functionally successful, other building work would also be needed. John Laing instinctively reacted against the unplanned development, with large housing estates far from jobs and shopping facilities,

---

*There were, of course, two sides to the matter. In his *Semi-Detached London* (Allen and Unwin, 1973), Alan A. Jackson writes of the housing surge, 'Both the waste of opportunity and the resultant ugly monotony are appalling to contemplate, and the damage done will take generations to repair. But,' he adds, 'there was also very real achievement. Finding a new home within their financial reach, many thousands had their living standards transformed: in a few short years, the sum of human happiness was immeasurably increased. Any alternative would have taken very much longer' (p. 323).

that marred so much of this period of London's growth. Perhaps it was the sense of a balanced community life that came from his experience of the smaller towns of the north-west, but he considered such opportunist development inhuman in its effects, and also commercially foolish. Unlike some contemporary developers, who went into the booming market under-capitalised and with an eye to quick returns, his Company had built up sufficient resources to be able itself to finance development of both shopping and factory precincts, where they did not already exist near to the new estates.

Accordingly, in 1929 he incorporated a new Company to work alongside his construction company—Laings Properties Limited, formed for property investment. He planned to build up inside this Company a portfolio of properties, mainly put up by the construction company. In this way, he served a number of purposes. He could provide his housing estates with the necessary ancillary facilities, and he could also plough back the efforts of his workforce into a growing holding of sound assets in which they could share, both by direct shareholdings and through suitable trust arrangements. His comments on the first accounts of the property company, for 1929, were characteristic: 'The policy of the Board is to secure property at the most reasonable price, and that the Company shall not be saddled with any expenses which can be avoided, and to make it gradually more and more substantial.'

At the same time, he launched into the first group of the great housing developments that were to make his name a household word of the thirties: two estates at Colindale (Colin Park and Springfield); two at Sudbury (Horsenden and Sudbury Heights); and one at Golders Green—all in north-west London—and a sixth at Woodford on the edge of the north-eastern suburbs. His chief managers from the Carlisle days, J. Lambert, G. G. Lowry and W. M. Johnson, were put in charge of the developments, and were joined by a Scot—also brought down from Carlisle, where he had worked on the St. Nicholas Bridge—G. B. Malcolm. These four men would meet John Laing for long weekly management meetings at which all works in progress would be regularly reviewed. John Lambert was a remarkable man of whom John Laing said after his death in 1956, 'We have never known him speak a cross word,' and who had built a formidable reputation for taming the most difficult of official clients. In charge of the sales arrangements and publicity was another Carlisle man who was to develop a considerable reputation in the field:

C. E. Penney, who had already supervised the sales of the houses at Esher.

The basis of John Laing's approach to housing was a simple one. 'Would I wish to live in this house?' He had great sympathy with ordinary people, and his own tastes were straightforward and uncomplicated. Having decided to go into private-housing development, he threw himself into it with great enjoyment, but he always disliked the aura of speculative building. 'I am a contractor, not a speculative builder,' he would say, and he wrote at the end of his life, 'Our experience in housing was one of the happiest and most successful parts of our business.'[5] If he sold a thousand houses, he hoped to have gained a thousand friends. 'Every class in the country wants a house,' he said in 1948. 'Once a man owns his house, he has a stake in his country. Else he is rootless . . . The man who is tenant of a house and garden can be very happy but never altogether satisfied . . . a flat is essentially for elderly couples, or spinsters and bachelors.'[6]

His advocacy of owner-occupation was more significant in relation to his times than we might appreciate today. In 1914, ninety per cent of houses had been rented from private landlords. After all the building of the 1930s, only twenty-nine per cent were owner-occupied even as late as 1951, whereas in 1973 the proportion had risen to fifty-two per cent, with five-eighths of the remainder rented from public authorities.[7]

His standards were high, and this meant that his houses were more expensive than others on the market at the same time. Yet he was concerned that people could afford to buy the houses he built:[8]

> My great desire was to build some houses in which the purchaser could pay a £50 deposit, and then his expenses for rates and interest would cost him only one pound a week. On one estate we achieved that. At one part . . . we let the houses and charged £1 a week, and that was the total payment the tenant had to make, but we had to increase that because the rating authorities said that if we agreed to let the houses for such a cheap rent they were not going to assess them on that and they put the rates up beyond what the £1 a week justified, and we had to increase the rent a little.

Stanley Graham, later City Treasurer of Carlisle, spoke of the working-class homes John Laing built in Carlisle at the same period. 'He built them for the working people to buy their own

houses. I could take you to houses in Carlisle they sold for under
£400. I trained in the Carlisle Council offices, and I remember that
he came to the old boss and said, "This is Laing. I want these
houses at the minimum rateable values, for I want the working
classes to own their own houses."'

The advent on the London building scene at this time of the
powerful new Company, with high standards of construction,
was of extreme importance. They brought with them, from the
more testing climate of the north-west, standards that were by no
means normal in the south-east. The common nine-inch solid
brick wall of the south-east was unreliable, and liable to damp
penetration. Most builders of the time dealt with this by
rendering the external surfaces. John Laing (and he had only a
few companions in this at that time) insisted on the eleven-inch
cavity wall that he knew from Carlisle. Foundations demanded
especial care, with deep concrete foundations to the walls,
including partition walls, and ballast concrete under the whole
house. The unfamiliar London clay had brought him special
problems and he took no risks. Damp courses had his close
attention for quality, and roofs had wide eaves; they were
adequately felted and of over-size timber; there was none of the
inadequately protected roofing that marred so much of the
speculative building of this period and inflicted annual winter
misery on the occupants of the houses. One man, later a director
of some of the Group Companies, told of a visit by John Laing to
the Woodford estate; dissatisfied with the bracing of the roofs, he
sacked all the carpenters and ordered the remedying of the work
(the men were re-instated the following day). Another, later to be
a director of the main Company, was in charge of a site, and was
reproved by John Laing on inspection, as he considered the
roofing unsatisfactory. The man pointed out that he had
consulted the architect, and that the architect would not
authorise payment beyond the specification. 'That does not
matter,' John Laing had replied; 'the firm's reputation will suffer
if in twenty years' time these roofs are seen to sag.'

John Laing had his own staff architect (David Adam) and
engineers, although some of his designs were by outside
professional architects, as he was jealous of good relationship
with the profession. His tastes were simple but practical and
were worked out as the estates developed. Elevations were of
brick, usually with rustic bricks, and with facing bricks on street
frontages. Roughcast he disliked intensely, for he liked to 'see the
quality of the brickwork'. After a few bay facings on the early

estates and some houses at Golders Green so treated 'to relieve any monotony', roughcast was strictly avoided. In the result, the houses have generally aged well; there were no mock-Tudor styles. He disliked high window sills; the occupant should, he said, be able to sit in his room and look out of his windows from his chair. Staircases should not be curved; it was dangerous for children and the housewife with a load of linen in her arms, and all staircases had therefore to be straight, with a proper landing at corners. By the early thirties, all flooring was tongued and grooved, with parquet in the halls of all but the least expensive houses, and quarry-tiled kitchens. Plumbing was by copper pipes; on one of the early estates there was a combination of copper piping with galvanised water tanks, and after a time some of the tanks leaked. It was an electrolytic reaction; accordingly every tank on the estate was replaced free of charge by a copper tank, and copper tanks were made standard thereafter.

It was by careful attention to such features that John Laing built his reputation. Although his wife was never apparent in the planning of the houses, there is evidence that he would listen carefully to her views. On one occasion he disapproved of a decorative scheme devised by an employee for a show house. Asking who designed it, he said, 'I will bring my wife to see it this afternoon.' Happily, Beatrice Laing approved, and the employee (who later rose high in the business) was exonerated! John Laing was delighted when estate agents, after a few years, began to advertise houses which came on the market as 'Laing built'. 'They have first-grade Estates,' wrote one London estate agent of long experience in 1977; 'have never built cheap and cheerful.'

This reputation was not won lightly, nor was quality obtained at the cost of efficiency. Before land was purchased for development, it was surveyed thoroughly. In addition to the builder's concern with drainage and the provision of services, the marketing essentials were given particular attention; transport facilities, local employment opportunities, shopping facilities had to be adequate, and in some cases Laing planned them into an integrated development. For one of the second group of estates, at Queensbury, he also planned and built two adjoining factory estates (a development later repeated at Elstree and Borehamwood).

Before the purchase of land was finally completed, the plans for the development had been drawn up and negotiations with local authorities were under way. At the Golders Green estate, the scheme had been approved, and the Company was actually digging for sewers, on the Monday after the completion of the purchase. At Canons Park, the first of the next group of estates, John Laing realised that some of the houses would be sunless; he had the whole layout redesigned in a week.*

The layout of each estate was designed where possible to preserve trees and to take advantage of natural features. Henry Harland had special responsibility for this, and controlled a staff of gardeners. Where other features were lacking, the layout might provide a central garden for the estate, as at Golders Green. Incoming houseowners were later given leaflets on the care of their privet hedges, and on some estates the earlier arrivals were invited to enter competitions for the best-kept front gardens—an obvious advantage in making the remaining houses attractive to new buyers. Properly made-up roads were put in at all estates, with wide main streets. On some quality estates, corner-site houses would have special treatment, and there would be restrained decorative brickwork on frontages, while variety was achieved by the use of different house-styles and a staggered building line.

Once work started on an estate, it was carefully controlled for both workmanship and cost. The costing system, after thirty years' development, was now an instrument of precision under the expert care of James Donaldson. The early work-study principles which John Laing had developed, evidenced in a rudimentary form in the notebook from the first years of the century, had already been applied in detail to the Easiform contracts of the mid-twenties, and an old surviving notebook from those contracts shows that operations were broken down and costed in great detail, the information being used both for management control and for calculating bonuses for the workers. A surviving handwritten note from 1931, prepared by John Laing to guide one of the younger site managers, shows that the manager was expected to estimate the cost of each item of each stage of the work before starting, and to report the result as soon as it was finished. In addition, every six months the cost of the

*Such speed was not only to catch the market: more important, it kept down costs. Great though the benefits of present-day planning control may be, the delays it has brought with it are extremely expensive; in times of high interest rates and high land costs, a year's delay caused by planning negotiations can add several hundred pounds in interest charges alone to the cost of a modest house, and that cost is borne by the purchaser. Add inflation and administrative expense, and delay can add two per cent a month to costs.

whole job was to be calculated by the manager and compared with the value of work completed, for his own guidance; the note set out a pro-forma calculation. The manager was to have the cumulative figures to date available each week.

These regular costing reports on each item as the work progressed were taken by the central office and recorded against carefully tabulated standards and targets for the work.[9]

> I always recommended that we had one costing surveyor to about every 100 men [said John Laing many years later]. Of course, certain jobs require less than this. This might seem extravagant but it gave me such control of everything and it kept me in touch with every manual worker . . . Donaldson received all the reports from the costing men. He visited them as necessary to see that they were efficient and he prepared for me a summary of each job as well as the details of each. This enabled me to visit the men who had done well and in a friendly way those who were not doing so well.

Detailed statistics were compiled for every type of house, recording areas in feet super, percentages of effective space and space efficiency, costings and cost per efficient square foot, with records of the dates and costs of each type of house built on the different estates over the years.

The actual carrying out of the building work was as closely supervised. John Laing was constantly visiting the sites and gained an uncanny reputation for going directly to the weak spots. Any form of waste was anathema to him, and anecdotes abound of rebukes for bricks left lying around; wall ties dropped on the ground; cement not stacked clear of damp; dirty equipment; but good work was noticed and approved. Safety was as strictly watched – the fitting of guard boards and toe rails – and accidents and injuries upset him badly.

In addition to the weekly meetings with the key managers, frequent meetings of all the staff engaged on the housing projects were arranged to discuss progress and consider difficulties and suggestions for improvements. Employees' dinners and get-togethers, weekly newsletters from the sales offices, the encouragement of staff to take part in selling the houses, all added to the team spirit at which he was aiming. He soon developed quality-control books for the estates. For each house a log-book recorded all the essential procedures: checking of foundations, the damp courses, cleaning of wall cavities, balling of chimney flues, spacing of wall ties, reinforcement of the lintels, roofing, adequate nailing of tiles—all were listed and had to be signed as inspected and approved by a supervisor, and ready for John Laing's inspection on each visit. All gutters had to be painted inside with red oxide before fitting; all hidden woodwork had to be primed.

When houses were eventually handed over to purchasers, there was a further pre-occupation check list. On the later estates, purchasers were given a twelve-month maintenance guarantee that was strictly honoured. Even a purchaser who was unreasonable might be given the benefit of the doubt. A senior executive remembers a lady who complained of damage to parquet flooring that was clearly the result of ill usage; yet the flooring was relaid for her. But there were limits. On one occasion John Laing himself went to see a particularly vociferous lady whose complaint was manifestly unfounded. To pacify her, he offered her a small rebate, to which she retorted, 'No businessman would reduce his price, unless he were at fault.' 'Madam,' replied John Laing, 'the offer is withdrawn. The interview is over. Goodbye.'

Marketing as a profession may not have been invented, but John Laing knew all about it. The inspiration which christened Easiform brought out the 'Little Palaces of Colindale' on the first major London estate, and soon 'Laing's little palaces' were appearing elsewhere in London. Local and national advertising made full play with the merits of the homes, though it was always accurate and forthright. Every press advertisement had John Laing's own jealous scrutiny. The houses were exhibited freely, at Olympia and at Alexandra Palace; in 1934 a detached show-house was built, complete to specification, in the forecourt of King's Cross station and floodlit at night (a happy childhood memory today for many children whose parents brought them to London). It was open at first from nine-thirty to eight, later until ten, and at this house details of all the estates were available; films of the housing were shown in the garage (John Laing was always a photography enthusiast); and cars were available to take serious purchasers to their chosen estates. Special 'housing money-boxes', in the shape of houses, bore the slogan 'Invest in a Laing house'.

By now, a second group of estates was in progress, and building was advertised in ten areas of the London suburbs. The six original estates had been sold out, but the Company was building elsewhere in the north-western suburbs (two at Canons Park, at Queensbury, at Sunnyfields and Parkside at Mill Hill, and at Booth Road, Colindale) and also at Cranford in the west, Southgate in the north, Shooters Hill in the south-east, and Purley in the south. The Sunnyfields houses were the result of open architectural competition; Queensbury was a massive development with two shopping parades, and two factory estates close at hand. Prices ranged fom £595 for a small semi-detached three-bedroom house with a shared car-run, to £1,300 for the most expensive detached house with four bedrooms and its own garage (at 1977 building costs about £8,750 to £19,000). Land, of course, was very much cheaper than it is today, and John Laing (who hated what he considered unearned speculation) took no profit on his land prices.

John Laing equally disliked the principle of the scale fee. His houses, he considered, should sell on quality alone, and estate agents who sold any houses for him did so at a fixed fee per house. Most of the selling was direct; each estate with its own site office remained open in the evenings and on Saturdays (but Sunday opening was strictly avoided). Staff were encouraged to man the offices on a voluntary basis in the evenings and on Saturdays, receiving a small commission for each house sold.

In February 1937 the King's Cross show house was supplemented by a new and bolder venture. The Minister of Health, Sir Kingsley Wood, opened for the Company a 'New Home Exhibition' inside a store building at 520 Oxford Street, by Marble Arch. Three full-sized show houses, fully furnished, were actually built inside the exhibition, advertised as 'the most wonderful permanent new home exhibition in England'; with them was a gallery of coloured house photographs, one-third full size, and an exhibition of materials and building methods. Opening from ten until eight on weekdays, the exhibition provided all the services to would-be purchasers that were also available at King's Cross.

Ironically, Kingsley Wood had just refused the Company's application to build some factories adjoining the Barnet bypass in the district of the Barnet Council. The Company had acquired 470 acres from Lord Strafford at Elstree and was planning to develop a garden-city estate there. The plans, professionally designed, set back the industrial development by a broad space from the main road; they ran carefully counter to the ribbon development of the time, and provided for balanced residential and industrial development. The scheme went ahead successfully west of the bypass, though interrupted by the war and subsequently greatly modified by planning regulations.

This estate at Borehamwood and Elstree was one of a group that formed the third stage in the Company's residential developments of the 1930s; others were at Edgware, Stanmore and Hatch End. By now the clouds of war were gathering, and several of these developments were to be interrupted by the war, but the gathering storm brought with it new challenges to the Company and to John Laing himself. These are the subject of another chapter. Despite his commitment to contracting on a severer scale, John Laing always looked with pleasure on his housing work and the related shopping and industrial construction. It was human in scale, and so much of it was near his home. He would delight to take his friends on a tour of the estates; his good friend Cecil Allen was with him on one such tour, and enjoyed his satisfaction. 'John,' he teased him, 'you sound like Nebuchadnezzar the king, boasting "Is not this great Babylon, that I have built?"'

During the 1930s, John Laing's business built about one in fifty of the houses put up by private enterprise in the London area, a proportion that is more significant in the highly fragmented construction industry than may appear. His influence on building standards, like his influence in the industry which will be explored in a later chapter, was immense, and the housing standards of building firms of this calibre, of which happily there were more than commentators often allow, had impressed themselves more generally on the market by the end of the decade, as the public learned to understand what it was buying. Conditions of the 1930s were, however, never to return; pressure on land, tighter planning regulations and changing social and economic patterns in the post-war world saw to that, and the decade of its housing estates can now be seen to have been an interesting digression from the main course of development of the Laing enterprise.

While London was yielding to the men from Carlisle (and there were other facets to the story than housing, as later chapters will show), Carlisle itself was not forgotten. If John Laing had been disposed to forget his native city, the formidable manager there, Thomas Wardle, would not have allowed him to do so. But he was still a Carlisle man, and his loyalties to his old advisers from the days of the Barrow troubles were unshaken. The Clydesdale Bank remained his banker; he was still taking pupils and apprentices from the Carlisle schools; and Tom Strong, his old Carlisle solicitor, still acted for him and dealt with the conveyancing of his London estates as he dealt with those in

Carlisle, backed from inside the Company by the 'most methodical man he had ever met', Andrew Anderson. John Laing's accountant and brother-in-law, Walter Harland, on whose advice he greatly relied, was required to take a season ticket from Stockton to London.

There was an even more striking token of his loyalty. The financial climate of the 1930s immeasurably assisted the housing boom, by channelling savings towards the Building Societies, whose coffers became embarrassingly filled. The consequent reduction in mortgage rates made house purchase available to many more people, and this trend was greatly stimulated by the development of the Mortgage Guarantee System (otherwise the Pool system) which cut down the purchaser's deposit to five per cent or less. John Laing strongly supported the system,[10] which made house purchase much more widely available, and his accounts as early as 1930 indicated a contingent liability to building societies for advances to house purchasers. Unhappily, the scheme led to collusion between unscrupulous builders and purchasers, and was rendered largely ineffective by the Building Societies Act, 1939.

Faced with strong competition from building societies seeking mortgage business, John Laing deliberately turned to the comparatively small society in his home town, the Cumberland Building Society (then the Cumberland Co-operative Benefit Building Society), the society which Jonathan Dodgson Carr had helped to found in 1850, and of which Laing's uncle, David Laing, had been a director for eighteen years. This society had hitherto confined its lending mainly to Carlisle and its surrounding area, and as the majority of house-building in the district was local-authority building, its growth had been limited. When the Woodford Green estate started, John Laing travelled specially to Carlisle to offer the society first choice of mortgage advances there: the local directors demurred at first, but eventually agreed, largely on the known reputation of Laing's building. It was an auspicious introduction which gave the society an introduction into the London market, and considerably aided its expansion.

Carlisle has one of the best records in the country for local-authority housing, in relation to its population, and a substantial proportion of corporation houses was erected by the Laing Company. Standards were enforced by John Laing's own inspectors on estates he built for others as rigidly as on his private developments, with weekly reports to him, independently of councils' own inspections. In addition, during the 1930s he developed some dozen private housing estates in Carlisle, enforcing standards as carefully as in London.

Thomas Wardle, the Carlisle manager and a joiner from Lancashire, was a tough and uncompromising man. He was utterly devoted to the business, noted for an implacable hatred of the smallest waste, loyal to John Laing's ways and methods, and extremely successful in their application; but, like many devoted followers of a strong personality, he seems to have combined many of his employer's severest traits with an absence of much of his humanity. One senior man who remembers him in the immediate post-Second World War period remarked, 'Carlisle was still doing jobs simply when we in London were going mad . . . Tommy Wardle was one of few men in the firm keeping his head . . . he didn't finish up with many friends, but yet there was no reason why he shouldn't. Once you got to know him, you realised there was a good side to him, but he upset a lot of people on the way.' The four great London managers were all able to earn the same sort of devotion from their workmen as John Laing himself received, but Wardle was a 'hard man'. 'I liked him all the same,' said one old joiner. 'I could please any hard man. He wouldn't give you any credit for anything. But I liked him all the same.' In the nature of things, most were not so charitable. It was characteristic that, when John Laing once visited Carlisle, one of the old hands, who knew him from the early days, appealed to him over Wardle's head. 'Oh, John Willie, please tell Mr. Wardle . . .' John Laing was (in the old Carlisle usage) 'John Willie', but the manager was always '*Mr.* Wardle'.

The depression hit Carlisle more seriously and earlier than London, and life there in the late twenties and thirties was tough. Joss Cartmell, champion bricklayer, started with the Company in 1927: 'Jack Hardy and I went to Workington and went round the pawnshops to find a decent jacket to go to our first job at Penrith in. I couldn't find one to fit me, but had to go to the job decent, and the first day I pushed a shovel through it. Timekeeping was very strict. If you were late you had to take it off yourself on your time sheet.' A worker from Blackwell brickworks said, 'I was coming out of that yard with only £3 a week: and there was three or four men lined up for your job.'

It was partly to help allay unemployment that John Laing started private housing on a relatively large scale in Carlisle, as he did in London, yet there were aspects of the industry where insecurity was endemic. Billy Allen was a self-employed lorry-driver who, like several companions, had bought a T-type Ford lorry on returning from the war, and hired it out on a daily basis. For seven or eight years he worked regularly for John Laing & Son, carting bricks from Blackwell to sites in the town, at first at nine shillings (45p) a thousand (it needed two journeys, and bricks were handstacked on and off the lorry). The price dropped later to seven and sixpence (37½p), and it took some tough bargaining with Wardle later, and the finding of alternative work, to prevent the price dropping still further and eventually to restore it to his nine shillings.

There came a day when the Company found other transport, and the eight self-employed contractors were out of work without warning. As self-employed men, there was no un-employment insurance for them.

> I came back home. I said to the wife – 'I've no dole, nothing.' I never gave my wife one pound note for thirty-two weeks: thirty-two weeks my wife had to do with nothing except what she had in the house. My boy was ten. She had stacked tinned food over the years. I used to say to her, 'You are a little squirrel, hoarding this and hoarding that.' When she was dying years later, I said to her, 'I used to call you a squirrel – thank God you were!' . . . At the end of the thirty-two weeks we had a coal fire there, but were down and out and didn't know which way to turn, just as if in a condemned cell with no sign of life, but the wife thank God she was a good Christian. She put three pounds of marrow bones on the fire one Sunday – that was the last meal and we never told a human being. She said, 'Let's get down and pray over it.' When that soup was on the fire we didn't know where the next meal was coming from. I went down to the Pentecostal church where we were members, and as I came out the minister shook hands and there was a pound note in it. When I got home my wife said, 'Oh, Billy, you've been backsliding' – she thought I had gone back to the old ways.

The Allens, as Pentecostals, shared the same evangelical beliefs as John Laing; it was ironical that they were the victims of an aspect of his industry that was, and still is, inhuman. John Laing always opposed the notorious 'lump' system of self-employed gangs of labourers; the self-employed haulier is a lesser problem, but as an individual he is even more vulnerable and desperately insecure.

The Laing organisation had made a significant mark on its native city before the move to London, as we have already seen. Some 7,000 of the city's 14,000 council houses were Laing houses. Percy Dalton, the City Engineer and Surveyor, on his retirement in 1949, wrote to John Laing of the city's various housing records between the wars, and added, 'This was only possible by your assistance and I shall always feel grateful for your firm's co-operation.' The private housing estates also added significantly to the city's housing, and of major buildings the Ashley Road schools, the electricity works, Garlands Hospital, General Post Office and St. Nicholas Bridge, had all been completed or were in progress by the time of the move to London. The later contribution has been even more significant. The Company's own offices and works have continued to grow, a substantial contributor to local employment and the careers of local men (though a Carlisle man returning from London in the early 1950s was happy to find that 'Carlisle was virtually what Mill Hill had been before the war – self-contained units where everyone would muck in and help everyone else'). Laings had been on record as 'Brickmakers' as long before as 1884: John Laing opened his works at Blackwell in 1921 and it remained in production, with a wartime period of closure, until 1948: during that period it produced over fifty million bricks. Other brickworks were opened at Brisco (sand-lime bricks), and in 1952 at Moorville.

In more recent days the Company has been responsible for the lion's share of major buildings in the city. Many of the local factories are of their construction and not least a substantial part, over the years, of Carr's biscuit works, and among other notable commercial buildings are the headquarters of the Cumberland Newspapers Group and the Cumberland Building Society. Public buildings include the new Willowholme power station in 1946; water and sewage facilities; the police and fire stations; the telephone exchange and the crematorium; churches and schools; the Technical College and the proud new Civic Centre in Rickergate. When the city, true to its progressive record, took urgent advantage of the Housing Acts of 1969 to modernise its old housing stock, the Laing Company was one of its major contractors, and by 1973, the corporation's last year as a separate authority, it had completed the modernisation of 1,500 homes. But the work in which John Laing would have most delighted would have been the painstaking craftsmanship of the masons during the restoration of the stonework of Carlisle cathedral during the twenty years from 1951. After careful study of work at

York Minster, a special team of craftsmen was formed for this task. In true medieval tradition, a head mason, Billy Campbell, is commemorated in a gargoyle on the cathedral. Important archaeological discoveries were made during the course of this work, and the work also served to shape some of the 'superb craftsmen' whom Sir Basil Spence used in the building of Coventry Cathedral.[11]

One day during the course of this work a Spanish visitor, with a companion who by chance knew John Laing, casually visited Carlisle cathedral. When the two men appeared, they noticed among the Laing workmen 'a hurrying and scurrying. Almost immediately the Clerk of Works appeared from his office and began to approach us. He came up quite close and then moved rather sheepishly away.' On enquiring the cause from one of the workmen, they were told that from a distance the Spanish visitor looked like John Laing: an interesting and unexpected tribute both to the regard in which he was held, and the extent of his involvement (he was then well into his seventies) in even a minor contract of the Company.

Carlisle is not likely to forget Sir John. Perhaps the most artless tribute came from a would-be apprentice being interviewed at Carr's biscuit factory. The applicants were given a general knowledge test, and one of the questions was, 'Who built the Roman wall?' Back came the answer from this lad: 'John Willie Laing!'[12]

CHAPTER 8

Church and Family

ONE OF THE three conditions for the situation of the new head office in London had been that it must be near a place where John Laing could help build a new church. Not far from the site in Bunns Lane, across the main railway line, the L.C.C. was in 1926 building the extensive Watling housing estate, straddling the new London Transport electric line to Edgware; a station had already been opened at Burnt Oak in 1924 (John Laing & Son Limited were to build the main structure of the station a few years later), and a large new community was coming into being.

On moving to London, the Laing family had for a time thrown in their lot with a small Brethren congregation at East Finchley some miles from their home. The arrangement was necessarily temporary: quite apart from the problems of distance, the energies and vision he brought from Carlisle could not easily have accommodated John Laing in an established church, with its set ways and traditions. Astonishingly, to one unfamiliar with the pressures of the Brethren tradition, it seems that he had even considered retirement from active part in the business to free himself for full-time Christian ministry; but so strong is the effect of Brethren idealism that such an urge would have been entirely in character. John Laing knew himself, however, and made a decision at this point that he would devote as much time to his Christian and charitable activities as to his business (a decision that, with his immense energy, seems to have resulted in a full effective working life devoted to each!).

At Finchley he met J. Fenwick Adams, a fellow member of the Brethren, with whom he became firm friends. He had already discussed the formation of a local congregation with three of the men who had come down from Carlisle with him and who had been members of the Hebron Hall congregation—William Sirey, Andrew Anderson and John McKay—and they later joined with two other local members of the Brethren, W. Alcock and W. J. Bull, meeting in Alcock's house for Bible study and prayer. Bull was a printer, whose son Geoffrey was later to become well known as a missionary and author; his book *When Iron Gates Yield* tells of his experiences as a prisoner of the Chinese communist regime after the revolution in that country.

During 1927 John Laing was able to start work on the building of Woodcroft Hall (today known as Woodcroft Evangelical Church). He had secured from the L.C.C. a prominent corner site adjoining Burnt Oak tube station, and had the building designed by Sir John Burnet, R.A. His own Company undertook the work, a picked team of craftsmen being chosen, and he himself contributed two-thirds of the cost. A parade of shops nearby was also developed by the Laing organisation.

On 21 January 1928, the church was opened with special services conducted by John Laing's old friends Dr. Bishop from Wylam-on-Tyne and Montague Goodman, and by Hudson Pope, another well-known speaker among Brethren and a worker with the Children's Special Service Mission whom Laing had met on a family holiday at Sheringham in 1926. The invitation letter was signed by J. W. Laing and his six companions. These opening services were followed by a children's mission conducted by Hudson Pope.

The result surprised even the seven. A crowd of children arrived on the Sunday, overwhelming the facilities, and soon the Sunday School numbered well over a thousand children (it was to reach fifteen hundred in a few years). Fenwick Adams proved himself an excellent superintendent, and urgent calls for workers went out to other churches, John Laing even calling in young men from the Crusader class he led at Mill Hill. The two main halls in the building were supplemented by overflow sessions in different rooms and annexes; the church was twice extended, and sessions were held in series. It was part of the last blossoming of a great Nonconformist tradition that the Second World War, with its evacuation and dispersal of families, was to destroy: a world of hard self-sacrificing work on the part of the bands of voluntary workers who staffed the Sunday Schools of the different denominations whose churches lay in the burgeoning 'cottage estates'; of great summer outings in hired trains or char-à-bancs to seaside or country; of prizegivings with piles of pious story-books, and sandwiches, cakes and scalding tea from urns. (C. S. Kent, a *Times* executive, was another from the Brethren who evoked a similar response in the thirties, on the still larger St. Helier estate in south London.)

The Watling estate had a population of almost twenty

thousand; although it developed a strong community association, the local authorities were slow to provide facilities, and even day-schools were woefully inadequate at the time Woodcroft Hall opened. There was little else for the children–unless it was the threepenny Saturday matinées at the Regent Cinema which opened a year later. St. Alphage Anglican church, on the southern fringes of the estate, had been built shortly before Woodcroft Hall, but otherwise it was the first church on the estate. There was much to be done.

John Laing and his wife took their full part in the activities of the church: he was one of the elders from the beginning and the other elders found him a dominant influence, but far from forcing himself on his colleagues. One elder, who joined a year or two later, remembers him as remarkably considerate and humble, yet quietly confident; another remarked, 'I never knew a less conceited man: yet he always took it that he was right! He was really unworldly; I never knew anybody less hidebound; he would do anything if he thought the situation warranted it.'

The estate was divided for visitation and general care among volunteer helpers from the church; a substantial congregation soon developed, and the church built up to some three hundred regular members within a few years, of whom sixty per cent were local accessions. John Laing, drawing on his long experience and his own enthusiasm for youth work, encouraged the formation of boys' and girls' clubs, of which more will be said later; he also for many years ran a men's club for local residents, inviting well-known speakers, some of whom remember his easy *rapport* with the members and the affection which he inspired. These club meetings would be held in the basement of the church building; there would be a meal, and a general discussion led by John Laing, and it was here that he most easily and naturally expressed his basic and down-to-earth faith. Sometimes he would preach in the main church services: although (as in Carlisle) he was by general consent not an eloquent preacher, his direct simplicity and honesty were as effective as in Carlisle, and there were often converts of his preaching. One elder of the church, who was also later a senior executive of the Company, remembers unexpectedly finding him in a side room of the church one evening, a group of a dozen or so boys about him, engaged in an artless discussion on his Christian faith–an entirely characteristic snapshot.

A high spot of the Sunday School came on 18 January, 1933, on the day when the local Watling Association opened its new

119

Community Centre. The Prince of Wales performed the ceremony at the Centre, but afterwards was diverted. In the words of the *Hendon and Finchley Times*:

When the Prince of Wales was about to leave the Community Centre he was asked if he would be good enough to visit 1,000 children who were taking part in the fifth anniversary and prize-giving of the Sunday School at Woodcroft Hall. Although the Prince was due at an unemployed meeting at Kennington, he said he felt unable to resist, and drove to the Hall, where a large crowd gave him an enthusiastic welcome . . . The Prince was invited on the platform by Mr. J. Fenwick Adams (Sunday School superintendent), and introduced to Mr. and Mrs. J. W. Laing, Mr. W. J. Bull (hon. secretary) and Mrs. Adams, as well as a number of teachers.

Afterwards the children subscribed for a special presentation Bible for the Prince, bound in royal blue leather and inscribed on vellum by Mr. Bull, and each subscriber received a special' commemorative postcard. With knowledge of John Laing's special flair, the inspiration of these events is not far to seek.

Some interesting characters associated themselves with the church. There were 'Curly' Reed, 'praise-the-Lord' driver from the Underground, who later became Pastor Reed in an independent chapel; William Smith from Irvine in Ayrshire, who came south because of the depression and took a job with the Company, and who acted as a pastoral visitor on the estate, later moving into the caretaker's flat and becoming a full-time church worker—a great pastor who could speak to the working man on his own level; and several other lads from the estate who joined John Laing's Company and rose high in its service. (Ted Richardson, who became a director of its South African operations, did a great Christian work in the black shanty towns there before dying of a heart attack in his late forties.)

John Laing's wide connections ensured that the church had some of the best visiting speakers of the day. Andrew Anderson, a methodical secretary, controlled the arrangements. Beatrice Laing was not only a leader of the girls' classes, but also ran, with the able assistance of the wives of other elders, an extensive and thriving women's fellowship that outlasted the wartime difficulties and could still mount large and greatly patronised summer seaside outings well after the war—events in which both the Laings would take enthusiastic part. Somewhat shy herself, she had a ready sympathy with the sensitive, and took a close and understanding interest in the members and their families. Where she gave help, it was given quietly and in confidence.

Woodcroft Hall was the foundation and centre of John Laing's Christian activity for the rest of his life, and until his final weakness in extreme old age he was regularly at the services, and in particular at the weekly communion. He told several friends that his life had held two important memories for him: they were Hebron Hall, in Carlisle, and Woodcroft.

Yet the work at Woodcroft was only a fraction of his activities. On moving to London, he had very soon enrolled as leader of the local Mill Hill class of the boys' Crusader movement; an evangelical youth movement founded in 1906, which in those days deliberately confined its activities to boys from the middle classes. The activities centred around a weekly Sunday Bible class, but this was supplemented by a variety of sporting and other leisure activities during the week, and regular annual camps and house-parties; the main thrust of its work was directed towards Christian conversion and commitment.

Approaching fifty as he was, he threw himself into the activities of the class with boyish enthusiasm; no facility of his own or of his business was too valuable to be used, if appropriate, to help the Crusaders. The Company's offices were a meeting-place for years, and later, when the Company had been mechanised, employees (not to say fellow Crusader leaders) were frequently alarmed at the latitude which their chief, normally so stringent over waste or damage, would allow to teenage high spirits on the Company's machines. He became a regular participant in the annual camps, which assumed a high priority in his life, and until he was seventy would be present as commandant or *padre*, taking part in every activity with the boyish enthusiasm he never lost. He eventually bought a house for his local Mill Hill class, and throughout the years he would be there, joining in the games and helping in the Bible study sessions, until age forced his retirement, not to inactivity, but to become a union leader, available widely as a speaker to classes for their special events.

Not long after his move to London he joined the General Purposes Sub-Committee of the Crusaders' Union, a sort of inner cabinet which met regularly each week over a sandwich lunch. For many years there were present at these meetings, among others, his friends Montague Goodman and F. D. Bacon (secretary to a leading London insurance brokers) and the

121

General Secretary, A. J. Vereker. Jack Watford, who succeeded Vereker in 1946, remembers John Laing at those meetings after the war:

> I could share with these men of affairs everything concerning Crusaders . . . John Laing was remarkable in that he would listen to a discussion and say very little and he would get out his black notebook and write very laboriously, and after everybody had had their say he would say, 'I rather think that the answer to this might be . . .' and he would bring out some simple solution. Everybody would say, 'Oh yes, of course, quite right.' He had a strong capacity for simplicity and didn't seem to get trammelled or snared by the paraphernalia of a thing . . . he had taken away the ifs and the buts and had seen the thing in its clear setting.

These men built up a close friendship and harmony that would show to advantage at the annual houseparties.

> I remember them at Bexhill in the early thirties at Easter together. We used to have fireside talks—about 200 of us—and he and Monty would ask each other questions and try to catch each other out. Frank Bacon would be in it too; the three of them would go hammer and tongs and it would be wonderful fun . . . He was a man of great simplicity; he had no deep theological capacity, it did not bother him at all. He would speak very simply, but the very genuineness of the man would come across. When he would talk to the boys in camp I would think, 'Oh dear, this is so elementary'—and yet they would crowd round him. He was approachable: a kind of father figure.

It was in the nineteen thirties that a young Crusader leader in Plymouth first met John Laing. A difficulty had arisen over a local leadership appointment, and inflexibility led to a clash between the central and local leadership. John Laing visited the group as a member of the London central committee; despite his strong convictions, he proved a genuine peacemaker, tolerant of other outlooks and broad-minded in his approach to the problems. It was the first link in a chain of events that led to Ernest Uren, a young Crusader leader and an incorporated accountant* joining

*The Society of Incorporated Accountants and Auditors merged with the Institute of Chartered Accountants in England and Wales in 1957.

John Laing & Son Limited in 1938. Uren was to be one of the Company's most significant accessions of his generation, and was eventually to become chief executive and to retire as a vice-chairman of the International Company.

Two of the Mill Hill Crusaders in succession became leaders of their local scout troop. John Laing gave his support and interest as generously to them, providing them with accommodation that stands today. Personally committed as he was to the strongly evangelical group, his sympathies were not sectional; still less were they so in social terms, as other developments proved.

During the summer following the opening of the Woodcroft Hall Sunday School, its superintendent came across a group of older boys outside the building. Why did they not join? 'What, me?' replied a boy. 'I'm fourteen!' Fenwick Adams discussed the reply with John Laing, who asked why the middle-class Crusader methods should not be available, and in a local church context, to lads from a different social background. Other church members had experience with uniformed organisations such as the scouts and the Boys' Brigade, but some had reservations over a uniformed group. What would best suit their own circumstances and abilities?

They decided on a club specifically for boys over twelve, John Laing outlining his ideas on the structure and methods needed if discipline and interest were to be secured. Someone, perhaps a Scotsman, suggested naming them Covenanters, and a badge–a plain red button with three-pointed gold crown–was chosen. After a false start of a month or two, John Laing offered to claim release for two years from the Mill Hill Crusaders, and to devote his efforts to the new venture, helped by William Sirey and a young assistant, Roland Webb.

Parallel with this, a similar girls' group was started, Beatrice Laing later becoming a leader, and the two groups grew steadily, several times (with the school) outgrowing their accommodation. Roland Webb was soon able to take over full charge of the boys' section, and each section eventually had some sixty to seventy members (each divided into three age groups) and six staff. John Laing arranged gymnastic instruction and donated the necessary equipment.

In 1930, while these groups were developing, Roland Webb heard from John Cansdale, a friend in Rugby whom he had not seen for some years; the letter brought the information that Cansdale was running similar boys' work in connection with a Brethren church there, under the same name of Covenanters.

This Rugby group had its own badge, and a group chorus based on Joshua 1:9, a biblical verse that had been a sheet anchor of Webb's for three years. A decision was made to associate; a new badge was designed, and the Covenanter Union (with its sister organisation for girls) was born, to grow steadily over the years as a church-based and evangelical youth movement, today with several hundred classes, attached to churches of most Protestant denominations.

Roland Webb for a time acted as honorary secretary to the new movement, to be succeeded as full-time secretary by W. T. Stunt, a solicitor from Chelmsford. John Laing remained a regular member of the central committee of this movement also, enthusiastic in his support, always with a vision of what the movement might achieve, and unobtrusively available with prudently considered financial support when needed.

Inevitably, John Laing's family were caught up in his never-ceasing activity, and at times (until they left for St. Lawrence College, Ramsgate, a year or two later) the two sons must have found life overwhelming. Beatrice Laing was as involved as her husband, but family life was by no means swamped, and the boys both grew into their parents' Christian faith. Like his father before him, John Laing had been nearly forty when his sons were born, and he was building plans for the future about them. As his mother had carefully instilled her own frugal prudence into her children, so he inculcated his own values by practice as well as by precept. He was generous with pocket-money, but insisted that it had to be earned–and sometimes by carefully calculated piece work on minor duties about the home. The boys were encouraged to follow their father's 'giving'; even income which was otherwise accumulated in trust had to have its appropriate portion given away. It was a reiterated principle that as much should be given away as was spent on oneself, and in this Laing was absolutely honest with himself. Ostentation or extravagance was strictly avoided. In one year a radiogram was bought, and it was the best available: but he also wanted a new car, and that had to be postponed (though he could well afford it), for two luxury expenditures in the one year would have been affectation.

In 1927 the family visited Spain to see Beatrice Laing's sister, who had married a Brethren missionary pastor in León, Thornton Turrall. They were able to make the occasion a family holiday. An incident from the holiday has remained in the minds of his sons. They had been bathing and had left their clothes with their holiday pocket money by the shore. One of the boys arrived back and disturbed a thief at work: his own money was saved, but his brother's had gone. When the incident was reported to their father, the lucky one was made to share his money with his brother. John Laing's sense of justice insisted that they had been equally foolish and must share the results equally.

A year or two later the family visited the Holy Land, a special event for which John Laing planned the best for them. In three weeks—it was before the day of aeroplanes—they had stopped off in Paris and visited the Louvre and other sights, travelled by boat from Marseilles to Port Said, and then by train to Jerusalem. For this special journey, John Laing's accustomed frugality was lifted. They stayed at the King David Hotel, hired a car, and thoroughly explored Palestine, visiting virtually all the accessible biblical sites except Damascus. On the return they had two days in Cairo, and a day each in Venice and Geneva. At the beginning of the journey he had put twelve-year-old Kirby, the older boy, in charge of the family money, the spending and the tipping, and signing the travellers' cheques for him on request. He was training his sons and himself in mutual confidence and understanding for the greater responsibilities of the future.

His customary careful prudence became legendary among both his personal and his business acquaintances. The practice of the Alfred Holt shipping family, for one of whom he had built a house in Cumberland in his early business years, appealed to him; this member of the family had told him that they had ploughed back into their business assets all the earnings from the ships themselves, drawing as a family only from their reserve funds. He himself was cautious to the extreme in his own business accounting, reckoning profit only when contracts were fully complete. Speculative profits were anathema to him, whether on shares or land. 'I find that the selling of shares to make a profit develops a mercenary habit which is against the spirit of Jesus Christ,' he wrote at the end of his life; 'the latter is a spirit of service, the former is a spirit of trying to get gains which are not a result of service.' On another occasion a competing company wished to buy a large piece of land on an estate they were developing. 'We could have made more profit by selling this land than we were making on the houses . . . but we were not snatching a quick profit; we wanted the pleasure of serving the purchaser and giving him value.'

At times his frugality became austerity. Extravagance of the type that is popularly associated with big business was foreign to him. On business journeys he would take packed sandwiches from his home (especially sweet ones—he had a sweet tooth) or eat in the site canteens. A site manager who provided a special meal for him was liable to be rebuked: what was good enough for the men, was good enough for him. Anecdotes are common of his walking out of restaurants because they looked too expensive for his taste. He was plainly conscious of his eccentricities in this direction, and a self-teasing humour is detectable in some of the anecdotes. On one of his visits to the Purley housing estate, he asked one of the staff for a pencil, and was handed a Royal Sovereign. 'This is a very good pencil—what did it cost?' 'Fourpence.' 'Now I know a shop where you can buy them for one penny'—and he gave the address: at Hendon Central (twenty miles away)! The same man saw him, in his eighties, mounting the staircase at his home two steps at a time. He commented on his youthful vigour, and John Laing smiled. 'Yes, and it saves the carpet!' The man added, 'I still am not sure how serious he was.' Wallace Haughan writes:

> Another instance of his dry humour was when in the war years he steadfastly refused to eat anything different from the ration. He was most strict about this, and when visiting contracts he would always eat at the canteen on the job. I am sure a lot of people will remember that the food was pretty poor; in fact, some of it used to be atrocious. He used to take his first mouthful and look up, and we always got the same remark, 'Isn't it delicious?', again with the famous grin.

His old athleticism was never lost, and he always conserved his superb physical fitness. In addition to the sport enjoyed with the youth groups, he took regular exercise on every possible occasion until an advanced age. Often he would drive his car in the morning, and leave it some considerable distance from his office, in order to take a brisk walk; very often, too, he forgot where he had left it, the staff would find his faithful driver, 'Billy' White, anxiously enquiring whether any of them had seen it on the way in. (This absent-mindedness also became legendary, and seems to have been inherited, for his father had often lost his bicycle in Carlisle in a similar manner; he was also notorious for losing his gloves, and the chauffeur kept a supply of spares for him, as he was meticulous about wearing them.) On one occasion a local resident saw a car stop near his home, and a man get out and move off at a brisk trot; he reported the incident to the police, who found that it was John Laing taking his morning exercise. A relative in Carlisle recalled how, on one occasion, he was speaking to a Bible class there on the prophet Elijah; at the incident when the prophet ran in advance of the royal chariot from Carmel to Jezreel (1 Kings 18:46) his enthusiasm mounted, and he expanded eloquently on Elijah's prowess and the importance of physical fitness!

Even on his journeys overseas, he looked for his regular exercise. One friend, who accompanied him to India after the war, remembers a refuelling stop at a desert airfield in the Middle East on the return journey in early 1949. John Laing asked the Iraqi Airways pilot how long they would be there, and was told 'fifteen minutes'. He looked at his watch, and went off at a steady run into the desert, turning back after precisely seven and a half minutes.

He was a golfer from his early days in London, taking regular rounds with friends like Fenwick Adams and, on occasion, William Sirey (no doubt realising the long hours the latter spent in the office), as well as with business acquaintances. 'I remember him at Colindale,' said one retired staff member. 'He came out and said, "I want to get back quickly, I'm having a game of golf with Mr. Sirey." It was a cold day–one of those days when the ground was white with frost–and he said, "Help me to paint these balls red," so he could see them.'

This fitness served him well for his site supervision; well into middle age he was able to do a job of physical work as well as any employee, and in his late seventies was alarming site managers by climbing, with the old rock-climber's head for heights, into the upper reaches of high-rise buildings under construction.

One feature of family life John Laing and his wife valued immensely. They were always supporters of systems of regular daily Bible reading, for which they used the Scripture Union notes, and a period of family devotions was a regular evening practice, to be shared by all visitors to the home. John Laing would disappear for a few moments and return with an armload of Bibles, one of which would be handed to each person. If a visitor were present he might be invited to choose a passage for reading, or the allotted portion for the day would be found. The party would then read, a verse each, around the circle. The proceedings closed with a short prayer by John Laing (who kept a methodical prayer list, dividing the week over his various interests, that was transferred from diary to diary at each year's end). As one regular visitor remarked, 'You always left, knowing what sort of man you had been with.'

There was a simple forthrightness and lack of sanctimoniousness about these devotions. Occasionally he might be detected chuckling to himself over something that had caught his sense of humour. His basic humanity was never overridden by mere piety. One visitor remembers an occasion when the chosen portion was from Psalm 37, and Sir John Laing's turn came at verse 25: 'I have been young, and now am old; yet have I not seen the righteous forsaken, nor his seed begging bread.' He paused and looked up. 'Well, Beatrice, we have seen them get pretty close to it!' He closed his Bible and added, 'I think we will read *Daily Light* tonight.'

As the nineteen thirties passed, John Laing was increasingly invited to lend his name (by now a formidable one) to Christian activities. Committee work and other activities did not appeal unless he could make a genuine contribution, and he therefore developed a clear strategy to govern his choice of commitments. Some activities with which he was in full sympathy, such as the Scripture Union and Children's Special Service Mission, or the Evangelical Alliance, he felt to be already fully and adequately manned; he supported them and they figured in his prayer lists, but he was not actively involved with them.

His basic loyalty remained to the Christian Brethren, and in particular to their evangelistic work and missions. Two concerns outside Brethren circles that were central to his strategy were youth work and Bible scholarship. As in business, he was far-sighted and looked constantly to the future. His concern for the rising generation lay behind the whole-hearted support, in time and money, given to the Crusader and Covenanter movements; it was paralleled in his business life by the emphasis on training. The concern for Bible scholarship reflects a deeper strategic feeling for vital areas that were not his own natural interest; again, it was paralleled in business life by a keen interest in technological development.

Although he was not a natural intellectual or theologian (he was far too much a man of action) his early reading, and in particular his youthful wrestling with the Darwinist challenge to his faith, had made him alive to the importance of the intellectual, and he was also conscious of the dearth of acknowledged scholarship among evangelicals. As his older son approached university age, and proposed going up to Cambridge, John Laing became interested in the evangelical voice within

Golders Green Estate: one thousand private houses *c.* 1929

Flats at Manor Fields, Putney Hill *c.* 1935 (p. 137)

Headquarters R.A.F. Bomber Command, 1940 (p. 154)

Concrete caissons for Mulberry Harbour, 1944 (p. 154)

universities. His attention was taken by the publication in 1934 of *Christ and the Colleges* by the Revd F. D. Coggan (the present Archbishop of Canterbury), a history of the Inter-Varsity Fellowship of Evangelical Unions,* of whose recently formed Business Advisory Committee his friend F. D. Bacon was already a member.

Bacon persuaded him to join the Business Advisory Committee in 1935. It was the beginning of what was to become one of his least-known, and possibly most widely influential, Christian involvements, and one by which he later made a notable unseen contribution to the subsequent flowering of conservative evangelical scholarship.

For a year or two John Laing was a quiet member of the I.V.F. Business Advisory Committee, watching and weighing the place of the Fellowship in his scheme of priorities. It was a critical time.

At this time [writes Dr. Oliver Barclay][1] the evangelical world was suffering an intellectual inferiority complex . . . Many were frightened of intellectual activity. The evangelical world generally seemed to be in decline. Many of its ablest young men and women were going liberal or losing their faith at university.

John Laing always looked for men, and he was a superb judge of the right man. His eye was particularly on the general secretary of the I.V.F., Douglas Johnson, an arts and medical graduate of outstanding ability who had first become honorary secretary of the I.V.F.'s fore-runner, the Inter-Varsity Conference, as long before as 1924. Johnson was to win Laing's full confidence as did few other evangelical administrators, and together they were to build a partnership that, behind the scenes, was a vital force in the growth of the Fellowship.

Most of this story will be for a later chapter. John Laing's most striking contributions during the nineteen-thirties were to buy and present to the I.V.F. the lease of premises at 39 Bedford Square which were to be its headquarters for forty years (characteristically, he asked that it should never be valued in the Fellowship accounts); to help reconstruct the Northgate Hall for the Oxford Inter-Collegiate Christian Union; to encourage the beginnings of an expansion in the numbers of travelling secretaries (to be followed up after the war); and to back the calling of a

*Now the Universities and Colleges Christian Fellowship.

great week-long International Conference of Evangelical Students at Cambridge from 27 June to 3 July, 1939. With over 1,000 participants from Britain and the U.S.A., from Scandinavia, Hungary, and other continental countries, the Conference was a vital public token of reviving Evangelical confidence. Sunday service in Great St. Mary's was broadcast by the B.B.C., and an open united service of Holy Communion there, held by special dispensation of the Bishop of Ely,* must have been one of the first such occasions to be overlooked by those august walls. Coming as it did just as the clouds of the Second World War were about to break, the Conference was a poignant and symbolic event: but it had been the kindled vision of John Laing behind the scenes which had insisted beforehand 'Let us do everything *well*', and had seen that the financial backing was there.

A second venture in evangelical scholarship – this time of a more directly biblical character – was conceived during the nineteen-thirties, but brought to birth towards the end of the war. A. J. Vereker of the Crusaders' Union had for several years been concerned with the need for an evangelical Bible college, based on sound scholarship, in the London area; his journeys abroad had increased his conviction, as he had seen such colleges in other countries, and he raised the matter among various of his London friends, including Douglas Johnson. The two men approached John Laing, who was later present with them and a number of evangelical leaders (including Montague Goodman) at a meeting on 25 May, 1939, which decided to proceed with the project. A planning committee was formed, on which John Laing served, but within a few months the outbreak of war caused the project to be halted. It was reborn before the war ended as the London Bible College.

Already there had been a foretaste of its post-war development, when John Laing had taken A. J. Vereker and Douglas Johnson over an old building at 19 Marylebone Road, formerly belonging to the Metropolitan Water Board, which his Company had acquired. 'This would be an excellent site for the new Bible college,' he had suggested, while leading them with aplomb over parapets that turned their heads, but not his own. The war intervened, and the notable post-war story will be told in a later chapter.

---

*It is pleasant to record that it was the influence of Canon C. E. Raven – not normally known as a friend of conservative evangelicalism – which secured this permission.

During all of this time, John Laing maintained support of Brethren and related activities, pre-eminently through the trust established with the Stewards' Company. Almost thirty per cent of dividends from his Company were being channelled through this trust throughout the nineteen-thirties (a high proportion of the remainder going to employee shareholders). The funds were allocated by himself as a result of deliberate assessment of needs brought to his attention: he had to be satisfied that the work to which he was giving, whether at home or overseas, was viable and adequately controlled. A stated scheme of priorities, both as to Brethren and non-Brethren work, operated within a carefully thought-out strategy. Wherever possible, giving was on the 'matching' principle, contributing one pound for every pound contributed by local interests—a principle applied especially to finance for new buildings, whether places of worship or premises for medical or orphanage work. All giving was carefully confidential; it was a product of his Barrow vow, and therefore a major and essential part of his private life with God.

Personal time also was carefully husbanded for those enterprises that were within his scheme of priorities. An executive of his Company, who was very close to him throughout his life after the move to London, found that his time was allocated as strictly as his giving:

> Though he was so keen and so exacting he was a wonderful example. You could always be sure of seeing him to discuss matters with him and get his advice and so on, even to the extent of his saying, 'I will see you at five o'clock.' . . . When six o'clock was come, he would say, 'Now that's it, no more business,' and before I was out of his office he had his drawer open and his Bible, and he was preparing for his meeting . . . He had a wonderful way of switching his mind: concentrating on the business we were talking about . . . How he could just stop dead like that and go on to the other thing—that's a thing I could never do.

Brethren evangelistic work figured largely in John Laing's thinking. He was in frequent consultation with the editors of the missionary journal *Echoes of Service*, who operated a clearinghouse for gifts to the missionaries and for information on their activities, and through them he kept in touch with activities overseas. At home, the old interest in the Cumberland and Westmorland tent work (of which David Beattie had succeeded him as secretary after his move to London) led naturally to his joining the group of overseers of Counties Evangelistic Work, a body which was concerned with supervision of similar activities in some of the southern counties. (It was later to expand to cover most counties of the southern half of the country.) He attended his first meeting of this body on 17 August, 1928, and became one of its treasurers. During the thirties he was directly concerned with the work in the counties of Hertfordshire, Bedfordshire, Buckingham and south-west Essex, and took a personal interest in the evangelists, helping also to supply and maintain some of their 'Bible carriages.' Later he was to serve on the central committee, on which he remained until the age of seventy: the involvement was close and generous: indeed there were years when ten per cent of the income of the work was provided by him.

He was also associated with the foundation of a short-lived magazine called *Onward* that circulated among Brethren just before 1930, and he contributed articles to it. There were a number of such small magazines at that time, and most in due course merged with a more widely circulating journal, *The Harvester*, of whose body of trustees John Laing was chairman for many years. Such magazines at the time were largely devoted to supporting and reporting on the work of Brethren evangelists and Bible teachers; they formed an obvious adjunct to the more directly evangelistic interests.

Brethren ran orphanages and schools at home and abroad to which Laing also gave support. Although the more significant associations came after the thirties, he joined the trustees of the celebrated Müller Homes for Children of Bristol in May 1937.

Perhaps John Laing's most notable contribution to the Brethren, however, was by extensive assistance in financing the building of new halls and chapels. When the Woodford estate was in progress, he offered the Brethren locally a choice of two sites: boldly, they decided that they could man both, and the Company built them. From Woodcroft Hall, two further churches in the north-western suburbs of London were formed, in 1935 and 1936. A third followed after the war. Many new churches elsewhere were similarly helped, always after careful investigation of their background and local support, and the building costs and plans. In all cases, financial help was given on the favoured 'matching' basis. Where the Company did the building work for such churches, it was invariably at bare cost; but where local builders were employed, Laing was equally interested in their work, and ready with approval of sound workmanship. He was also actively interested in the work of non-denominational inner-London missions, such as the Bethnal Green Medical Mission and the Lansdowne Place Medical Mission in South-wark.

Houses on several of the estates were set aside for the use of missionaries temporarily in the country on furlough; in Honey-pot Lane, Edgware, twelve flats were provided in six houses to be available for retired missionaries and full-time workers. Beatrice Laing took a close interest in these houses, and ensured provision for the practical needs of their residents.

The openness and vigour of Brethren churches generally were always matters of close concern to John Laing: he was not a party man, but he was anxious that they should share his own unsectional concern for the Church at large. 'Are they going on in a good *open* manner?' would be a frequent enquiry. 'He was bothered because the Brethren got so inward-looking,' said another friend. 'He longed for more outward expression.' It was a concern shared with his friend, Montague Goodman, and perhaps this non-sectarian attitude explains why the main emphasis of his support for biblical education and scholarship was always inter-denominational. But Brethren scholars always had a very special place in his interests, and figured on his personal prayer lists, as one in whom he had taken a particular interest since they met in 1929 writes:

In the long, difficult years of study in Germany, he was always ready with a word of understanding and of encouragement. He saw so clearly the need for conservative Christian scholar-ship of a quality as high as he set for himself in business, and unimpeachable in its credentials.

John Laing was a man big enough to see beyond himself, and to encourage others who could go where he could not.

CHAPTER 9

Industry and Nation

All the office in a skitter and a scurry,
All the office in a flitter and a flurry,
Hither and thither distracted run;
A hundred and one
Things to be done
Ere set of sun
And done
No matter how
NOW!

EVERY OFFICE HAS its wit, and the young lady who left that jingle behind her after a short time at Mill Hill in 1928 no doubt had the picture with that sharpness that is the gift of her kind. Certainly she caught a number of her colleagues with vivid little vignettes, and added feelingly about herself

The gift of observation
Has its compensation;
But too much clarity
Does not add to popularity.

The Company was fortunate to have a group of senior executives who would drive themselves to the limit in its service. The senior men were frequently working long hours far into the evening; John Laing's unfailing energy put a severe burden on his administrative staff. Yet he was a man of great heart, who inspired and stimulated them, and won an unquestioned loyalty from them. His personal secretaries found themselves caught up in his charitable interest: the charitable giving from the first was systematic, large and widespread, but above all confidential. It was a strict rule that John Laing's name must not appear, nor must a regular pseudonym, and the personal secretary would have the task of selecting a wide range of anonymous cover for any published lists that societies might issue. Normally this would be a biblical reference: John Laing would always be interested to approve or disapprove of the chosen verse, and the secretaries' biblical knowledge was undoubtedly increased hugely! Sometimes Laing's giving was impulsive (despite his customary caution), particularly where some personal tragedy had caught his attention: one of the early secretaries, then a fairly young girl, remembers being sent out, at short notice, on such errands, even on one occasion to investigate a case that had been reported in the press from a remote spot in East Anglia. It was in 1931 that John Laing was joined by the remarkable Miss Emily Ridout Byrnell, who remained his secretary for the next twenty-eight years, and in 1952 summed up both John Laing and herself: 'Always setting the example, he expects the impossible and usually gets it'.[1]

Despite the onset of the economic slump, the great housing estates were by no means the only work available. Air Ministry contracts continued to be a regular part of the Company's work; there were also contracts for housing for local authorities, schools and other public works, shopping parades with their residential flats, and a considerable number of factories for the growing light industry of the London districts (many of the last two categories for the property company). After being fairly stable on average for some years, turnover took a sharp leap in 1930, largely because of the private housing estates and related developments, and it topped a million pounds for the first time. Building costs had been constant since 1923 (they were to fall slightly during the mid thirties), and in 1977 terms this sum would represent about fourteen million pounds: still a size which, to John Laing, was capable of personal central control. Most work outside the Air Ministry contracts was now in the London or Carlisle areas.

The largest contracted work during the first half of the thirties was the construction of the great Middlesex County Hospital at Shenley in Hertfordshire, a project which has taken its place in the collective memory of the older Company hands. The securing of this substantial high-grade work (the first stage to the official opening in 1934 cost £800,000, and the second stage which followed added a further £700,000) in fact proved of first importance to the later development of the business, for it meant the retention of a proved and efficient working team throughout the depression years; it was not for nothing that one veteran recalls of Shenley (as of Catterick in the twenties) that 'practically everybody went to Shenley'.

This contract was the first to see the regular use of contractor's mechanical plant, though on a small scale in comparison with that of today—and horses and carts were still much used. The Company's first excavator, an Insley, was in use there, driven by Neville Reece who, during his time with the Company, was to man excavators (up to the vast machines used on the post-war open-cast coal workings) on sites throughout the country. Reece had joined the business in 1927 as a result of John Laing's personal powers of observation; he had been working with his lorry on a job near the Company's offices in Bunns Lane and was one day approached by John Laing. 'I like the careful way you look after that lorry of yours—would you like a job with me?' He was to stay for the rest of his life, one of the Company's most trusted workers, whom John Laing would visit for a brief talk on every visit to a site where he was working. 'Laings were everything to him,' says his wife.

The quality of the work at Shenley was after John Laing's own heart. Situated on high ground, with separate buildings connected by subways, and planned by the County Architect, W. T. Curtis, it took the best advantage of its magnificent site, on the Porters Park estate that Middlesex County Council had acquired some years before. When it was fully completed it had accommodation for two thousand patients with all the necessary staff and facilities that made it a self-contained small town, with an outlying colony a short distance away. The brickwork and masonry were of high quality, and the Company's most skilled men were employed on the work.

Although successive work there lasted for a decade, the main contract required the hospital stage to be handed over in two years, ready for furnishing; in fact not only was it furnished, but also patients were in residence twenty-two months after start of the work. During that period, 50,000 cubic yards of earth had been excavated; 2 miles of reinforced concrete subways and 37,000 yards super of reinforced concrete roads were put down, with 7½ acres of reinforced concrete paving and over 9 acres of suspended concrete floors and roofs; no fewer than 13 million bricks had been laid. The great square water tower, 140 feet high, was a special feature of the contract; eight skilled bricklayers raised the tower five feet every day, with special wage rates for the work.[2]

The superb organisation of the contract was in the charge of W. M. Johnson, remembered by one brought up under him in the Company as 'like a father; next to the governor he had a remarkable way with men, tough but with absolute integrity and never unjust—very like Sir John himself'. There was the closest co-operation and trust between the architect and the team. As on the housing estates, detailed records of production were sent each day to the Company's office, whether of measured concrete or brickwork or of the use of the plant, and the cost of the work was known in the office by the end of the day. Both quantity and costs were checked against targets, and John Laing himself closely monitored progress; he was also frequently at the site, usually arriving before work started at 8.00 a.m. Visitors were proudly taken around the site; the then secretary of the Cumberland Building Society, visiting London for an Association meeting, was one who remembers spending two hours on the site with his chairman and John Laing.

The first section of the contract, the main hospital, was opened by King George V on 31 May, 1934, the seventh of John Laing's contracts to have received the accolade of a royal opening.

Other work in the thirties of especial interest was the development for investment of a substantial scheme of high-quality residential flats at Manor Fields, Putney, in south-west London, on the estate which had once belonged to the great Lord North, not very far from the very different L.C.C. Dover House development of a few years previously. Meticulously designed and landscaped around the existing trees and contours, the scheme became known as one of the finest in the country and attracted widespread interest. Henry Chapman Harland himself lived there for a period to supervise the progress and execution of the project. This development, which has matured well, was followed by similar schemes in Hampstead.

Turnover climbed steadily during the thirties, doubling in the period up to 1936, and more than doubling again by 1939 as the airfield projects multiplied. The staff at the beginning of the decade was still extremely small, with not more than twenty-five to thirty in the office at Bunns Lane: estimators, buyers, surveyors and accounts staff. One of the staff, whose office adjoined that of John Laing, remembers them working at long benches on high stools. The office was divided by glass partitions, and when the new-year's calendars arrived the largest would sometimes find its way on to the partition between the office where this man worked with his colleagues, and his chief's next door (only to be quietly removed after a few days. 'Do you *really* need such a large calendar?'). Houses for the staff were built on the land adjoining the offices, so that many of the head-office men were within short walking distance. A sports club was started informally in 1927 when John Laing and David Thompson opened a tennis court adjoining the offices with a token knock-about; it was constituted more solidly in 1933. Share-holdings in the Company were owned by men from all grades of employees, and attendances at the annual general meetings were already about sixty.

John Laing became interested in the National Savings movement, which appealed to both his patriotic instincts and his sense of thrift, and in 1928 he arranged for his Company to contribute towards every national savings certificate bought by its employees—a small step, but an important lead in an industry where the movement had previously gained little support. This association with the National Savings movement was to be extended and emphasised during the Second World War.

Production bonuses, as we have seen, had already been instituted by the mid-twenties, as a corollary of the detailed works costing. An old notebook of Easiform costings from those years includes standards for bonus calculations at Exeter and Woolwich and, later on, joinery at Colin Park. On the housing estates in the mid-thirties a target cost was set for the bricklayers' labour on each house; if there were a saving on this target, the men would receive a proportion of it. The plan seems to have varied in detail; old employees remember receiving the whole saving from a tight standard, or a proportion of saving from an easier standard. The traditional Christmas gifts were also later supplemented by merit bonuses—in this case largely applicable to the administrative staff.

Productivity at the contracts had always been high. Glaziers at the Easiform estates had a norm of 200 panes of glass (11 × 8½ inches) fitted by a man and his assistant in ten hours (a steady average of one pane every three minutes) and there is a note of a man and a boy actually fitting 350 panes in that time. A pair of semi-detached Easiform houses would be felted and tiled by two men in a little over two days: one day to felt and lath, one day to tile, and six hours to ridge and hip. At Shenley, Joss Cartmell, a skilled bricklayer, once laid 1,100 bricks in three and a half hours on a straight run; the normal average was 800 to 1,000 a day.*

*Taylor Woodrows were said to expect their skilled bricklayers to lay a thousand bricks a day in 1931 (quoted from Alan Jenkins, 'On Site 1921–1971' in *Semi-Detached London*, Alan A. Jackson, 1973, page 105). The wartime standard fixed by the Ministry of Works for the payment-by-results system—admittedly at a time when skilled labour was very scarce—was said to have been only 400 a day.

Everything depended, of course, on the type of brickwork.

John Laing's own semi-whimsical watch on productivity was the subject of many stories. One joiner remembers how, a year after he started his apprenticeship at Carlisle in the mid-twenties, John Laing visited the works; he had not seen him for some time, but remembered him by name and came and talked to him; the lad was mortising door stiles. 'How many do you do in an hour?' 'Eighteen.' 'Oh, no! Twenty is the number, Joe, twenty an hour; and *every* hour.' During the slump of the thirties men were joining the Company from far afield; there were constant letters seeking employment for men out of work. John Laing's reputation among the Brethren naturally brought many such letters from his co-religionists, and one man had joined as a painter. Soon after he joined, he heard that John Laing was visiting the site where he worked, and as the visiting party approached, the man could be heard loudly humming a familiar hymn tune. Now in some districts Brethren have a tradition of extremely slow singing, and this man was working in time to his tune. John Laing stopped by him. 'Ah, you must be Mr. So-and-so.' (His customary knowledge of even the new men was much in evidence.) 'Now this is how you should do it,' and taking the brush from the man he began humming the national anthem at a very brisk pace and wielding the brush in corresponding time. Neville Reece remembers seeing him at a wartime aerodrome contract watching the navvies working, then stopping them. 'This is the way you use your pick,' and John Laing (then well into his sixties) was down in the trench demonstrating vigorously.

His insistence on quality of workmanship was equally strong. He was regularly on the sites in the early morning, and would customarily carry out vigorous quality checks. Wallace Haughan remembers him ordering the demolition of two houses on one of Laing's own estates that were already roofed and ready for plastering, because he considered them below standard. One member of the staff had been promised that his house would be built to allow space for a garage; by oversight the building was wrongly sited, with no garage space, and again John Laing ordered its demolition when it was well advanced, and a re-start in accordance with his promise. In Carlisle similar stories were common talk. On another factory contract, he found the approach being concreted. Calling for the specification, he checked the thickness at several places, then turned to the general foreman. 'We are giving the client a quarter of an inch less than he is paying for and I want you to take up all this area.'

Control of materials bought and used was just as meticulous. He relied on absolute honesty on the part of his staff, and any breath of corruption was immediately stifled. (This rule applied in every aspect of his dealings.) For a period, all executives were required to sign a declaration that they had neither sought nor given any form of inducement, before they received their Christmas bonuses (though John Laing was later to put on record that he had never been very happy about this procedure).[3]

> In visiting contracts I always made it a rule to visit the checker to show that he was an appreciated member of the firm. I realised that he was exposed to great temptation. He was usually in a little office at the entrance to the site, and therefore was a lonely man. By that personal contact I got to know a number of checkers and appreciated them very much. I tried to encourage them to tell me about their home and family in the short time available.

The checking of deliveries to the sites was stringent in the extreme, and regular traffic returns were made to head office for recording and checking.

In other important aspects touching his employees' welfare he was also a pioneer. In July 1931, John Laing's *aide-mémoire* for a forthcoming meeting with his accountant Walter Harland read: 'Pension Fund–£10,000 invest in Property Company . . . For hardship to men, not had opportunity to save, who have done valuable work for firm and served considerable time, not squandered their funds by extravagant method of living. For sickness, old age or relatives. All to be *ex gratia*.' The discussion led to the formation of the Laing Benevolent Fund in the following year, as a charitable trust for employees; the Fund owned shares in the Companies and received regular covenanted donations from the Company. Built up steadily by John Laing over the years, the trust was eventually combined in the nine-teen-seventies with the Laing Charitable Trust (formed in 1962 for more general charitable objects); the combined assets of the two trusts (which by then were quite distinct from the main pension fund for employees, and from Laing's other charitable foundations) at that time totalled over two million pounds. The income was applied entirely to employee welfare and to more general charity.

The Holidays-with-Pay scheme which he instituted in his

Company in 1934 was a leader–quite possibly the first in the industry, and years in advance of both the general building industry scheme of 1942 and the still later legal requirements. One old worker remembers how he heard the news at the Blackwell brickworks in Carlisle.

> We used to go in to chip the boilers during race week, which was a general holiday in Carlisle. We used to get time and a half, but this year we went in–and no time and a half. We went to Mr. South the manager. 'What about this time and a half?' He says, 'Oh, with the machinery breaking down, Bob' (That was my brother) 'It's run away with all the profits.' Bob asked, 'When is John Willie coming?' He said, 'He is coming next week.' 'Can I talk to him?' He said 'Most certainly.'
>
> So when Mr. Laing came on the Monday morning we all came up and he said, 'What's this, Mr. South; a strike?' 'No,' he said, 'they want to see Mr. Laing.' So he came over to us and said, 'You've a grievance about this time and a half. You can all go back to your work; you will get it, but this is the last time. I am bringing in a new scheme.' He was willing to pay the workers for race week, but the other small builders wouldn't agree to it. His scheme was that his shilling and our shilling went from one year ahead to the next. This would have been about the early 1930s. He was doing it before any of the industry.

It was the favoured 'matching' principle again. In its earliest and simplest form, one shilling a week was deducted from a man's pay; the Company added another shilling, and so a week's paid holiday a year was provided. It was a modest start, but it pioneered the paid holiday for operatives at a time when it was unheard of in the industry, and it was a fore-runner of all that has followed since. It must be seen in the context of days when holiday arrangements in commerce generally, even for staff employees, were meagre by today's standards. A pupil under the pupillage scheme at that time received two weeks' paid holiday a year, but on moving out of his indentures to a supervisory position his allowance was reduced to one week. Indeed, John Laing's own exacting view of supervisory responsibilities was apt to make holiday arrangements for the more senior employees more rather than less severe. Perhaps it was a further sign of the conflict between a harsh industrial ethos and the 'external reference point' we have discussed in an earlier chapter.

These innovations were all trail-blazers, in fields where the Company was to remain an industry leader. From 1932, pensions were provided for some established employees, on an *ad hoc* basis, from the Benevolent Fund, supplemented by other contributions from the Company.* This somewhat paternalistic arrangement was superseded when regular superannuation schemes for both operatives and staff were set up independently as the Second World War was ending. They have since been regularly revised to keep abreast of the most advanced contemporary practice. The current operatives' scheme is the largest in the construction industry.

On the broader front of the industry at large, there were other developments. John Laing contributed occasional articles to the technical press, perhaps on a general subject such as housing development policy, or on a specific technical matter such as the method of drying timber for use in centrally heated buildings (a special research feature of the large joinery works he had established at Mill Hill). The latter contribution was based on the Company's own careful research tests, and they offered information to other contractors: this was an early fore-runner of the extensive research and development department to be set up by the Company immediately after the Second World War. The Company was beginning to share in the growing technical sophistication and mechanisation of the industry; a mid-thirties film shows concrete still being mixed and tamped by hand, but steel reinforcement was being used, and the film spoke of fifteen large excavators in constant use, with mechanical rollers and other equipment. Expenditure on vehicles was growing. At this time, the film said, the Company was building some thousand houses a year, in addition to working on eight large contracts; some three thousand men were employed.

The numerical record of the private house-builders in the nineteen-thirties was immensely successful; in England and Wales they raised output from 127,000 houses in 1931 to an average of 250,000 a year in the years 1936 to 1938 (in addition to local-authority building, which rose from 55,000 in 1931 to 101,000 in 1939).[4] But the quantitative output was accompanied by a great deal of criticism of building quality, some of it in the professional press, and by some damaging litigation that harmed the reputation of the industry as a whole.[5] The leaders of the

*The Company's chief (and friendly) rival announced with its 1935 accounts that it was starting a staff pension scheme.

industry were sensitive to these criticisms, and in 1935 the press could report plans afoot for the establishment of required model building standards, and of a register of house-builders complying with them. Sir Raymond Unwin, the architect friend of John Laing from Gretna, was prominent in the discussions, and chairman of the Standards Board. In January 1937 the Minister of Health was able to announce the formation of the National House Builders Registration Council (today known as the National Housebuilding Council). The Council was to maintain a register of builders who were prepared to undertake to build their houses to the model specification; it would inspect the houses carefully during construction, and the builders would give a two-year maintenance warranty.

John Laing himself was an active participant in arrangements so precisely in accordance with his own ideals, and he served on the Specification Committee under Sir Raymond Unwin. In 1939 he was called on to show his support for the scheme in a very practical way. The Council wished to obtain statutory recognition under the Building Societies Act, 1939, so that purchasers of houses certified under the scheme could receive favourable mortgages. A Treasury condition of recognition was provision of an indemnity against loss caused by a certified house not conforming with the standards. Because of the novelty of the concept, no insurance company was prepared to underwrite the indemnity at a reasonable premium, and John Laing, together with J. G. Gray of Coventry, personally underwrote the risk. It was a striking testimony both to his own confidence in the industry and to his own personal standing in the eyes of the Treasury.

The formation of the Council led directly to the founding in 1939 of the Federation of Registered House-Builders (now The House Builders' Federation), on the council of which John Laing served for many years, and on which he was, with others, to play an important part in the post-war rehabilitation of the private house-building industry.

One other development of this period in the organisation of the construction industry was also helpful to developments he was encouraging. He was a pioneer of the use of quantity surveyors within the English industry, a necessary adjunct to a contractor's negotiations with his clients. As the competence and importance of those engaged in this function within the industry grew, the question of formal qualification inevitably arose. To raise it, however, was to run headlong into the complications of that

143

search for professional recognition that has engrossed so many of the ramifying proficiences of an increasingly complex society during the past century. The chief existing body in the field insisted on training and practice inside the office of an independent practising quantity surveyor, and the purely 'contractor's surveyor', could not obtain membership or he was obliged to vacate a membership already held.* By the late thirties the number of quantity surveyors employed inside the industry had grown sufficiently to lead to the formation, in 1938, of the Institute of Quantity Surveyors, a body which was fully incorporated on 9 August, 1941, and has since painfully won full professional recognition for itself.

The members of John Laing's Company who had been so deeply involved in the elaboration and refinement of his methods were eager to take advantage of these developments, which fitted excellently with the Company training scheme, and John Gregg (later to be vice-chairman of the Company and president of the Institute) was one of the active early members of the Institute, and a succession of senior Laing men has since contributed to its affairs.

On the Jubilee Day of King George V, 6 May, 1935, John Laing left Croydon airport with a companion, E. H. Broadbent, for a visit to Russia. Broadbent, a well-known teacher among Brethren, had, in the course of his ministry, travelled widely in Eastern Europe and Russia before the First World War and had built up a close knowledge of the Baptist and Brethren-type congregations of independent Christians in those countries. He was also deeply versed in the long and obscure histories of many of the dissenting, and often .persecuted, Christian minority movements of the German and Slav lands. The purpose of the visit was to see if he could re-establish contact with some of the Christian minorities he had known in Russia before the war.

The two men flew from Croydon to Berlin in a Lufthansa plane and spent a day in that city, visiting a Brethren prayer-meeting in the Hohenstaufstrasse, where John Laing preached briefly, Broadbent translating. On the following day they flew on to Moscow. There they were taken by the woman Intourist guide on tours of factories, houses and recreation gardens, seeing very many aspects of the people's life. The Moscow Underground was within a few days of opening, and they joined with the crowds that were being given free introductory rides, and were

*The rule was lifted by the Royal Institution of Chartered Surveyors in 1967.

impressed by its fine stations. They saw the great concrete multi-storey apartment blocks that were replacing the old one-storey wooden houses, and visited the tomb of Lenin. Later they travelled on a great arc, visiting Gorki, and then down the Volga to Kazan, Saratov in the German-speaking area, and Stalingrad, from which city they went by rail to Rostov.

From Rostov they travelled into the Caucasus, visiting Ordzhonskidze, Tiflis and eventually Erivan, capital of Soviet Armenia, within sight of Mount Ararat. Returning, they reached Batum on the Black Sea coast, took a coastal boat to Yalta, Sevastopol and Odessa, and finally returned by train to Kiev, from which city they returned via Warsaw to England, arriving on 4 June.

Broadbent was a skilled linguist, fluent in Russian and German, and a previous traveller in the country. As a result he and Laing were able to speak with large numbers of the people they met in trains, boats and markets, sometimes apart from their guides. Their conversation both with guides and others often fell naturally to matters of religion, usually to elicit a stock profession of atheism, which they turned to a long discussion of Christian teaching, and sometimes informal readings of the Bible. They greatly enjoyed these conversations, and met a few Christian believers, but usually they were approached cautiously by any believers, for these were the years of the great religious repression immediately following the Stalinist laws of 1929. On one or two rare occasions they were able to make contact with old Christian acquaintances of Broadbent's, and to find them strong in their faith.

John Laing's curiosity and interest were unrestrained. Broadbent describes how they were taken on tours of new factories, collective farms, and new housing estates. Laing would ask to be shown the newest workers' homes; having been taken to the selected block, he would tell the car to stop near some other block and ask to see that too. The guide would protest against an unannounced visit, but John Laing was already knocking at the door. From there his famous smile and charm conquered; sometimes his rule would come out of his pocket, and into his notebook would go the measurements, numbers of people living in the apartment, and often details of earnings, the work done, cost of rent and food, and a mass of similar information. Similar details would be collected from other persons of all classes whom he met. All was absolutely in character with his customary interests in Britain, but, in Stalinist Russia of the mid-thirties, the pair of travellers must have been in considerable danger of arrest on espionage charges!

On one occasion they were, indeed, briefly arrested. Approaching a Volga quay in the German area, John Laing took one of his many photographs, of a group of peasants waiting for the boat. They were arrested on landing by a zealous young official, and eventually released only after strenuous explanations and much showing of official papers by the guide.

John Laing, unlike many Brethren, took an active political stance. Reared in the Free Trade principles of old-fashioned Liberalism, he had early revolted against its effect on the agricultural workers he knew so well in Cumberland and its support by the industrial manufacturers of the north. It was natural that, with his fervent belief in individual enterprise and the response of free men to fair incentives, he should turn to a progressive Conservatism, and he had joined his local constituency party. But he was far from blind to the human failings of the capitalist economic system, and there were aspects of the Russian experiment with which he could sympathise (he confided to a Carlisle friend his approval of the fact that the fruits of their labour went to the workers, not to *rentiers*). But other features of the Russia he saw impressed him more deeply: the lack of personal liberty, the ubiquitous fear that he sensed, the inculcated distortions that twisted the natural friendliness of the people into an obsessive suspicion of the motives of other nations. The sheer crudities of the pervasive anti-religious propaganda revolted him still more than the wasted churches. Above all, the freely expressed ruthlessness of the Stalinist system, and the open triumphal declaration of the more ardent Communists he met that Britain would soon fall to them, convinced him that he was in touch with an all-pervading conspiracy – a conviction he never lost.

Another result of his visit to Russia had a profound influence on his practical thinking. The tower-block form of living was already being popularised in the west by the thinking of architects such as Le Corbusier; to the municipal or government planner it might seem to offer economies of cost and of space. But Laing had seen the great blocks of Russian flats with their communal kitchens and facilities, and had contrasted his own housing estates, where every man could have his own garden and every woman her kitchen (modern concepts of the roles of the sexes hardly affect the basic argument!). Some Russian had replied to him, 'A woman will never be a good Communist if she

146

has her own kitchen,' To John Laing, the concept was inhuman; to him, the family with its own garden plot and home had its personal stake in its native soil, and its members were the likely loyal citizens. Flats might be suitable for the well-to-do (as at Manor Fields), or the unattached. The effect was to reinforce his dislike of popular high-rise housing, which he always opposed where he could. In this, as in other matters, his straightforward humanity has been justified by events.

One man, then a bricklayer, remembers how John Laing visited the estate in Honeypot Lane, Edgware, not long after his return from Russia. This man, with several companions, had been sent to London from Carlisle because of lack of work in the north, but T. Wardle had asked for them to return. Asking the site manager, George Malcolm, to wait on the ground, John Laing mounted the ladder to the scaffolding where they were working, to break the news to them; he remained there some time, chatting happily about all he had seen in Russia, and enjoying his constant personal interest in all his employees. Another former employee remembers joining the typing pool at the age of sixteen in 1936. During the first week Mr. Laing himself sent for her.

> I knocked on the door, and after the customary 'Come in', knees knocking, went up to the large desk by the window. 'Do sit down,' was the request. I looked at the only seat, which was a *very* high stool—I shall never forget it—how I managed to jump up on to that stool I shall never know. 'How are you enjoying your first taste of office life?' This was the last thing I had expected to hear! However, I was in that room for at least thirty minutes, and in that time was welcomed to the firm, and had a friendly chat . . . I was sent back to my office feeling much happier and having a feeling of belonging to a big happy family, which lasted until I joined up.

The Company was at this time out-performing several of the big national rivals that have grown with it to the top of today's construction industry: in terms of comparative status it was already a leader, small though it still was in relation to its present-day size. Several other businesses were also given a helping hand, either by direct financial investment or by commercial association. John Laing was for a time a director of John Line & Son Limited, the paint and wallpaper manufacturers. The most fruitful of these associations, of which there were

147

several others, was that with Square Grip Reinforcement Limited, a company in whose technical innovation in the field of concrete reinforcement he was very interested, and which grew in friendly relationship with the Laing Group to be an industry leader, making an important contribution to airfield construction during the war. This association also brought John Laing himself into friendship with the head of Square Grip, Frank Henmán, and with the latter's brother P. S. Henman (later chairman of the Transport Development Group), with whom he was to be closely associated in Christian activities and giving.

In 1936 a bold step was taken, and one of the few in which John Laing's ambitions were to be frustrated. For a hundred years the Westminster Hospital had stood on its site off the south-west corner of Parliament Square, behind the Middlesex Guildhall. It faced Westminster Abbey across Broad Sanctuary and looked out at the Houses of Parliament. The hospital was to be moved to new buildings in Horseferry Road, and the site by Parliament Square was put on the market. John Laing bid for it, and bought it at a price of £330,000 and costs. The purchase caused a press sensation, but John Laing had planned carefully. One of his sons asked him how he could face a deal of such a size without losing a minute's sleep, when he had known him spend a restless night over some minor waste of bricks on a building site. He replied, 'I have done my sums so far as Westminster Hospital is concerned, and I believe that it is all right. If I didn't think so, I wouldn't have bought it. However, as far as the bricks are concerned, that is symptomatic and it shows my managers don't really pay attention to detail and that worries me very much indeed and causes me to lose sleep.'

He had indeed made many careful calculations, as surviving records show. The whole project was expected to cost some £800,000 including the land (the £500,000 building costs being equivalent to 1977 costs of some seven million pounds). In the gothic setting of Parliament Square, Ruskin's earlier influences on Laing were revived. He admired intensely Saint Louis's Sainte Chapelle by the Palais de Justice in Paris and hard by Notre Dame, and took Sir John Burnet's partner, Thomas Tait, to view it. As they looked at the slender pillars and great areas of glass that John Laing admired so much, a young Australian known to Thomas Tait approached them. 'Is not this building delightful? It will serve as a pattern for a new type of architecture to which civilisation is moving forward.' Tait was commissioned to design a modern building for the Westminster Hospital site, under the influence of La Chapelle. John Laing was a little disappointed with the result, but it was approved by the Royal Fine Art Commission.

The Carlisle builder of a mere ten years' standing in London had touched the nerve centre of the established order. Controversy broke out, and in 1939 the war intervened. When it was over, the site was compulsorily acquired from him, statedly for a new Colonial Office. A new design was commissioned, and then plans were changed again. The official mind dallied, and for nearly half a century the nation has gazed at an unsightly hoarding-girt blank, adjoining its most prestigious square, and facing its supreme national monument. Few realise that the blank site is also a memorial to Sir John Laing's disappointment.*

The purchase of the Westminster Hospital site had another sequel, which indicates again both the independence of mind of this committed Conservative, and his concern for basic human values. On 1 June, 1936, *The Times* carried a letter from him which read:

> Sir: The purchase of Westminster Hospital site, for which my firm was happy to pay about £350,000, as compared with its value of £6,000 100 years ago, should focus public attention on the necessity that all land should belong to the nation in order that the increase in values which is continually taking place through the nation's effort should be reaped by the nation. In the case of the Westminster Hospital, fortunately, the benefit goes to a most worthy charity, but in the majority of similar cases the benefit goes to individuals who have done little to cause the increase in value. Further, if all land belonged to the nation, beneficial schemes for improvement and development could be carried out without difficulty or expense. If a district became obsolete, the Government could arrange that as soon as the lease expired the whole district should be rebuilt, with new arterial roads, to meet the requirements of the time. This is a benefit the value of which cannot be fully appreciated. It would clear away slums and make our towns beautiful and healthy.
>
> The great and beneficial change from private ownership to public ownership of land could be carried out if there is good will, in a very easy and undisturbing manner. Let all property

---

*As this book goes to press, plans have been announced for the development of the site as a conference centre.

and land be freed from rates and income-tax for one year, and the benefit of this relief go to the owner of the land, to be considered as a sinking fund which would pay for the freehold in 60 years, and at the end of that time all land, including the sites of buildings, would belong to the nation.

Different classes of property vary in their land values, but on calculation it will be found that this relief payment, used as a sinking fund, would be reasonable payment for the land. In many cases the relief payment is considerably too much, and in a few cases it would be rather too little, but such a large problem, the solving of which would be of immense national benefit, needs to be viewed broadly by all parties. Many would receive too much, but even those who receive rather too little have the benefit of securing the undisturbed use of their land for nearly three generations, and property is not so sacred that we need look so far ahead. We have all experienced investments which lose their value in a short time. There would be certain difficulties of detail, but these can be overcome in a right manner. To try to deal with them, however, is beyond the scope of this letter.

I make these suggestions as a Conservative and a landowner, after considerable experience and thought, and I earnestly ask that they should not be dismissed as impracticable, but that they should be carefully considered and further explored.

I am, &c.,

J. W. Laing.

The letter, as one might expect, was a nine-days' wonder. A gentleman from the Carlton Club responded indignantly that it was a 'blatantly Socialistic statement that the owners of land values have done little or nothing to increase those values,' and another who signed himself *Valeat Quantum Valere Potest* pointed out that, if the sum originally paid had been invested at four per cent per annum compound, 'it would have greatly exceeded the sum paid last week by Mr. Laing'. The latter would have had a point, if it had not been for the fact that the owner of the land had already enjoyed the income, or the equivalent in its use, throughout his ownership. On 5 June another correspondent (who obviously did not know John Laing) opined that he was neither a countryman, nor a lover of the land. Meanwhile, other papers seized on the letter. The *Daily Express* gave it a leading article; the *People* took it up, and *John Bull* (not surprisingly) approved.

John Laing was again shrewdly in the van of affairs, as the

appointment of the Uthwatt Committee on Land Compensation and Betterment five years later showed. Forty years later, the powers-that-be (of differing political colours) have made at least four attempts to grasp the nettle.* If John Laing's solution was over-simple, it could hardly have been more clumsy than theirs. These measures have several times dried up the supply of building land, with resultant hardship to ordinary men and women looking for homes, and they have once contributed to a collapse of the property market, with near disastrous economic consequences. In addition we have over the years seen a vast diversion into property speculation of resources that might have gone to productive industry.

Unpalatable and visionary as John Laing's far-sighted simplicity might have been (perhaps *The Times* correspondent who declared that the idea was 'not one of practical politics' was inexorably right; for he over-estimated the long-term stability of government resolve, and we might also speculate what inflation would have made of the arrangement) we may yet be forgiven for wondering whether what we have had has been any improvement.

---

*The expropriation of development value under the Town and Country Planning Act, 1947; the Betterment Levy under the Land Commission Act, 1967; the Development Gains Tax under the Finance Act, 1974; and finally the Development Land Tax under the Development Land Tax Act, 1976, combined with the Community Land Act, 1975.

CHAPTER 10

Second World War

IN 1937 JOHN LAING was invited by the American Government and the New York Chamber of Commerce to visit the United States. A speech he made to the New York Building Congress was later said to have had a considerable influence on American thinking on private housing estates,[1] and he also addressed a conference of Government officials at Washington. It was characteristic of John Laing that his chief memories of this visit, on which he was accompanied by his son Kirby, were of 'the kindness of the builders of New York and the government officials and . . . especially a voyage down the St. Lawrence river at the beginning of the autumn and seeing the marvellous colours of the leaves.'[2] 'He was the most delightful of travelling companions' wrote a close friend after his death; 'His capacity for enjoyment was unbounded. Everything lovely and beautiful thrilled him.'

The chill of approaching war was already in the air; in the business it showed itself by the increasing tempo of work for the Air Ministry. Contracts had been awarded to John Laing & Son continuously since the end of the First World War, but from 1935 they multiplied, as construction of airfields began to take on a considerable urgency. The work was still of high peace-time standard, with superb fittings in some of the quarters, but the number of fields put in hand grew each year. W. M. Johnson moved from Shenley to take charge of much of this work. The contracts were eventually of the average order of half a million pounds a time, some six to seven million pounds in 1977 terms.

The Company's long association with the Air Ministry had led to a relationship of mutual respect between John Laing and its successive directors-general, and he (with one or two other leaders of the industry) was in the confidence of the Ministry. With the urgency of re-armament, the usual lengthy procedures of competitive tendering that are normally insisted on by Government for its contracts became impractical, and discussions took place between these men and the Air Ministry over alternative methods. John Laing himself had always disliked the cost-plus type of contract, which had been extensively used during the First World War; he considered it to be inefficient, destructive of enterprise, and open to questionable practices. He took a leading part with the Ministry in developing for these and later wartime airfield contracts a system of 'target costing', in which his thinking on production bonuses for his own employees is clearly in evidence.* A target cost would be set for the contract, and if the actual cost of labour and material proved to be less than this target, the contractor was paid cost and profit, plus a sliding-scale bonus based on the saving: if he exceeded the target he was penalised. Variations from specification were related to the original target.

The system was crude at first, and plainly depended for its effectiveness on the accuracy of the original targets, but as experience was gained it became possible to replace the target by a price based on a known norm and a schedule of quantities. Other queries obviously arose, relating to such items as whether maintenance of non-mechanical plant was included in the set cost or was an extra, or how standing time for mechanical plant should be treated, and the system led to the Ministry itself being closely involved, through its surveyor, in the actual running of contracts. Continuous costing was necessary, and the long years of John Laing's development of his own contract-costing techniques began to contribute effectively to the wider national interest.

In 1938 the approach of war was heralded by urgent instructions to begin work on sites for protective balloon barrages. The first fourteen emergency sites were divided equally between Wimpey and Laing, the seven Laing sites in the south and midlands being under development by the Company early in 1939; eventually eleven contracts in all were placed without previous negotiation. The Ministry gave outline plans, but all detailed work, including surveys and drawings, was the Company's own responsibility. In all this work John Laing himself was closely involved, supervising the progress from the drawing-board through to the sites.

The most important of all the Company's contracts in progress at the outbreak of war was the construction of the highly secret new headquarters for R.A.F. Bomber Command, with its

*Official circles had known somewhat similar procedures during the First World War, and in the production of respirators for Aden and Malta during the Italo-Ethiopian crisis.[3]

innocent 'village' of buildings—so natural in their surroundings that they had no camouflage throughout the war—surmounting the nerve centre, the operations rooms deep underground. The completed headquarters was handed over to the Royal Air Force in March 1940.

When Britain declared war on 3 September, 1939, John Laing was just three weeks short of his sixtieth birthday. Full though his life had been hitherto, he was entering on its most strenuous period. Already the volume of work passing through his business was more than four times what it had been ten years before; in the next three years, despite the cessation of house-building, it was to double again in money value (an increase of nearly sixty per cent in volume) and the workforce was to increase more than threefold. Because the new wartime work was scattered through-out the country, the physical effort and organisational complexity of the larger volume of work was immeasurably increased, and that against the background of shortages of materials and skilled labour, and the disruption of communications by the needs of the war itself, aggravated by the heavy bombing attacks of those years of war. His two sons, by now actively engaged in manage-ment, were to leave to join the forces, Kirby going to the Royal Engineers and Maurice to the Royal Air Force (in which he was present as a glider pilot at the crossing of the Rhine). John Laing and his men rose superbly to the occasion. 'He seemed to work like a machine in the war,' wrote one man who was a leader in the wartime team. 'He gave everything he had to the war effort, arriving at jobs at 7.30 a.m., and he was then sixty-five years old. What a man and what a leader!'

The demand for skilled construction workers inside the Forces soon depleted the Company's own resources. One executive remembers how he had applied to join the Royal Air Force at the beginning of the war, although listed in a reserved occupation. Before the reply came he had a telephone call from C. B. Hancock at the Kirton Lindsey aerodrome site: would he join a 'Laing Company' being formed in the Royal Engineers? A balanced list of different classes of tradesmen was prepared and he, with a colleague, visited the sites throughout the country seeking volunteers. More responded than were required, but the correct proportions of the different tradesmen had to be achieved and on 16 February, 1940, No. 683 General Construction Company, Royal Engineers, was formed at Chatham, with about three-quarters Laing men, under Major C. B. Hancock. Others of the large contractors formed similar companies; as the war con-

154

tinued, the personnel were dispersed, in the nature of things military, among many units, but the Company served throughout the war until disbanded (by then 683 Artisan Works Company) in 1946.

At first intended for Norway, the Company's first posting was frustrated by the evacuation of that country, and it was sent to the Orkneys and Shetlands for its first two years, for the construction of military camps and defences on the many remote islands of those groups—working at pressure throughout the winters, in the teeth of the gales, with the minimum of equipment. 'The only black mark gained during our stay was on one occasion when the outfall from a septic tank was discharged into a stream which supplied the local distillery. Several thousand gallons of whisky were ruined!'

John Laing made the long journey to visit the Company at Easter 1941, joining in the concert for local troops and the informal church services arranged in the local cinema. He stayed at the Company's officers' mess, and was reported (entirely in character) as having persuaded the officers—who included some pretty hard-bitten men—to join him during that time in an informal prayer-meeting in their quarters.

Another early initiative arose directly from his experience in the First World War. Remembering the hutting produced in Carlisle, he set David Adam, the Company's staff architect who had contributed so strikingly to its housing developments, to research into the construction of military hutting. The experiments were closely watched by John Laing himself; he was continually reviewing and testing the products, and was obviously fascinated and inventive in relation to the technical problems—thermal insulation, weather-proofing, economy in labour and materials, sectional construction methods, portability and ease of erection, dismantling and re-erection. His own early plans were for a hutting factory on twelve to thirty acres, near to the timber ports and accessible to London, in a reasonably safe area, but close to a town where labour and accommodation could be found. Eventually the production was carried out at Elstree, where he had bought the land for his factory estates, and it led to country-wide contracts with the War Office and Air Ministry.

Foreseeing transport needs, he had bought a number of new Bedford trucks shortly before the war started. Soon after the outbreak of war, an order commandeering the vehicles was issued. John Laing, conscious of the great urgency of the work on which the Company was engaged, refused to let them go. The local police had their own talent for tactful dealing, however, and one Saturday an officer called on him at his house. Under no circumstances, Laing insisted, would he let the lorries go; the contracts on which they were employed were of vital importance to the war effort (which was very true). The police officer looked at him with a smile. 'Then, under the circumstances, I have no alternative but to arrest you and to keep you in detention over the weekend. I wonder what your friends at Woodcroft Hall will think?' The vehicles were released after very little more discussion!

He took what helpful interest he could in local civilian needs, despite the clamant call of the military contracts. Company facilities were made available, where possible, for canteens, shelters and other necessities. The children from the Woodcroft Hall Sunday School had been evacuated with most other London children to safer parts of the country, and the large basement accommodation in the building was strengthened against possible bomb damage, and turned into a large rest centre and shelter for local people.

The Company had by the outbreak of war built up a considerable expertise in factory development, and it was natural that a substantial part of its activities during the war should consist of the construction of ordnance and aircraft factories, of which over fifty were built in different parts of the country. Two enormous projects were in Cumberland: the three-million-pound Royal Ordnance Factory at Sellafield in west Cumberland, which was in production within twelve months of work starting in February 1942, and a great factory for High Duty Alloys and the new Ministry of Aircraft Production that, in 1941, also went into production within a year of the work starting. This factory contained what was probably at that time the largest power hammer in the world—a 500-ton Erie that rested on an intricately designed 3,000-ton concrete foundation forty-eight feet deep. During the first three years of the war the Company also completed extensions to Carlisle's new power station by the River Eden at Willowholme. Nearby, it built large ordnance and equipment storage depots for both the R.A.F. and the War Office.

Undoubtedly the largest contribution by the Company to the war effort—as with other contractors—was in the construction of airfields. It is difficult today to appreciate the sheer magnitude of the work involved in the airfield construction programme in those days, when Britain was the only base available to the Allied forces, facing the whole of the occupied European continent. In 1942, with the arrival of the U.S.A. forces in this country, Air Ministry construction absorbed one-thirty-second part of the total daily war expenditure.[4] Demands on available manpower were a constant source of friction between the government departments affected. Hugh Beaver, Director General of the Ministry of Works, complained to Ernest Holloway of the Air Ministry in May that he was trying to carry out more construction than there could possibly be labour to man efficiently. Ernest Bevin, Minister of Labour, pointed out to the Air Ministry in December that there were already 502 completed operational air-fields,* with another 120 on the way to completion and 20 others starting, while sites were being sought for another 43; the programme was competing for labour with the repair of bombed houses. Yet during the whole of the period 1941 to 1945 the Air Ministry was pressing for a greater allocation of labour.

No fewer than 444 airfields in total were built by a wide variety of contractors for the Royal Air Force between 1939 and 1945, at a total cost of over 200 million pounds excluding buildings, with another 36 for the United States Air Force. (It should be remembered that building costs during that period averaged about one tenth of 1977 figures.) In 1942 one new airfield, on average, was being completed by one contractor or another every three days, in addition to sixty-three major extensions of existing fields.[5] Construction was not a simple matter of laying concrete on an empty field. Every airfield meant major surveys of drainage and topography, and vast earthworks and preparatory excavation. At times a million cubic yards of earth might need to be excavated and disposed of: three 50-yard-wide concrete runways (during the period doubled in length from 1,000 to 2,000, and sometimes 3,000, yards each) would be laid at angles of 60 degrees, with a 50-foot perimeter track surrounding the field. These, with the hard standings, would use some 130,000 tons of ballast and cement, and 50 miles of drainage pipes and cable conduits. This was before any of the airfield buildings were taken account of. While the construction was in progress—usually in a remote country district—the workforce of hundreds had to be housed, fed and supplied, and materials transported on time and to schedule, for all works were undertaken under conditions of extreme urgency.[6]

The technology was unfamiliar, and there was no time for tests

*This would have included the pre-war airfields.

or experiments. Until the war, all airfields had had grass surfaces. Not only was it now impossible to lay or grow a suitable grass surface in the time available, but also the advent of larger and still larger aircraft made hard surfaces essential. The stresses on concrete or tarmacadam by the take-off and landing of heavily laden aircraft were at that time unmeasured, and had to be learned by hard experience. No sooner had one set of lessons been mastered than the advent of a new generation of heavier planes (culminating in the great American Flying Fortresses) brought fresh problems. When the runways were laid, water would lie on the impervious surfaces, leading to fresh problems of drainage, and of the disposal of the water from the courses into which the drains discharged.

Some of the results, where less efficient or conscientious contractors were in charge, were bad; the reputation of the construction industry began to suffer as it had during the housing boom of the thirties, and with the same concern to its leaders. By contrast, the reputation of the more satisfactory contractors grew, and several firms in this period built reputations that were to take them to the heights when the war ended.

Among these firms, Laings were one of the most marked. 'They were probably the best and most conscientious company in the industry,' said one man responsible for the technical supervision of the airfield surfaces on behalf of the Air Ministry. This reputation was directly the product of the close personal supervision of the work by John Laing and his long-trusted managers. Despite the distances and the vast increase in the volume of work, the rigorous control procedures of the pre-war contracts were as strictly enforced, though much of the costing and clerical work had perforce to be decentralised to the airfield sites. John Laing's own inspections had by now become legendary, and the inevitable grape-vine of warning would operate as he was on his way. He still had the uncanny knack of spotting faulty work; still there were the careful personal checks, and instructions to take up and re-lay inadequate surfaces. A friend tells the story of one such visit:

On the occasion on which I was taken along, we left at 7 a.m. It was probably an hour's drive to the first airfield. We drove straight to the manager's office. From there on he went round on foot. Mr. Laing may not have known an old proverb once familiar to farmers, 'The eye of the master fattens the ox, and his foot the ground', but he practised the wisdom of it. He would watch a tamper at work and view with a critical eye the new roadway that followed in its wake. If the noise was not too excessive there would be a cheery greeting to the operator and then on to view another section. On one site there was an enormous concrete mixer with its hopper 20 or 30 feet above the ground. The gravel and cement were being hauled up manually to feed it. The manager was asked for the figures for the total amounts to be used on the site. After considering the information for a few moments in which he obviously made a rapid mental calculation, Mr. Laing asked, 'What would it cost to build a ramp so that the lorries could unload straight into the hopper?' The Manager gave a rough estimate of £2,000. 'Well,' said Mr. Laing, 'I think you had better have it done.' And then he carefully wrote down some notes in the inexpensive type of jotter that he always carried with him and used constantly. I felt certain, if we had returned to that airfield a week later, we would have found that ramp already erected. We covered, perhaps, four or five airfields under construction. At each, his eagle eye seemed to take in every detail. At the last one we were still there after the men had gone. The manager took us to see the repair facilities on the site. We found a mechanic still working on repairs to one of the machines. Here was obviously an indispensable and key man who was no clock-watcher. As soon as we were well away from the building, Mr. Laing said to the manager, 'How much are you paying that man?' He was given a figure, that for those times sounded well above average. Mr. Laing said, 'That man deserves to be well rewarded for that kind of service.'

His own interest in concrete technology had been awakened long before with the early Easiform houses, and he encouraged every advance during this period. The urgency of the work on the airfields also gave a great impetus to mechanisation. No longer was there time or labour for concrete to be laid and tamped by hand, or even mixed in the standard mixers. As the war went on, great excavators and scrapers, mechanical rollers and trenching machines were brought into use, and the first continuous concrete-mixing plants were introduced, combined with careful quality-testing on the sites, and the use of large mechanical spreaders.

In the three years before the war, the Company had built more than a dozen R.A.F. airfields: from 1939 to 1945 they built fifty-four more, together with three Royal Naval Air Stations—

and these included some of the largest in the country. It was an immense contribution to the national war effort, but it also put the Company in the forefront of the industry in many technical fields. The experience of those years was also vital to the post-war growth of air traffic.

In 1943 the first plans began to take shape for the invasion of Europe, and work was put in hand, under the code-name Mulberry, for the construction of the artificial harbour that was eventually to be used for the landing at Arromanches on the French coast. A special branch of the Ministry of Supply was formed in September 1943 to carry out that section of the project which involved the construction of the six miles of floating caissons and the concrete pontoons for the ten miles of floating bridging, that were to be towed across the Channel to form the harbour. A labour force of 20,000 was engaged on the project, and a general embargo placed on all new construction work within thirty miles of the scattered sites, to avoid competition for labour—an embargo that included the whole of London. A team of twenty-six contracting companies and six firms of engineering consultants was engaged for the work, John Laing & Son Limited constructing ten of the largest caissons, code-named Phoenix, and forty of the floating pontoon 'Whale' units. David Adam again came to the fore, and in his office was designed much of the shuttering used by the different contractors, to be made in the Company's joinery works. The project was given first priority for all transport, and work continued by day and night: materials to be transported for use included 700,000 tons of ballast, sand and cement, 30,000 tons of reinforcing steel bars, and 20,000 tons of timber—with a further 250,000 tons of rubble for the dock bottoms. The eventual harbour was twice the size of Dover harbour.

Following the success of Mulberry, the group of contractors engaged on the Phoenix caissons joined for mutual planning of post-war pre-fabricated house construction, again work in which the Company, and Adam in particular, were closely concerned, the Company in fact building the prototype house. This, however, takes us into the subject of the next chapter.

Other significant developments of the wartime period, in open-cast coal mining, war-damage repairs, and the planning of the post-war housing drive, also belong to the next chapter, but before passing to them we must look at John Laing's own personal involvement with matters of national planning during the war years.

On annual staff outings, by coach, rail and 'Royal Eagle'

Visiting the M1 motorway contract (with Montague Goodman)

Foundation stone, Tyndale House, Cambridge (p. 190)

SOLI DEO GLORIA
BIBLIOTHECAM TYNDALIANAM
STVDIA SACRA FOVENDI CAVSA
DICAVIT
IOHANNES W. LAING
A:D: XI KAL: MAI:
ANNO SALVTIS MCMLVI

Already, in March 1940, the Building Research Board of the Department of Scientific and Industrial Research had set up a committee on Alternative Materials and Methods of Construction* (later to be renamed the Committee on Wartime Building) under the chairmanship of George (later Sir George) Burt, the chairman of John Mowlem & Co., Ltd. John Laing was appointed one of the first members of this committee, which was active until January 1943, its task being to advise on alternative materials and construction methods in the face of wartime shortages.

The wartime shortages of materials and labour, with a large proportion of skilled men drafted into the Forces, soon made necessary some centralised control over building and civil engineering. Accordingly, the Ministry of Works was created in October 1940 from the former Office of Works, the first Minister being Lord Reith, who was succeeded in February 1942, by Lord Portal of Laverstoke. The director-general of the Ministry from April 1941 and throughout the war was Hugh Beaver, who became Sir Hugh in 1943, a civil engineer and chemical engineer who had been a partner in the well-known firm of Sir Alexander Gibb & Partners.

There was a measure of mistrust in the early days of the Ministry between itself and the industry's own representative bodies, the National Federation of Building Trades Employers and the Building Industries National Council (both under Sir Jonah Walker-Smith, John Laing's acquaintance of ambivalent memory from Barrow, who had himself been director of housing in the Ministry of Health twenty years before.) This mistrust seems to have been heightened by the formation of the Builders' Emergency Organisations in 1941. Formed for the allocation of work on a fair and economical basis, and for the mobilisation of resources in bombed or invaded areas, these organisations tended to mobilise the smaller builders, and the industry's federations were concerned as to their status. †

In May 1941 Lord Reith, the Minister of Works, set up the Central Council for Works and Buildings. Consisting mainly of representatives of both employers and labour, nominated by the Minister rather than by the representative bodies, it was envisaged as an independent and experienced body to advise the

---

*Not to be confused with the Burt Committee of 1942 (see next chapter).

†John Hughes, who had been a director of the Laing Company in the early twenties, was chairman of the North Wales Builders' Emergency Organisation.

Minister concerning the industry and its part in the war effort. Hugh Beaver was chairman, and Sir Ernest Simon deputy chairman. John Laing was nominated as one of the industry's representatives on this council.

He also served on a number of specialist sub-committees of the council: on the Schedule of Prices Committee and on the Education Committee, both of which published reports in 1942, and on the Placing and Management of Building Contracts Committee which reported in 1944. The Education report, a detailed survey of the training situation and needs of the industry, was produced by an important group under the chairmanship of Sir Ernest Simon,* and looked very much to the future. It was a striking indication of the extent to which the Government and the industry were concerned with the post-war situation even in the darkest days of the war, and it is described more fully in the next chapter.

An aspect of national planning which was related directly to the immediate needs of the war arose from the Essential Work (Building and Civil Engineering) Order of 1941. The Government made it obligatory for all undertakings or sites listed to introduce a system of payment by results for workers. Targets of output were fixed for specified operations, and bonuses, shared in a stated proportion between foremen, craftsmen and labourers, were paid if the targets were exceeded. Although the unions at first opposed the scheme, and the Employers' Federation disagreed about its form, they co-operated after the Order was brought into force. The preliminary work on the scheme had been undertaken by J. W. Laing and Howard Farrow, and John Laing's thinking is very apparent in its form. Once the Order was in operation, the Ministry of Works formed an advisory panel, presided over by Sir Hugh Beaver, with representatives of workers and employers. Henry Chapman Harland of John Laing & Son Limited served on this panel throughout the war, with Sir George Burt and others well known in the construction and civil engineering industries.

Introduced at first for excavations, concreting and bricklaying, the scheme proved effective and was extended to other operations, though not to permanent housing. The Mulberry Phoenix components and airfield construction were among the successful applications of the scheme, which thus made an important contribution to victory.

*Mrs. Barbara Wootton was drafting secretary. See also page 166.

After the American entry into the war, and the realisation that a German invasion of Britain was now unlikely, eventual victory seemed certain. By the later part of 1942, planning for post-war housing construction took definite shape, to be interrupted by more serious immediate problems when the flying bomb assault began on 14 June, 1944. In both these developments John Laing and his Company were deeply involved, but the account must be deferred to the next chapter. Increasingly, he was taking an important part in the higher deliberations of both Government and the industry, a part marked by his election in 1943 to the Council of the Institute of Builders, on which he served until 1949.

Possibly the most quietly influential involvement in Government processes was, however, on an informal and personal level. When Lord Portal succeeded Lord Reith as Minister of Works in February 1942, he felt the need of expert personal consultation with leaders of the industry, apart from official committees and formal bodies, and a friendship grew up between him, John Laing and Godfrey (later Sir Godfrey) Mitchell, Chairman of George Wimpey & Company Limited. He relied on and consulted these two outstanding men on numerous occasions during his service as Minister (he was succeeded by Duncan Sandys in November 1944). When the Laing Company published its own history of its wartime work in 1946, Lord Portal contributed a foreword, acknowledging John Laing's help and willingness to meet him during that time, and acknowledging also the help of Henry Harland.

In its wartime history, and in its company history of 1950, the Company claimed that 'during the first four years of the war, one five-hundredth part of the total National Effort, measured in monetary value, was carried out by this firm.' The calculation seems to have been a simplistic one, dividing the total government defence expenditure by the Company's turnover, on the basis that virtually all that turnover during the relevant period was defence work for the Government.* When it is remembered that airfield construction alone absorbed approximately one-hundredth of the total defence expenditure,[8] the claim seems reasonable, on the information already discussed in this chapter. The Company's long service to the Air Ministry was marked symbolically when Marshal of the R.A.F., Lord Tedder,

---

*Total defence expenditure from 1 April, 1939, to 31 March, 1945, was £22,846 million.[7] The Company's own turnover during the period was £45 million.

contributed the foreword to the Company's centenary history, *Team Work*.

Yet, through all this intense effort, John Laing forgot neither his Christian activities nor his personal friendships. The fuller story will be told later, but one small incident can conclude this chapter. In October 1943, one of his former Crusader boys was repatriated as an invalid from a German prisoner-of-war camp, and John Laing heard that he was in hospital near Maidstone. In a letter to Sir Maurice Laing after Sir John's death, the former prisoner of war (now a minister of the United Reformed Church) recalled the sequel:

> Your father visited me. It was a cold, wet and windy day and during the course of our conversation your father asked me if I would like some butter. He said his wife had packed some with his sandwiches and he wished me to have it. I welcomed the offer as butter had not been on the P.O.W. menus, and he left me for about twenty minutes, returning eventually, thoroughly wet, with a small pat of butter! I greatly appreciated his gift and since then have often reflected upon this kind and simple act. It was an expression of humble Christian love.

John Laing adamantly refused, as senior executives remember, to accept any 'off-the-ration' farm produce, even when visiting country sites. There is no doubt that the little gift came from his own wartime ration.

CHAPTER 11

Reconstruction

So SUCCESSFUL, IN terms of quantity, was the inter-war housing boom that by 1939 one-third of all houses in England and Wales had been built in the previous twenty years. During the six years of the Second World War, when new housing construction was virtually at a standstill, the clock was precisely put back. One-third of all dwellings (not, of course, the same third) were damaged or destroyed by bombing during the war.[1]

By the autumn of 1942, the shape of the future need was already discernible, although the violent assault by flying bombs and rockets was still two years ahead, and as yet unforeseen. It was plain that a major effort would need to be concentrated on local-authority housing. The new construction between the wars, successful though it had been in numerical terms, had been predominantly of houses for owner occupation. Destruction during the war, on the other hand, had especially hit the working-class areas of the cities, and the replacement of the lost houses for renting must in modern conditions rest on the public authorities.

Housing policy had always been the responsibility of the Minister of Health, but after the formation of the Ministry of Works from the old Office of Works, the planning responsibilities of the Ministry of Health had in June 1942 been transferred to the new Ministry (the Ministry of Town and Country Planning was to be formed later, in 1943). Accordingly, in September 1942, an inter-departmental committee was set up by the two Ministries, under the chairmanship of Sir George Burt (who was chairman of the Building Research Board and a member of the Ministry of Works Central Council, to consider materials and construction methods for the building of houses and flats, and to make recommendations for post-war practice. John Laing, as a member of the Central Council, was appointed to the committee on behalf of the Ministry of Works at Sir George Burt's request. The committee reviewed construction methods available, including prefabrication, and paid particular attention to those methods of construction which would circumvent the expected post-war shortage of bricks and skilled bricklayers; the Easiform method was one of those examined and reported on satisfactorily. Technical considerations reviewed included the consumption of labour and materials, and the practical criteria of strength and stability, moisture penetration and condensation, thermal and sound insulation, fire hazards, maintenance and durability, and liability to vermin infestation. The committee rejected the traditional nine-inch solid brick wall as unreliable against damp penetration, and put forward recommended design standards for future house-building. Its preliminary report was published in October 1943,[2] but it continued very actively in being, and issued no less than ninety-nine separate reports on a wide range of constructional topics between March 1944 and September 1945. John Laing continued as one of its most active members.

The Education Committee of the Ministry of Works Central Council, on which John Laing had also served, had already published its *Report on Training for the Building Industry* in 1942. This report, too, had undertaken a thorough review of post-war needs—this time of manpower—and had regretted that the housing policy which had followed the First World War had not been governed by any long-term programme. 'Upon the building industry,' the report had stated, 'more than upon any other single industry, will rest responsibility for national welfare after the war'—a prediction that the fierce post-war housing debates, arising from widespread and desperate needs, more than justified.

The committee had not been able to satisfy itself that training in the industry, in general, was substantially better than it had been in 1926,* although it had acknowledged the apprenticeship schemes which had been instituted. It had made far-reaching recommendations relating to training and education at all grades, both the special action needed to meet the short-term post-war crisis, and the more permanent requirements of the industry. It had also recommended long-term planning of the industry itself and of its intake of workers, and the introduction of a guaranteed week for operatives.

Prime Minister Churchill issued a directive on 19 October, 1943, endorsed by the War Cabinet two days later, laying down, as priorities for post-war reconstruction, education, social

*See page 89 of this book.

insurance and housing, and the War Cabinet was increasingly concerned with preparations for the return to peace (the unplanned sequel to the First World War of only twenty-five years before was still fresh in men's minds). The Beveridge Report outlining the Welfare State had been published late in 1942, and the Uthwatt and Scott Reports on land finance and use were also available. While the immediate problems of demobilisation, food and employment were to have priority, plans for rebuilding and for social services were intended to be brought to a high degree of preparation during the war. A Ministry of Reconstruction under Lord Woolton (with a seat in the War Cabinet) was created in November 1943.

Lord Portal, the Minister of Works, was already consulting with John Laing and Godfrey Mitchell on matters affecting the construction industry, and about this time a senior surveyor of the Laing organisation, with ten years' experience of their system,* was seconded to the Ministry, which under Sir Hugh Beaver, its director-general, set up its directorate of post-war reconstruction to plan the future housing programme. The Ministry was thus able to develop detailed costings and standards for house building, under the personal guidance of the two great contractors,† and with the full benefit of John Laing's long development of his system. Eventually this planning led to the appointment of the Cost of Housebuilding Committee under J. G. Girwood, on which John Laing served, and which reported in 1948. It was John Laing's suggestion which led to the Ministry producing the 'yardstick house', a standard for brick-built houses against which all costs and new developments could be measured.

Other committees on which he served at this time were the Ministry of Works Standards Committee, and the Department of Scientific and Industrial Research Plumbing Committee of the Building Research Board; both were under the chairmanship of Mr. Sydney Tatchell, and reported in 1944 (the second published a further report in 1947). He also served on the Building Industries Sub-Committee under Sir Ernest Simon, on the Processes Panel under Mr. Wynne Edwards (both convened by the Ministry of Works Scientific Advisory Committee), and on the Ministry of Health Prices of Building Materials Committee

*The executive concerned was later to rise high in the Ministry of Works, and to be awarded the O.B.E.
†See page 87 of this book.

167

under Sir Isidore Salmon, and he gave evidence for the Central Housing Advisory Committee's 1944 Reports on Design of Dwellings and Private Enterprise Housing.

The urgent planning for the post-war period was suddenly and rudely interrupted when, on 14 June, 1944, the first German V.1 flying bomb crashed on London, to be followed twelve weeks later by the first V.2 rocket. The air raids of the whole of the earlier blitz had destroyed nearly 85,000 houses in London and had damaged more than one and a quarter million. In two months the new onslaught had damaged another million houses, 21,000 of them beyond repair: casualties by the end of July already totalled over 35,000, including nearly 5,000 killed. In August, at the height of the attack, houses were being damaged at the rate of twenty thousand a day. Gradually, the flying bombs were brought under control by Royal Air Force balloon and fighter operations, and from September the rate of damage eased, but there was no protection against the rockets. Throughout the winter the onslaught continued, to be stepped up after Christmas to an average of thirty rockets a week. March 1945 showed signs of an increasing tempo. Each incident would destroy or damage another six hundred houses, and they were to continue until the Forces invading France over-ran the launching sites.[3]

The situation in 1944 was critical. Southern England was a vast military camp, with two great armies in urgent concentration on the invasion of France.* If the attack on London led to a sudden rush of homeless refugees on to the roads—still worse if civilian morale broke—the whole plan of operations could be disastrously disrupted. The prompt emergency repair, wherever possible, of all damage was absolutely essential. Incredibly, the London building labour force (only 21,000 men had been available to the Ministry when the first flying bomb fell) had been able to keep pace, in broad terms, with first-aid repairs during the first few weeks of damage. A labour force of 60,000 at the end of August had exhausted all available hostel accommodation, yet somehow another 60,000 men were found by December, some 45,000 coming from the provinces. Sir Malcolm Trustram-Eve, the chairman of the War Damage Commission, acted as chief of staff to Lord Woolton, the Minister of Reconstruction (thus involving the inner War Cabinet in the operation), and with the Ministries of Health and Works he had set up an emergency twenty-four-hour service with its headquarters at

*D-Day, the start of the invasion, was 6 June 1944.

Drake House, Dolphin Square. Eighty thousand houses were repaired sufficiently to make them habitable during the autumn of 1944. H. C. Harland, as current president of the London Master Builders' Association, was very much involved with organising the emergency service for the whole of Greater London.

These were, however, essentially emergency measures. By November it was plain that more substantial action was needed. Hundreds of different small building firms were engaged in the work; much of the labour was of necessity unskilled and strange to London; the supply of materials, and the feeding, transport and housing of the labour force (now nearly 130,000 men) presented unparalleled problems, and through it all there was the constant disruption of fresh rocket explosions and new damage. Second-stage repairs were becoming urgent on many of the houses already dealt with.

Duncan Sandys, Chairman of the War Cabinet Committee for defence against flying bombs and rockets, succeeded Lord Portal as Minister of Works on 21 November, 1944, and on 1 December the first meeting of the newly-formed London Repairs Executive was held under his chairmanship. Sir Malcolm Trustram-Eve was vice-chairman, and representatives from the Ministry of Labour and the Ministry of Health also served on it.

On 9 December the Executive approved proposals to place the work in each London borough under a Joint Repair Committee, drawn from both sides of the industry, with the work in each borough under the organisation of a major contractor as agent of the Ministry of Works. Mowlems were appointed in Camberwell (the proposals aroused some disquiet within the Building and Civil Engineering Industries Advisory Council, and Trustram-Eve seems to have handled them gingerly, reporting Mowlems' appointment as an experimental measure). The organising contractor was to co-ordinate work in the borough, supervise programmes and estimates, balance the labour forces, and ensure proper advance ordering and supervision of progress.

John Laing & Son Limited were invited to take charge of the large and severely damaged Borough of Lambeth, the Norwood division of which was Duncan Sandys' own constituency. Two of their very senior managers were brought in to control the work, and a team of their most trusted supervisory employees was drafted to Lambeth. Some 250 different firms were engaged on work there, with a labour force not far short of 10,000. Over 40,000 damaged houses still awaited attention. The Borough

Engineer was known, also, to be a strong character with firm ideas of how things should be done.

John Laing later recounted how he had called together the representatives of the firms working in the borough and explained his Company's function, and sought their co-operation. Morale at the time was very low, and the task in front of them was frustrating and endless, but within a few weeks output was multiplied many times and the programme was running successfully. A man involved in this work later wrote vividly in the Company's house journal:[4]

> We had no lack of callers of all kinds, ranging from the seedy-looking individual who wished to sell us sets of door furniture which he had *picked up*, to the elderly gentleman who came slowly up the steps muttering comments which the editor refuses to print, but which were plainly audible to our receptionist, and which he hurriedly explained were references to his wife.
>
> These callers had all manner of troubles and questions, and tried every method to get priority for their own houses. They came up our stairs in a never-ending stream, young and old, rich and poor, labourer and director, smiling and tearful, cajoling and threatening . . . Then there were the letters . . . one of the more unusual letters, after several pages of complaint, finished off with five pages in Chinese!
>
> Investigation of complaints often led one into strange and depressing places and showed that some people had a peculiar idea of bomb damage, as evidenced by the gentleman who complained of a leak which was traced to his habit of emptying the tea-pot out of the window. The gutter was blocked with tea-leaves!

But John Laing's own most vivid memory was of the cheerful gratitude of one family of four, left uncomplaining in a house to which there remained only a scullery some seven-foot square, with a sack over the vacant window space, and one gas fire.

On 9 April 1945, when the onslaught was over, the Mayor of Lambeth wrote a warm letter of thanks to John Laing.

On 7 May 1945, the German forces surrendered to the Allied armies. A new world was to be born, and the plans so carefully formulated over the later war years were to be tested in operation. Involved as he had been in national planning, John Laing had not overlooked his own Company. Remembering the end of the First World War, he had had the Easiform specifications re-examined, had seconded a senior manager to work on improvements and refinements, and had spent considerable sums in preparing formwork before the demand was known.

In July polling took place in the first General Election for ten years, and by the night of 26 July it was known that Churchill was no longer prime minister and that Britain had a Labour government. The Minister of Health in the incoming administration, who was also in charge of housing, was Aneurin Bevan, a man strongly disliked by Churchill and the object of widespread suspicion because of his supposedly extreme left-wing views. He was certainly believed to be no friend of the private house-builder. Moreover, many of the powers that the wartime Government had put in the hands of the Ministry of Works were now transferred back to the Ministry of Health. It was inside the former Ministry that so much of the planning for the post-war situation had taken place, and how much of the detailed wartime work was lost in administrative change must be an open question.

The caretaker Government earlier in 1945 had put forward a plan to build three to four million houses in twelve years or a little longer, including half a million for slum clearance and the relief of overcrowding. Three hundred thousand houses were scheduled for the first two years, together with 200,000 temporary prefabricated houses. It was an over-ambitious plan. It was one thing on paper, but another to transfer into action in the face of extreme shortages of materials and the painfully slow build-up of skilled manpower that was the obverse of the scrupulously fair demobilisation system. Priority was given to the repair of war-damaged dwellings, and the requisitioning of unoccupied premises: 116,000 families found homes by January 1946, but new house-building got off to a painfully slow start, and private house-building was forbidden except under licence. Bevan's first big speech on housing in October 1945 was a great success, but by December he was facing a vote of censure, in which he was viciously attacked by Churchill. But the country was desperate for housing, and misery was aggravated by a severe winter. Bevan was to remain the object of severe criticism by opposition and press throughout his term of office, which ended with his resignation in April 1951. It must therefore be remembered that by the autumn of 1948 he had achieved the target of 750,000 houses which the wartime Government had estimated to be sufficient to provide every family with a separate house. That this was a gross under-estimate that failed to foresee the post-war boom in both marriages and births, and rising expectations, was Bevan's misfortune, but hardly his fault. During 1948 he achieved an overall total of 284,000 houses (including temporary housing)—no mean achievement in relation to pre-war figures, within three years of the war ending. By then the country had run into serious financial problems, and cuts in expenditure crippled the programme for the remainder of the Labour administration.

John Laing did not share Bevan's political views. In 1945 he became first president of the Hendon North Conservative Association, on the constituency's formation out of the old Hendon division (an office he held with distinction until 1968, when he retired to a vice-presidency), and he deplored publicly the determination of the new Government to build four-fifths of its housing through local councils, a course which he considered doctrinaire and uneconomical.

After the war, he was one of five council members of The Federation of Registered Housebuilders* (Sir Jonah Walker-Smith was another) who negotiated with the Ministry of Health on the re-establishment of the private house-building industry. Then, in 1946, he was to his surprise appointed chairman of the Housebuilding Committee of the National Federation of Building Trades Employers, and therefore the spokesman of the industry in meetings with Aneurin Bevan. He later recalled how he had gone to the first meeting expecting hostility, only to find an extremely courteous reception. He returned to tell one of his senior executives that he had found Bevan a remarkably pleasant man, despite his reputation.

To one of his Carlisle friends he described how, at an early meeting, Bevan had 'banged the table a bit' on his socialist views, and Laing had responded, 'Excuse me, I am an industrialist, but I happen to be a bricklayer, and you—a politician—can't tell me how to lay bricks: but I will give you all the help I can.' John Laing was first and foremost a patriot: the country's need for housing was paramount, and his full influence and loyalty would be thrown behind the man responsible for meeting the country's needs. For his part, Bevan responded warmly to John Laing's practical support (something which must have been of real value at a time when, politically, Bevan was the object of much

*Now the House Builders' Federation.

172

unconcealed hatred), and their relationship became as close as that which John Laing had enjoyed with previous ministers. On 12 July, 1947, during a speech at the opening of the first Easiform house at the Coldharbour Farm Estate, Woolwich, Bevan said, 'Of all the building contractors in Great Britain, one of them with the warmest place in my heart is John Laing & Son Limited, and they have really played the game.'[5] It was only one of numerous visits he paid to Laing estates, and the happy personal relationship between the two men became very apparent.

The two men, the miner from South Wales and the descendant of a line of stonemasons from Cumberland, must have sensed many common feelings, despite their opposite political views. The innate courtesy of Bevan, of which his biographer speaks; his preference for discussion and debate rather than confrontation; his habit of listening to a case without interruption and then testing it by incisive probing enquiry; his stress on first principles; his concern for high building standards and his strong visual sense of design – they were all traits that John Laing shared and understood. And we can imagine some of Bevan's non-partisan words meeting with the warm approval of John Laing: 'The purpose of getting power is to be able to give it away,'[6] or 'After all, you know, a man wants three houses in his lifetime: one when he gets married, one when the family is growing up, and one when he is old; but very few of us can afford one.'[7]

It was no surprise, therefore, when in 1948 Bevan appointed John Laing to the Central Housing Advisory Committee of the Ministry of Health, which he chaired himself. He had already drawn freely on his experience and advice, one example of John Laing's influence being the memorandum on direct labour circulated to local authorities by the Ministry in November 1946.

As we have seen, the Laing Company, with the experience of 1919 in mind, had anticipated the need for a new Easiform house to be available when the war ended, and the house, one of the first off the mark, was soon in considerable demand. Some of the earliest enquiries were from local authorities who wished to replace bombed Easiform houses built in the twenties. At Plymouth, the Laing representative visiting the estate there was gratified to hear a tenant shout to the official accompanying him, 'Give the man an order!' Easiform was no temporary design: the factory-built prefabs, of which so many were erected in the emergency years, may have been designed for a fifteen-year life only, but Easiform houses were built for a guaranteed sixty years.

Much of the research was directed to improving the quality of the inner wall of clinker concrete, which gave rise to technical problems. The thermal insulation properties of this type of concrete were attractive, but the laboratories were constantly seeking to improve it. The appearance was varied by new design features, roofing and finish. Other study concentrated on the improvement of the flow of production and the working rhythm, essential features of successful large-scale production. An important advance was the introduction in 1949 of central concrete-mixing facilities at the estate sites; central mechanical 'batching' of the concrete not only improved output, but produced a more consistent and better quality. Mechanical plant was introduced for the erection of the concrete shells and the preparation of joinery. The system also proved adaptable to other uses, and not only fathered a second generation of other types of system building, but was also modified to other types of construction work requiring concrete walling. It has led on to radical new types of construction, using on-site factory facilities (and then fully industrialised off-site factory production), and to modular building systems that assimilate advanced international thinking. Some of these have proved less satisfactory than the simpler Easiform itself.

The Easiform system made an even greater contribution to post-war housing than it had after the First World War. John Laing continued to take a close personal interest in its progress, and the Company's house journal, from its first issue in November 1946, prominently featured progress and statistics, on sites widely scattered throughout the country. By 1947 half the Company's labour force of 7,000 were engaged on the Easiform housing drive. The method was licensed to other contractors, and by June 1949, 10,000 Easiform houses had been put up; 15,000 by September 1950; 20,000 by November 1951. In December 1951, 131 completed houses had been handed over in one week. The count mounted; several hundred local authorities used the system, the defence authorities called on it, and there were numerous overseas enquiries. Eventually, by 1968, over 100,000 Easiform houses had been built throughout the country since the Second World War.

During his ministry, Aneurin Bevan took a very real personal interest in the system and frequently visited the sites. In 1946, opening a small estate of fifty houses that had been built near Bristol in five months to accommodate residents displaced by the new Filton runway, he described them as 'first-class houses built of concrete, and [provide] an answer to those sceptics who say you must build houses of bricks and mortar'.[8] In July 1949, he praised them as 'seemly, simple, convenient, dignified and ample'.[9] In November 1950, the site in progress at Swindon was visited by the then Princess Elizabeth, who inspected a completed and occupied house.

Easiform was not the Company's only contribution to the post-war housing need. They continued to build traditional houses for local authorities, and took a considerable part in the development and construction of the British Iron and Steel Federation steel house.

Another urgent need of post-war reconstruction which also bulked large in the Company's programme at this time was the production of coal by open-cast mining. They had begun work in open-cast mining in 1942 to meet wartime needs, but the major developments took place after the war. In 1947 and 1948 the country was producing some five per cent of national coal output from open-cast workings.[10] John Laing & Son Limited worked a number of these sites. The great Carrington's Coppice site, at 178 feet the deepest open-cast site in Britain, was started by the Company on 23 April, 1947. Over four and a half million cubic yards of overburden had to be removed, by the largest machines available, to get at the coal, and at the peak of production the work was proceeding twenty-four hours a day. Like others of the Company's sites, it several times held production records; it was worked out by the end of August 1949, and the land was reinstated for agricultural use by August 1950. The Company was winning some million tons of coal a year at this time, approximately ten per cent of national open-cast production.

John Laing's personal contribution to the industry's councils continued undiminished. He remained an active and enthusiastic member of the Building Research Board of the Department of Scientific and Industrial Research, which in his own words 'guided and shepherded' new forms of construction, and from 1946 to 1951 he was chairman of the Building Research Committee of the National Federation of Building Trades Employers. He was also largely responsible for delicate negotiations, which overcame suspicion and mistrust, to achieve the uniting of the house-builders' organisations and the affiliation of the House Builders' Federation to the N.F.B.T.E. He felt keenly the damage of poor workmanship to the reputation of his industry and was behind any development which would improve its product.

It is pleasant to record that Sir Jonah Walker-Smith was

instumental in securing Laing's services as chairman of the Specification Committee of the National House Builders' Registration Council, which brought up to date the recommendations formulated by Sir Raymond Unwin's committee on which John Laing had served before the war: this appointment made him *ex officio* a vice-chairman of the Council. The new specifications, published in 1948, remain the basic modern standards of house-building. After some years in this position, he was succeeded by J. H. Melville Richards, a past president of the Institution of Municipal Engineers. He was also a member of the committee of the south-east section of the Federation of Civil Engineering Contractors and of the British Standards Institution and Road Research Board, and, in 1952, of the Bailey Committee on House Interiors set up by Harold Macmillan as Minister of Housing.

It can have been no surprise when, in the New Year's Honours List of January 1951, John Laing was appointed C.B.E. He found himself waiting with a number of others before the investiture; there was a short delay, and some nervousness. The occasion brought him its own reminder of expectations long nurtured by his deep and simple faith. Turning to a man standing beside him, he remarked, 'I have been thinking what it will be like when we assemble before the throne of our Lord Jesus Christ. What shall we be thinking; and do you hope to be there?' By a coincidence, his neighbour, a stranger, was also a convinced Christian, and the brother of the secretary of a Christian society John Laing knew well. 'Thank God,' the neighbour replied, 'I hope to be there, through what Christ has done.' John Laing had borne his witness, and found a brother.

CHAPTER 12

Metamorphosis

IRBY AND MAURICE Laing had been appointed directors just before the war started, but in the short time before they each joined the Forces they had been completely pre-occupied by day-to-day management of some of the urgent rush of work which the war had brought. When they returned, it was to a business requiring critical decisions. John Laing was then approaching seventy; the considerable growth of the war years had been on work directly related to the war effort which was now finished, apart from the continuing open-cast coal mining, some remaining permanent airfields, and the prospects of Easi-form. The business would need a complete re-direction. With his long experience, John Laing knew that the spurt in house-build-ing would not continue consistently. 'The boom will break,' he constantly warned his sons.

In personnel, too, the face of the Company had changed. John Laing had suffered a severe loss when, in December 1941, his fellow-director and personal friend, William Sirey, had died suddenly. Sirey's place, both as chief estimator and on the Board, had been taken by his young, able and equally hard-working colleague, R. H. Woolliams. Of little effect in the Company, but of personal note none the less, a name from the distant past had been lost the following year, when John Laing's old mentor from his earliest days in the business, John Rigg, had died in Carlisle. Walter Harland, his brother-in-law accountant and adviser, died in May 1946, and Henry Chapman Harland, though still a director, was on the verge of retirement. John Lambert had retired in 1943, and David Adam in 1948.

There was a substantial foundation for the future. First and foremost, the Company's excellent reputation, perhaps formerly unduly attached to the pre-war housing record ('Why have we won no power station contracts for many years?' John Laing asked on one occasion. 'Because you are known as house-builders,' an executive had replied, and precipitated a change in policy), had been enhanced by its airfield construction experience, which pointed back into civil engineering, where John Laing's original objectives had lain. Its workforce, or at least its core of regular employees, was equalled in loyalty and reliability by few. Financially, its base was absolutely secure, thanks to John Laing's lifetime of careful prudence, backed also by the substantial property portfolio he had built up inside the Property Company.

John Laing's judgment of the times was as accurate as ever. He realised that with the ending of the war, and in the reaction brought about by the loss of wartime objectives, it was essential to concentrate on sustaining the morale of his workforce. He therefore began to emphasise his favourite theme of teamwork in action. When the starting of a house journal was suggested to him in 1946, he gladly accepted the suggestion, and the journal was duly christened *Team Spirit*, a name it has retained ever since. A carefully thought-out and highly professional production, it emphasised from the first both the current objectives and the record of contracts actually in hand, and also the long past history and tradition of the business. Tables and acknowledgments of contemporary achievement were matched by stories of past personalities and events, and by vignettes of individuals past and present of all grades who had spent their lives in the Company's service. The 'team' motif was extended into every possible aspect of the Company's publicity. The history of the Company that was published a year or two after the centenary celebrations of 1948 (themselves an important feature in the process) was called *Team Work*, and every encouragement was given to employees to see themselves as part of a living organisation with united objectives.

In this process, the employee shareholdings assumed a considerable importance. Numbers of employees attending the annual general meetings as shareholders were to grow steadily in the following decades. The accounts prepared for shareholders were accompanied by the statutory directors' reports, which were also used to emphasise the theme, and the Company's commitment to training and welfare of its employees. An important feature of earlier years was revived and extended after the war, in the annual employee outings. These dated back to the Carlisle days—as long before as 1922 there had been a staff outing to Ullswater—but in the immediate post-war years they took on a special significance. John and Beatrice Laing would be present, and they would use the outings as a special opportunity to meet the employees in a relaxed atmosphere, taking part in their activities and thoroughly enjoying themselves. To many of the participants the outings were a highlight of the year's activities, and it seemed (as was very nearly the case) that the Governing Director and his wife knew all the employees personally; they took a close interest in their circumstances, and would discuss family affairs on a basis of individual friendship.

In 1947 there were six separate staff outings from different areas of the country. The London district took twenty coaches to Clacton-on-Sea, and feeding the party presented no small task. The executive responsible remembers his problems in finding suitable accommodation; and a somewhat bewildered manager of the biggest of several restaurants used, after providing 400 persons with tea, asking John Laing whether he was satisfied. 'Oh yes,' the Governing Director had replied, 'everything was very good—although table × could have done with another plate of bread and butter.' On such attention to detail is success founded!

1948, the centenary year, saw a special outing down the Thames to Margate, for which the *Royal Eagle* was chartered. On the journey, the Laings made every effort to speak to each member of the party, and there was a presentation to them on board, with a speech by John Laing, in a sentence or two of which he again declared in simple words his own deep religious belief, and what it had meant in his life.

But if he saw clearly where the Company's morale needed reinforcing, he also realised that organisationally it was time to begin to hand over to a new generation. Unlike so many creators of large-scale enterprise, he had two extremely able sons to take over and develop the business to which he had devoted his life. He probably found the process no easier than others have done, but his judgment of timing was as sound as ever, and they were brought fully into direction from the time of their return in 1945. Another important step had been taken in 1944 when Ernest Uren* had been made chief accountant to the Company. He was to prove himself an administrator of great ability. Despite the tested and vital system of cost control on the contracts, the overall financial organisation of the Company left much to be desired, if it were to move from an era of personal control to the corporate structure of a larger organisation. As the size of contracts increased, it became more and more difficult to keep the costing accurate and on time. The disruption and scattered work of the war years had aggravated administrative problems. Uren

*See page 122.

struggled with the financial and costing records first; when these were fully integrated and mechanised and running on an accurate and up-to-date schedule, the base for the financial control of future organisational expansion was secure.

In the technical field, the Company had already become a leader in concrete technology, and the development of a new generation of permanent airfields for the Royal Air Force and the United States Air Force, as the war was ending, consolidated its experience. It had also learned a great deal concerning the development of other forms of specialised concrete for industry, on projects such as the Sellafield munitions complex.

The management was alerted to the need for the most advanced mechanisation by a general Air Ministry embargo on the use, for high-grade work, of a particular type of continuous concrete-mixer that had been a mainstay of contemporary bulk-concrete production. This machine was capable of turning out large quantities of good-quality concrete, and had done so in the hands of the Company's expert workforce, but in general use elsewhere in the country it had proved unreliable. Maurice Laing left for the U.S.A. in October 1946 with a senior executive, to study new types of equipment in use there, and American concrete technology in general. He returned with some of the most modern machinery available, including concrete-plant with sophisticated automated mixing facilities, capable of highly intensive production, that gave the Company facilities second to none in the country. Shortly after this, the Company engaged the services of one of the leading technical specialists in concrete.

In 1946, a Central Research and Development Laboratory was opened, with sections engaged on continuous research into new materials and methods, as well as the testing of production while contracts were in progress. In 1950 a new Central Plant Depot was opened on part of the site at Elstree where John Laing had planned his pre-war housing and factory complex. Over the next few years, departments were established to study mechanisation and plant development, materials technology, soil mechanics, architectural, mechanical and electrical engineering design, as well as a large civil engineering design department. With the advice of industrial consultants, the first work-study department in the industry was established.

These developments were in the hands of others, but as the years went by John Laing continued his close personal interest and pride in all that happened, well past normal retirement age.

One of the significant new products of this era was the result of introductions in which he had played an active part immediately after the war. It was pre-shadowed by a note in the Company journal concerning the Research Laboratory, in May 1948. 'It is expected that during this year at least one new construction material will be brought to the production stage, and, from indications given by the laboratory experiments, this material appears to have very great possibilities for all types of building.' He had always been interested in the possibility of a lightweight but strong building material that might be developed from light aggregates, and there had been experimentation in Carlisle as early as the mid twenties. A visit by John Laing himself to Sweden early in 1948 stimulated the work already in progress at Mill Hill, and in 1950, after three years' research, the Company was ready to launch Thermalite. This was a form of light-weight aerated concrete, developed from pulverised fuel ash, that created a strong and weather-resistant building material, much lighter than traditional materials, with high load-bearing qualities and a very considerable thermal insulating value. The Company claimed that three inches of this material were, in thermal efficiency, equal to thirteen and a half inches of brickwork.[1] A special company was formed in 1950 to exploit the new product, with its own factory, and later a link was formed with Ytong, the similar Swedish product.

Thermalite was a breakthrough in industrial terms, and has remained for many years unsurpassed in a field which has attracted a great deal of competitive research. In block form, it was very soon being used in construction work of all types, and houses constructed of the material were already on the market in 1951. The high relative humidity and unpredictability of the British climate had meant that few of the similar materials already developed (mainly overseas) were entirely suitable for general use in this country, and the new product had been specifically designed to meet local conditions and to use locally available materials.

On their return from the war in 1945, Kirby and Maurice Laing had found themselves with a stark choice: retrenchment or expansion. They chose expansion, and emphatically. The developments described laid the administrative and technical base for this expansion, but its implementation depended on human factors, and the acceptance of change by the persons immediately affected. In 1946 W. M. Johnson, by now the most senior of the prominent pre-war and wartime managers, and

J. Gregg, the chief quantity surveyor, joined R. H. Woolliams on the Board of Directors. It was a significant step. On the retirement of Henry Chapman Harland shortly afterwards, employee directors equalled in number the three family directors, and of these three, John Laing himself was nearing seventy. Not only was the base for decisions widened, but also the path to the top was now visibly open to any employee. Kirby and Maurice Laing became joint managing directors later that year.

The intended expansion of the Company into the new post-war world of vast industrial organisation was becoming plain. While airfield contracts continued as a regular commitment, the civil contracts that heralded the new phase of the Company's life were of national significance, and several of them were natural developments from the expertise in concrete technology. In 1946 came the contracts for construction of the two-mile runway at Filton, near Bristol, for the vast (and later aborted) Brabazon civil aircraft project—the 110-ton Brabazon 1 was the largest land airliner projected to that date—and for Paton and Baldwin's immense Darlington factory, the largest knitting-wool factory in Europe, on a site of 140 acres, with a spinning shed that alone covered 21 acres. It included its own power station, a million-gallon reservoir and water-treatment plant, forty staff houses and nine miles of roadway, in addition to the great factory and the administrative and recreational complex. The loss of the Heathrow airport contract was a deep disappointment to John Laing himself, but later the firm was to build at Prestwick and Glasgow. In January 1948 came the contract for the country's first plutonium factory at Windscale, on the site of the wartime Sellafield factory, a contract of formidable high technology, and under deep security wraps that have still not been loosened—though a senior executive remembers meeting there two of the top foreign scientists who later defected to Russia. In the same year work was in progress on a large new conventional power station at Plymouth, and a substantial section of the huge steel mill at Abbey Works near Port Talbot in South Wales, as well as the new cement factory for Associated Portland Cement at Shoreham in Sussex. Later there was work at the new oil refinery at Coryton in Essex, and building-work at the refinery at Fawley in Hampshire.

That John Laing was still taking very great interest in the progress of contracts at this time, and that he had lost none of his old flair for human relationships is shown by an anecdote of the Shoreham contract, told by one of the present Laing staff:

In 1949 I was a young secretary on the Cement Works Project we were constructing just a few miles inland from Shoreham-by-Sea. We had a small structure where the men sat to eat their lunch after they had queued up in the canteen. This was made up of second-hand corrugated sheeting, and there were holes in it from the nails that had been previously driven into it. When the weather was fine, the cement dust blew in, and when it was wet the rain seemed to pour in; added to this, the food produced was very second-rate and there had been a lot of grumbling about it. We were informed that Sir John was coming to visit the site and would be there for lunch. Sid Smith, the site agent, arranged that luncheon would be served in his office. I brought in a table-cloth, decent cutlery, plates, etc. I even made a flower arrangement for the table and provided a water-jug and glasses. The food was prepared by the canteen and kept warm in my office on the stove. We had suggested 12.30 to Sir John for lunch, and when that time came he was missing. He eventually turned up about 1.00 p.m. and said, 'I've had my lunch.' He had put on an old raincoat, joined the queue of men and got his lunch. When he was sitting eating it, one of the workmen said, 'I believe the old man is visiting the site today. I bet he isn't sitting in this rotten canteen eating this rubbish.' He didn't let on who he was, but the very next day we got a new roof and the quality of the food was greatly improved from then on.'

For the expansion, managerial style had to be significantly altered, and the Company developed its own structure of delegated authority and decentralisation, in a form which would retain the local initiative and incentive that John Laing's emphasis on team spirit had fostered, while providing the backing of a strong central organisation. In 1948, the early form of this new style of management structure had W. M. Johnson as director in charge of contracts at Head Office, with three district managers (two of whom later became main Board members), and under them five area agents. Andrew Anderson and Ernest Uren joined the main Board in 1951. As the growth of the Company continued, the structure was steadily expanded, with regional offices and directorships, and a steady promotion to the main Board of executives through all grades of management.

In 1952 the Company 'went public' by obtaining a Stock Exchange quotation for its share capital (the quotation was obtained through a holding company with a considerable number of operating subsidiaries). A special class of 'employee shares' was created for the flotation, and continued in use for several years, before being merged with the ordinary share capital; the comparatively small proportion of shares under this name obscured the extent of the total employee interest in the Company at that date; this was mainly by ordinary shares (of which twenty-three per cent were held by employees immediately before the flotation, and another thirty per cent by the charitable Stewards' Company, only twenty-six per cent remaining in the personal names of John Laing and his sons).*

The regular labour force passed its wartime peak, and by 1950 it reached 15,000 men, and was still expanding fast. The Mill Hill headquarters expanded unrecognisably – at first, until building permits could be obtained, in temporary refurbished hutting. Increasingly, an expanded front-line force brought expansion of supporting services. The Company had established its own catering organisation during the war, and with it other on-site welfare facilities; by 1949 the department was running nine canteens and five residential camps (thirty-five other canteens were being run by contract caterers), and in a year it had served two million meals and three and a half million hot beverages. Later, the Company's own printing works was established. Increasingly, businesses grew within the business.

Growth itself brought a stimulus to further growth. As suitable staff came on within the Company, it became necessary to provide them with increased incentives and opportunities. The Company's attention had turned to overseas work at the end of the war, when it won a contract for rebuilding the bombed King George V Memorial Hospital in Malta for the Missions to Seamen. The contract had John Laing's own special interest (although largely financed by the Scottish Branch of the British Red Cross Society, it was announced at the opening that he had himself made a generous gift to the rebuilding), for the Society was one that he regarded affectionately, as he did also the Royal National Mission to Deep Sea Fishermen. He and his wife were both present at the opening by Countess Mountbatten of Burma on St. Andrew's Day 30 November, 1948.

The first substantial expansion overseas came in 1947. In the previous year, John Laing had visited South Africa with his son Kirby. Maurice Laing had completed part of his Air Force training in that country, and was interested in opportunities there, and his father and brother travelled out to survey the possibilities of

*Most of the remainder were held by a number of trusts that included extensive charitable objectives.

184

opening a branch there. In 1947 a branch was opened at Johannesburg, and an organisation was established that rapidly ranked among the largest building and civil engineering organisations in Southern Africa. The Company soon extended to Rhodesia and Zambia, where road construction was quickly in progress, and eventually the business there became larger than that in the Republic.

The Company was interested in the possibilities of improving housing for the black population. In January 1948, a contract was signed, in conjunction with a local contractor, Roberts Construction, for the largest housing scheme ever attempted in South Africa: 5,100 houses, 3,400 of 324 feet super and 1,700 of 216 feet super, with domed concrete roofs cast on the site. Laings were later building housing in Zambia, and undertaking extensive contracting in many places on the continent. No less than 30,000 houses were completed by 1955, in addition to other major contracting. But eventually it proved necessary to close down operations, the 1962 accounts recording that the Southern African activities had been brought to an end 'as a result of political unrest and its effect on capital investment'.

The South African extension was only the first of increasing interests abroad. By 1951 there were contracts in Mauritius, a power station at Benghazi in Libya, and harbour works in Syria. But the most extensive contact of the immediate post-war years started in 1949, when work was undertaken by the Company for the Duke of Westminster on his private estates in different parts of Britain. From that contact grew a partnership with Grosvenor Estates that has led not only to considerable developments in this country, but also to extensive joint projects in British Columbia, and for a time to a large operation in Vancouver which John Laing himself was able to visit while he was still active.

The later development of the Laing organisation, in Britain or overseas, is not part of this biography, except for one or two exceptions that remain for the next chapter. The present-day concern (in terms of constant building costs, seven times the size of the expanded business when John Laing reached his seventieth birthday in 1949*) is, in size of real turnover, some 1,600 times as large as the business with which John Laing struggled at Uldale and Barrow in his twenties. The extent to which, from that tiny beginning, he laid the foundation for what has followed, the reader of this biography can judge.

---

*The Company history of 1950 rightly concluded, 'the story ends on the threshold of a new age.' (*Team Work*, p. 108.)

CHAPTER 13

'The Power and the Glory'

THE POST-WAR EXPANSION and re-organisation of the Companies released John Laing from detailed responsibility and from his personal dominance over their activities, but it also gave him greater opportunity to develop his religious and charitable interests. The business remained a major concern and involvement, and he continued to visit the head office and contracts daily. Even in his seventies he was said on one occasion (when ladders were not forthcoming quickly enough) to have clambered up the scaffolding of houses under construction for a surprise inspection, and in his nineties he was still visiting the offices at Mill Hill and attending the annual general meetings.

He relinquished the chairmanship of the active construction and property companies to his sons in 1954, but retained the chairmanship of the public holding company until 1 January, 1957, when he was succeeded by his son Kirby. It was significant timing, for he had just signed the contract for some work that crowned his business life, and of which more is to be said later. Announcing the change in *Team Spirit*, he was emphatic. 'Let me say at once, I am not going to retire.' (He was 77!) 'I have always got pleasure from my work, although at times it has been hard, but those hard times often bring their reward.' He was appointed president of the Company, this being amended to life president in 1975, when he was approaching ninety-six.

We turn now to pick up the threads of his non-business activities from the wartime period. His widespread donations were partly known by rumour within the Company, but details and their full extent were known only to a few confidential employees, except when, as one senior man remembers, 'When I returned to London about 1942, my office must have been one of the nearest to his, because I got all sorts of jobs. On one occasion he was buying some houses to put people into and I had to ring up all those estate agents and find sizes and prices. It was homes for various people–he was always doing that sort of thing.' The

186

tradition has continued: today over half of the dividends paid out by the public company go to charitable objectives.

During the war years he became friendly with a New Zealand industrialist who visited this country for an extended time; this was Robert Laidlaw, a man of similar background and principle to John Laing himself. John Laing developed a high regard for Laidlaw, who was a successful evangelist and an advocate of planned Christian giving, and while he was in this country persuaded him to attend as a leader the Crusader camp which (despite the war years and absence of younger men in the Forces) he continued to run. The memory of the two men together as officers of the camp is still a powerful one for men now in middle age.

John Laing continued leading his boys' camps until his seventieth year. In 1947 his adjutant at a camp at St. Bees on the Cumbrian coast was a well-known London solicitor, just returned with the Military Cross from distinguished war service, who had attended several camps with him before the war. This colleague remembers the Laing lorry (driven by 'Bill' White, John Laing's trusted personal chauffeur) which took the boys on their climbing trips into the hills. On the first day John Laing – nearly sixty-eight – took them all on a 'quickener': it was a mountain walk on which many of less than half his age found themselves struggling to keep up with him. He was as fit and as full of fun as ever, joining in all activities with the old enthusiasm.

Speaking to the boys at the camps, John Laing was simple, homely and brief, never talking down to them, but drawing on his own experiences of work and family life, with sound common sense and practical advice on the affairs of life. He would advise them against early marriage; every man needed the 'adventure years', when he could be free to travel, to take 'manly holidays' and enjoy his youth. Yet there was no censoriousness about him. One young officer was believed by his fellows to be spending rather more time than they approved with one of the girl cooks. Did he not think, they asked, that as commandant John Laing should reprove the young man? Not at all. John Laing had noticed, 'but he had thought how good it would be, if as a result of serving her Lord in the cookhouse, the girl met the husband of His choice.' Another young man had approached him rather earnestly about how to find a wife with all the virtues, which the young man enumerated. John Laing replied, quietly, 'You see, the difficulty is that none of these qualities have you got yourself.' He was punctilious, too, in inculcating a respect for obligations; one camper remembers receiving a letter reminding him to return a collar-stud, borrowed and forgotten!

> 'Another thing that impressed us,' said another fellow-camper, 'was his readiness to take on anything and everybody. He would love to go on a slippery pole with a pillow case and knock everybody off with great glee. He'd always enter into the fun of it; he was a boy at heart . . . Genuine, warm, simple-hearted and with no airs.'

His attendance at the Crusader general committee meetings continued well after he no longer attended the boys' camps, and in his eighties his interest was still strong. His fellow members remembered him as quiet and always ready to listen to others, always ready with his little black notebook and never forgetting a promise. He never sought to dominate the committees, and was always ready with a perceptive contribution. As the years passed and his perceptions clouded a little, he took the sometimes rude rebuffs of brasher newcomers in good part. The years brought no 'state of anecdotage'. One colleague, who knew him well and had served on Montgomery's staff in the African campaign, found in him the same straightforward directness, the same ability to pick out the essentials of a situation and not to be confused by detail, as he had recognised in the great war leader.

At the Crusader-leaders' conferences, John Laing's contribution was always a personal one, and men would talk to him who found other prominent leaders less approachable. His concern was to find future leaders, to bring them on in leadership and to give them his own love of the Bible.

His colleagues state that they had no consciousness of any attempt to control proceedings by financial strings; support was there, but they were never made aware of it, nor was it liable to be withdrawn because of some passing pique—his giving was without manipulative undertones. His most spectacular gift to the Crusaders' Union immediately followed the war. Some four hundred Crusaders had been killed during the war, and the Union had built up a small memorial fund from gifts sent in by their friends and relatives—sometimes the accumulated savings of a young man who had died in service. The General Committee discussed how they could most appropriately use the fund, and someone suggested acquiring a permanent camp site. 'Oh, but it must be better than that,' John Laing had said, 'not just a camp site—these fellows gave their lives for us.' He set his property experts hunting, and they found on the market a small country estate on the Isle of Wight, with twenty-eight acres of woods and gardens. So he was able to present Westbrook to the Union, others of his colleagues fitting the house out to provide a splendid permanent centre, with facilities for tented camps in the summer months, which has been one of the most constructive and fruitful bases of the Union's work. In 1948 he led one of the last of his boys' camps there, with his old friend Frank Bacon as padre, and photographs show him sitting at the camp mess tables with the lines of boys, thoroughly part of the proceedings.

In 1942, at the height of his wartime activities, John Laing had become chairman of the Inter-Varsity Fellowship Business Advisory Committee, to continue for nearly twenty years until succeeded by his friend, P. S. Henman. It was a vital period of imaginative extension by the Fellowship. He was at its head-quarters in Bedford Square regularly for an hour or two every week, quietly enquiring and encouraging about all aspects of the work.

His first emphasis was always on personnel. 'Find the right men and women, and we can soon put roofs over their heads.' He encouraged the building up of wider financial support and interest, that would remain when he himself had gone, and so his 'matching' system of giving would frequently be brought into operation. Perhaps a talented young man or woman would come to his notice, to be backed financially as a member of the growing team of travelling secretaries, or additional capital was needed for expansion of the programme of publications. There were other donors who joined with him (it was another friend who bridged the publication of the first edition of *The New Bible Commentary*, and a further friend from the publishing trade who guided the growth of the booklist), but always at the back of the operation there was quiet support from John Laing.

He would arrive for his weekly visit with his characteristic smile. 'How many students and graduates have come to the Lord Jesus?' and, writes one who knew him intimately in those days, 'the emphasis on *Lord* was such that the Lord of Heaven and Earth might well have been looking over his shoulder!' Then he would visit all the staff, quietly questioning, examining the progress of the publications and enquiring into their costings, listening to the latest progress report of a university mission or a discussion of some particular problem, until he left and 'all the staff felt that they were being encouraged by the business Managing Director—yet he never once interfered with any policy or other decision of the Student Executive or Graduates Fellowship Committee.'

When the work expanded beyond the capacity of the premises in Bedford Square, it was John Laing's foresight and generosity that secured the lease of the site behind, in Morwell Street, and backed, on the 'matching' basis, the cost of the building work there – to provide a headquarters in the joint building that was an essential contribution to the ongoing and expanding work through thirty years of unprecedented growth in the numbers of students in Britain. In combination with his support for the growing field team, it was an act of vision as opportune in its own field as any of his far-sighted business decisions.

An equally significant and timely contribution to Christian growth in the post-war years had its roots in wartime developments. A high percentage of first-class Cambridge degrees in theology began to be won by men who supported the evangelical Cambridge Inter-Collegiate Christian Union, and conservative theology began to gain a much-needed self-confidence. It was felt that a centre for scholarly research, near to first-class facilities, was becoming essential, if the new tendency was to develop on firm foundations, particularly as men known to be conservative evangelicals often found their way to research posts and grants blocked by influential opposition. A few of the handful of conservative theological and biblical scholars had consulted together, and John Laing was brought into the discussions. In 1942, they found suitable premises in Selwyn Gardens, Cambridge, and established Tyndale House; John Laing helped largely with the purchase, and later built there one of the finest of purpose-built and equipped residential libraries for biblical research, on his usual 'matching' basis of giving. He also endowed subsequent scholarships. The nucleus of the library itself, formerly that of an Oxford Old Testament scholar, was purchased by funds he provided.

The subsequent influence of Tyndale House on evangelical scholarship has been incalculable; it was not for nothing that in March 1958 John Laing could write to the scholar whose influence had been strongest in persuading him in support:

I had meant to say in my letter of yesterday how much we owe to you in two things (and lots of other things): you inspired me with the thought of Tyndale House, and the great value it might be for Evangelical Bible Scholarship, and second,

Donald Wiseman always points out that it was you who inspired him to go in for scholarship.

In January 1943, John Laing became a member of the executive committee appointed by the Council of the infant London Bible College, charged with finding premises suitable to provide for both offices and lectures. Within weeks,[1] 'the chairman reported the offer of generous financial help from J. W. Laing–the first of his many benefactions to the college'. Shortly afterwards, the College started a few classes in temporary premises, but in September 1945, John Laing offered the use of the building at 19 Marylebone Road, that he had introduced to his two friends before the war, rent-free for a period of three to five years, pending the erection of a new building.

The offer was warmly accepted, and the necessary work of adaptation put in hand; again, the Laing Company (still a private company) undertook the work at cost, spreading payment over an extended period. The College was opened with a formal ceremony of dedication on 31 October, 1946, with Montague Goodman in the chair and John Laing leading in the dedicatory prayer. John Laing's friend, P. S. Henman (who shared substantially with him in the cost of the subsequent expansion and rebuilding) was treasurer of the College. In 1953, John Laing joined the Board of Governors.

The College grew beyond expectations, quickly building a considerable reputation under its first principal, the Revd E. F. Kevan. The premises were soon outgrown and, despite strict contemporary restrictions on building, a new building was urgently needed. Long-drawn negotiations with the authorities followed, and it was not until February 1956 that John Laing, who had lent his prestige and expertise to the conduct of the negotiations, could report final approval of the plans. He had already offered to sell the site to the College for £15,000 less than cost (very far indeed below its current market value), and, in addition, he and his wife would donate the first £30,000 to the building fund, and his Company would put up the building at cost, he himself reimbursing the Company for the profit foregone.

Work on the new building started in the autumn of 1956. John Laing was unsparing in obtaining the best possible bargain for his client. A senior executive of the Company remembers no less than twenty-seven different prices being worked out for the job before he was satisfied. While in progress, the work had his close attention and regular personal supervision. (A characteristic sidelight on another well-known trait—his rather fearsome driving—is thrown by a story told of one of his visits. The site manager found that his car had been damaged on the site, and that nobody had reported the matter. Indignant, he called in the police—who reported after a few days that he could charge the offender if he wished; it was his company chairman!). Eventually, on 20 January, 1958, the College moved into the new building, the formal opening by John Laing and the dedication service following on 10 May.

Again, it was a strategic gift to the evangelical churches. The building continued in use by the College until 1970, when further expansion made necessary its removal to the premises formerly occupied by St. John's College at Northwood—a move largely made possible by its possession of the first-class building in Marylebone Road. The London Bible College is now well established as a key factor in British evangelicalism. In 1959, Sir John Laing was appointed president of the London Bible College, and later endowed the annual Laing lecture, the first lecturer in 1971 being F. F. Bruce, Rylands Professor of Biblical Criticism and Exegesis at Manchester University.

Another vision of those days was to prove abortive: that was for the establishment of a London centre for united evangelical work, a building serving as headquarters for many of the contemporary evangelical societies. Evangelical individualism defeated even Sir John Laing's enthusiasm in this, and perhaps that very individualism is after all a major strength of evangelicalism. Perhaps, also, he was ambivalent in this vision: he was always insistent that men are more important than buildings, and in 1959 declined an invitation from the Archbishop of Canterbury to join the steering committee for the building of a headquarters of the World Council of Churches in Geneva, 'not being in favour of large buildings for such purposes',[2] while expressing to a friend a desire to see more of the Council's relief work.

Another interest which had engaged both him and his wife for some years was the work of the British and Foreign Bible Society. He had been an active member, and for some time president, of its local Mill Hill Auxiliary; in 1948, he joined the headquarters General Committee and in 1954 became a vice-president, the Society expressing its appreciation of his 'keenest interest in every aspect of our work, and your wide knowledge of public affairs and ever-ready help'.

He did, indeed, give high priority to the Bible Society, telling a

The Cathedral Church of St. Michael, Coventry

Sir John and Lady Laing on their golden wedding day, 1960

Talking to children about his coat of arms at a village tent mission (p. 214)

friend in 1958 that 'in my case the main work will be brethren work, next to that I.V.F., Crusaders and the Bible Society'.[3] He served on several sub-committees, not only on the more expected Property and Production sub-committees, but also on the Overseas (later Asia) sub-committee, and in 1953 and again in 1959 (just before his eightieth birthday) he visited India on its behalf. The earlier of these two visits had been to investigate possible sites and premises for a Bible Depot in Bombay; he was later, through his Company, responsible for the construction of Bible House in Salisbury, Rhodesia, and also for the internal reconstruction of the Society's headquarters at 146 Queen Victoria Street, London. He was active in small matters of detail as well as large, and the Society regularly benefited from its own substantial share of his financial generosity.

Among the Society's translation work, a project in which he took an especial interest was the production of an Arabic translation of the whole Bible by a Brethren missionary in North Africa, Captain E. G. Fisk; Laing was proud to possess a presentation copy of this Bible, from the Society. It is indicative of the range of his concern that a friend who visited him in connection with Bible Society business knew also of a needy old native Christian worker in a North African country, who also received regular personal help: 'a really great man', this friend described Sir John, 'in his delightful simplicity and beaming warm-heartedness'. In 1961, Sir John became a member of the Joint Council set up at Lambeth Palace in celebration of the 350th anniversary of the Authorised Version of the Bible and the publication of the New English Bible New Testament.

As the letter to his friend just quoted shows, his first interest remained with Brethren evangelistic and missionary work of all kinds. In 1945 the local home evangelistic committees combined in an enlarged Counties Evangelistic Work, and he served on Joint Oversight from its first meeting on 10 July, 1945. He was one of a committee that rejected proposals to wind up the work in 1947, and he later played an important part in its development. As interested as ever in photography, he encouraged the production of a series of regular films documenting the work, giving technical instruction through his Company's publicity staff. These films helped to gain respect and support for the work; they have earned notice for it on the B.B.C. as well as in more specifically Christian media, and have encouraged similar work as far away as Australia.[4]

Later, he made a room in his own Central London offices

available for the regular meetings of the Counties Work Executive Oversight. Of pre-eminent value, however, even beyond his regular financial giving, was his humane and extremely generous personal help and advice given to officers and committee at a time of deep internal crisis in the work. He continued his regular involvement with 'Counties' until his eightieth year, when he asked to be relieved of regular responsibility, while continuing his very real interest in its progress.

When he helped with the building of a new meeting hall, he was on his own ground. If ever he visited a hall put up by a local builder, whether he had helped finance it or not, his interest would always be aroused by the design and workmanship. One executive of his Company who was also a member of the Brethren, accompanied him on a visit to a local church in Kent, where he was due to speak. Questioning him on the proposed subject for his talk, the executive was surprised to find that he had with him a Company film on open-cast coal workings! But he based on it a simple practical talk. Afterwards, discovering that the congregation had put up their own church building, he asked to be taken on a tour of inspection, sharply inquisitive on all details of cost and design. At another church building (also in Kent) in 1963, where Sir John had helped with the finance and was invited to the opening services, he startled those present by getting down on hands and knees–he was then eighty-three–to inspect the new underfloor heating. Modern expectations took him aback a little (the sanitary ware was of a quality 'much better than we usually use for Brethren chapels!'), but afterwards he asked–to the confusion of those present–why the builder had not been invited. On his return to London he wrote the builder a personal note, congratulating him on the quality of his workmanship.

W. T. Stunt, the solicitor who had been general secretary of the Covenanter Union, had become an editor of the Brethren missionary magazine *Echoes of Service* in September 1947, an appointment which made him *ex officio* one of the administrators of the Bath clearing-house for gifts to Brethren missionaries. In December 1948, John Laing, with William Stunt, left Britain on one of the first of his post-war journeys abroad to visit Brethren missionaries. It was a 17,000 mile trip to India, Pakistan and Ceylon, and Stunt has left some vivid recollections of the journey. They flew out in one of the old flying boats, and found themselves delayed on the flight:

Those old flying boats were very comfortable and they had a lounge, and he asked the pilot whether, as it was Sunday, we could have a service. The pilot was surprised but very co-operative and it was announced that on the appropriate time on Sunday morning there would be a Christian service in the lounge. Eight or nine of the travellers came: he asked me to read a passage of Scripture; he then prayed, read another passage of Scripture and then prayed . . . Sir John said, 'Now, I think we ought to join in their games . . . they have come to our service.'*

The famous notebooks were much in evidence during his travels, and every piece of information, whether from Indian crossing-sweeper or high Government official, was carefully noted. When visiting a mission station he would again be noting costs, measurements and building methods. There was a careful evaluation in the notebook both of the work and of the individual workers, each marked against a standard list of ten or twelve criteria. All this information would be available to guide him in allocation of the very substantial annual sums he was giving to the work.

William Stunt remembered how, in the little village congregations established by the missionaries, largely of outcaste people, John Laing would speak simply through interpreters, telling homely stories of his childhood and parents, his emotion showing plainly on his face. The listening people were fascinated and captivated.

Laing and Stunt visited one village by local bus:

The meeting in the village was in what seemed like a tumble-down cowshed. I think there were about four hundred people crammed in there. First we were taken to lunch by the schoolmaster, an outcaste man. His house was a hut about half the size of this room, divided into two, one was the kitchen. The dear lady explained to Mr. Phair (the missionary) that she had made it nice and clean for us by daubing all the walls and floor with cow-dung, and we sat down on the floor with our feet crossed; and he put in front of us a plate made of banana leaves sewn together with grass, and an enormous pile of most beautifully cooked rice, and on top of it some curry. The dear

*While this book was printing, a friend of Sir Maurice Laing met the captain of this flight, who recounted this same incident, describing it as 'one of the most memorable times in my life'.

man explained that he had told his wife that English people did not like hot curry and she had made it as cool as she could. He brought us some boiling hot water in which peppers had been boiled and we drank it and it took away the heat of the curry. We ate the rice and curry with our hands, and it was delicious. When we finished, the 'plates' were given to the goat outside.

Then we went to the hall: there were about four hundred people present. At first the Gospel was preached and then . . . about forty of us sat down round a cloth on the floor and Mr. Laing and I sat with our backs to the wall. At one time Mr. Phair said, 'Do you know what the caste people outside have said – one of them said to the other, "but there is no god there; I thought these Christians were worshipping their God", and the other said, "Well, that's the strange thing about these Christians: you cannot see their God, but they believe that when they eat the bread and drink the wine like that, their God is with them".'

On another occasion the missionary seemed to be an inordinate time translating: leaning across to William Stunt, John Laing whispered, 'Am I giving this talk – or is Phair?' He had illustrated his talk by the story of his being fog-bound outside Barrow harbour as a young man, and of his relief at eventually seeing the harbour light: the problem, of course, for the translator, was that the hearers had never seen the sea or a harbour.

During the return journey they visited one middle-eastern capital, where Laings were discussing some construction projects. Stunt was present when it became clear that the official to whom John Laing was talking was suggesting some 'pay-offs' for himself and the contractor. He remembers Laing's abrupt reaction. 'We do not do business like that!' The interview finished forthwith.

They arrived back in Britain on 20 May, 1949, but it was only the first of several journeys by John Laing to the Indian sub-continent, in which he continued to take a close interest. The leaders of the newly independent States had his respect. 'Nehru,' he recorded on one occasion 'is a good man' (though he disapproved of his Kashmir policy), and Ayub Khan he admired as 'free from all suspicion of bribes, godly and tolerant'. As we have seen, he visited India in 1953 and again in 1959, and in 1958 was largely instrumental in financing the formation and building of the Delhi Bible Institute, a foundation that clearly had the success of the London Bible College in mind, and in which he continued afterwards to take an active interest. His vision for India was much what it had been for Britain twenty years before, and he was anxious to encourage both the local production of Christian literature and an indigenous biblical scholarship, actively supporting work of both classes. He realised, however, that human resources were as yet scarce among the Brethren congregations: 'Of course, it would be a great advantage if, in addition to their standard teachers,' he wrote to one scholar friend in March 1960, 'they could occasionally have some scholarly teachers giving what you and Professor Bruce could give, but how could we get that type of teaching in India?'

In 1959, shortly before his last visit to India, he had met Chandhu Ray, then Suffragan Bishop of Karachi, and had been greatly impressed by him—'one of a dozen men who I would put in the very first rank, among others such as Messrs. Goodman and Laidlaw'. Although he was nearly eighty, his notes of the meeting show a precise interest in the facts and figures of the contemporary refugee problem in Pakistan, and he was able to assist towards the schools programme which the Bishop was setting up, with the backing of his Government, in the new townships there.

In the late spring of 1952, he was also able to visit Algeria, Morocco and Spain, with another of the editors of *Echoes of Service*, this time visiting isolated mission stations in remote places where transport was only by mule. In March of that year the first general meeting had been held of the Missionary Technical Fellowship, a group of businessmen and technicians who were prepared to put their skills, on a voluntary basis, at the service of overseas missionaries who might need them. A report had been received of buildings in a sad state of repair at one of the remote North African stations, with no local help readily available. Two businessmen, one a builder, were prepared to leave their businesses for a time to undertake the work, but they needed a full report on the buildings. John Laing and his colleague were travelling in the area and visited the station (the last stage of the journey required a two-hour mountain ride on donkey or mule. The station, incidentally, was manned by three gallant English ladies) and a full report was sent by them to the volunteers, enabling the appropriate materials to be got together, despite the formidable transport problems, and the two volunteers were later able to journey out and effect the necessary repairs. They found the three ladies living in buildings where all the water they required had to be carried by donkey from fifteen minutes' distance from the house, by means of jerry cans strapped like panniers on the animals' backs. After his return, John Laing was present at a meeting in October when the completion of that work–and the urgent need for more–was reported to the Missionary Technical Fellowship in London. On this journey, John Laing was also able to visit his missionary relatives at León in Spain.

In 1953, he visited the Middle East on a holiday-with-business trip, seeing the closing stages of the harbour work at Banias in Syria. The Company's staff, he wrote in *Team Spirit*, needed 'the patience of Job, the wisdom of Solomon, the courage of Joshua and the persistence and determination of St. Paul, and with these virtues, they have managed to overcome all the difficulties'.[5] During this journey he visited with great interest the impressive ruins of Baalbeck in Lebanon and the ancient rock city of Petra in the desert of Jordan.

His programme of travel during this decade was strenuous enough for any man in his seventies, but it reached a climax as he approached his eightieth birthday. In 1955, he was away for six weeks in North America. Wallace Haughan remembers how in Vancouver he caught his finger in the door of a car, and practically took off its top. Ten days later, in his San Francisco hotel with W. M. Johnson's son Clifford, 'He turned to Clifford and said, "Clifford, I am pushed for time; I haven't got time to go to the hospital; will you take these stitches out for me?" That was one time when Clifford Johnson refused to do what Sir John asked him to do!' On 30 December, 1957, he left to travel round the world in thirty-two days, visiting Singapore, Sydney, Auckland, Fiji, Honolulu, Vancouver (where he inspected Company contracts) and Amsterdam, calling on the work of Christian organisations in which he was interested. Returning to Britain, he was still actively enquiring into Christian and charitable work that had been brought to his attention, and engaging in correspondence with his scholar friend on current topical debates in the churches he loved; but to an executive who enquired of his journey he merely said, with a twinkle in his eye, 'the surf-bathing in the Pacific was marvellous!' 'I can just say that life is fully as happy as it has been in any previous period of life,' he wrote in a letter in September, 1958, 'and I think our Heavenly Father just grades our pleasures to fit our ages.'

In his eightieth year he was writing with relish to a friend who was to visit the Continent with him, discussing the business contacts he could make in Germany, the buildings and engineering projects he should visit, planning the details of the journey:

> What would interest me most would be if about one-third of our time was spent in brethren assembly work; one-third in interdenominational Christian work, such as the Bible Society, or Christian Radio work, or Christian educational work on the lines of the I.V.F.; and one-third in Building and Civil Engineering work.

At Hamburg he visited the great Christian hospital and met its founder-director, Friedrich Heitmüller. In Berlin he met some of the city planners and toured many of the new developments. But his friend's most vivid memory was a visit to a motorway bridge under construction across a deep valley:

> The work was perhaps not more than two-thirds completed and there were still here and there on the roadway great squares unlaid with a drop of several hundred feet to the floor of the valley. Sir John seemed to be in his element and kept moving from place to place, while I followed like a petrified dunlin. In particular, he wanted to know all about the pillars, of which one could have a close view through adjacent unlaid squares. They were hollow (if I remember aright) and he wanted to know about the nature of the pre-stressed concrete used, the method of shuttering used with such pillars, and other technical details, all of which had to be translated into German, and then the answers into English. On a later visit to this contractor I found that his family always referred to the bridge as the 'Sir Laing Bridge'.

A month or two later, back from this journey, he was off again on the visit to India already mentioned.

During this period he was promoting many other prominent evangelical developments. On 18 December, 1945, he had called and taken the chair at a 'tentative meeting' at the Mildmay Centre in London. A young New Zealand Air Force pilot, Murray Kendon, had suggested that the flying skills learned by Air Force personnel during the war might well be used for the benefit of missionaries working in the more remote areas of the world. So was born, with active support from the Laing family as well as other leading missionaries and their supporters, the Missionary Aviation Fellowship, to be of incalculable value over the years in widely separated areas of the world. One of John Laing's first acts was to make a significant contribution to the cost of the first plane, a twin-engined Miles Gemini, 'Mildmay Pathfinder'.

Two leaders of student evangelicals had visited the Moody Bible Institute in Chicago after the war and seen there a notable religious natural history film, *The God of Creation*. They brought a copy back to this country and approached John Laing, whose interest in the use of film in evangelism was known to them. It was in the cinema at his company's premises in lower Regent Street that the first showing took place before a small audience, to be followed by a wider showing to Christian leaders at the National Club. As a result John Laing became one of the prime movers in the launching of Fact and Faith Films in this country.

Other notable contacts followed in the next ten years. In October 1952, he was present at the Council of Reference meeting that invited Dr. Billy Graham to London for his first Harringay crusade, and advised on its promotion. He actively supported the crusade, bringing many guests, and acting as a counsellor. Later he recalled how he had counselled one man from a leading building contracting firm who was deeply involved in corrupt business practice—with some sadness, the man concluded against committing himself as a Christian because he could see no way out of the practices.

There was an enlightening sequel to this involvement with the Graham crusades. When the 1966 Earls Court crusade was being planned, the telephone of the director (an old Crusader from the Mill Hill class) rang: it was Sir John Laing. Where would Billy Graham be staying when he came to London? Was it the Hilton Hotel, as he had heard? (His own simplicity of living was well known to the director.) The director assured him not. Then, said Sir John, if, and only if, he could be definitely assured that Billy Graham would *not* be staying at the Hilton, he would send a gift to the cost of the crusade. The assurance was forthcoming, and a substantial cheque arrived in due course.

In 1954, he joined the Council of the Scripture Gift Mission, a smaller Bible Society specialising in portions and extracts from the Bible in many languages. It was a timely accession, for in 1956 the Mission's premises were destroyed in a tragic fire that took one life. John Laing's advice and experience proved invaluable in the reconstruction work, to which he devoted much time and interest. The then General Secretary recalls how, when Sir John first came up for re-election after his eightieth birthday, he visited him to see whether he might wish to retire, only to receive a searching examination on missionary work in all parts of the world that would have been exceptional from a much younger man.

> I have seen him [he added] close his eyes in a Council meeting after lunch and have thought 'there is an elderly man taking his after-lunch nap.' But not a bit of it—his mental computer had been working and he would suddenly open his eyes and produce figures that were well in advance of the rest of us.

On the Board of Trustees of the (Bristol) Müller Homes for Children, John Laing's advice through times of problem and change in the post-war years was also welcome and humane. One generous proposal he made in connection with the re-modelling of the work (when the original great orphan houses proved unsuitable to modern needs and conditions) was frustrated by changing national policies in relation to the methods and character of children's homes. He also served as vice-governor of Barnardo's Homes and vice-president of Mr. Fegans Homes, both children's works dating from Victorian times, with Brethren influence in their founding. Several Christian foundation schools benefited very considerably from his donations, and he served as governor of some of them. He served, too, on the Committee of the Mission to Lepers and actively helped the Royal National Mission to Deep Sea Fishermen and the Missions to Seamen. His personal influence was also brought to bear, where it could be effective, to obtain a fair hearing for evangelicals on radio and in the media.

But a continued enumeration of the societies in which he took an interest become wearisome. One evangelical leader, more discerning perhaps than many from whom the donations were hidden, was accustomed to refer to him as 'The Five Thousand'. Another friend, involved with a society in which he took a great deal of interest, remembers how substantial gifts would sometimes reach his society with the request that they be passed on anonymously to other works, which were never to know the identity of their benefactor: he was concerned that the breadth of support of voluntary works should be maintained and increased, and was cautious lest a work should become dependent on one large donor.

The early post-war years saw other personal charities established as channels for giving: a trust fund for biblical scholarship in 1947, and the Beatrice Laing Trust in 1952. Within the Company, the pension fund was rationalised and extended in 1952 to permanent employees of all categories with five years' service with the Company, and a welfare fund was established to supplement the older benevolent fund in the same year.

In 1955 and 1956 contracts were signed for the Company that to John Laing symbolically crowned his work, and united his two worlds. By a strange coincidence, the second contract was signed at almost the same hour of the same day as an announcement that the Company had been awarded a contract for building and civil engineering works at the proposed Berkeley nuclear power station – a conjunction that became known in the Company as 'the power and the glory'.

For the two contracts were for the successive stages of the building of the new Cathedral Church of St. Michael at Coventry, to replace the cathedral destroyed during the wartime air raids. From the time he had known that the contract was to be awarded, John Laing had set his heart on winning it. His ambition was not easily realised: even after his Company had won and signed the first contract, for the foundations, on 10 January, 1955, it was far from certain that they would be appointed for the super-structure. Sir Basil Spence, R.A., the architect to whom the opportunity of designing Coventry Cathedral was the fulfilment of a life ambition, has described in his book *Phoenix at Coventry* the debates which took place over the acceptance of the tenders; Spence himself strongly backed Laings, and on 13 December, 1956, John Laing signed the second contract, probably his last major act before retiring from the chairmanship of the Holding Company on 1 January following.

Sir Basil Spence has put on record how, after the decision to award the second contract to John Laing & Son Limited (who had been 'pleasant to work with, business-like, and, of course, superb craftsmen'),[6]

> I was delighted and telephoned the news to Maurice Laing. Next day I got a letter from him saying that his firm considered it a great honour to be entrusted with this work and that at the end of the job they would give all their profit back to the Cathedral. He asked me not to publish this decision as it would detract from the spirit of the gift. I hope the Laing family will forgive me for breaking that promise now.

It was the first cathedral to have been built in Britain as a single planned operation for 300 years. The old cathedral had taken 125 years to build, and had been destroyed in one night on 14

November, 1940, leaving only the tower and spire and scarred
outer walls, which Basil Spence was to incorporate in his inspired
design. Laing's fine team of craftsmen was available, including
the masons who for five years past had been working on the
restoration of Carlisle cathedral; the construction of the slender
sixty-foot columns alone would demand great things of their
experts in concrete technology. But John Laing can be allowed to
describe the work, and his feelings, in his own words:[7]

When told that we were to undertake the building of Coventry
Cathedral, I was filled with gratitude. My sons and I conferred,
and resolved that a building for the worship of God and our
Lord Jesus must be done without any profit motive, and that
everything must be of the very best quality.

Our next consideration was to choose a very experienced
project manager who must be a man of character and who
would consider it a great privilege to spend five years of his life
on such a worthy building. We chose Mr. Adam Stocks, who
had been in our employ for thirty-five years, a considerable
part of that time having been engaged on buildings of very
high quality, such as universities. He considered it would be an
honour to be responsible for such a contract, and he had the
same feeling of privilege as we all had.

We had a most reliable and devoted man in Harold Ratcliffe,
the foreman stonemason. The foreman bricklayer, Eric
MacLeod, a most conscientious worker, started with our
company as an apprentice thirty-eight years ago, and he built
with his own hands the whole of the inside lining of the
cathedral.

In November 1956, a letter was sent to those people
connected with the building of the cathedral holding responsible positions, saying that we wanted everyone engaged in the
construction of the cathedral to bear in mind that this was to be
a building which should endure for more than a thousand
years, and from the standpoint of beauty it should compare
with the cathedral built about the year 1200.

With this thought in mind, we should be very careful to see
that everything was done thoroughly, and that the materials—
especially the stone—should be selected for endurance. The
story was recounted of Sir Christopher Wren and St. Paul's
cathedral. Sir Christopher personally examined the stone
round the coast of England and found that which stood up best
to the effects of tide, frost and sun, and he selected his stone

accordingly. We should be equally careful in everything we had to do for Coventry Cathedral.

During the carrying out of this contract, we are thankful to record that there were no serious accidents; the few accidents there were were of a minor nature.

We have been much impressed by the small number of men employed on such a work of magnitude and quality, and the reason was that the workers—even the humblest—felt a sense of devotion in being engaged on such an outstanding building.

It was a great pleasure to be shown round the cathedral by Provost Howard just before his retirement. His face glowed as he described the scheme of Sir Basil Spence, the architect, which expresses a twentieth-century parable of human life. On entering the cathedral, the windows cannot be seen because they are so arranged (with the exception of the great baptistery window) to throw their light forward, but in the distant foreview are the Altar, the Cross and the Veil of Glory. As we moved forward, each successive window came into view with its motif to illustrate a stage in the journey of life, the first being childhood, next adolescence, then maturity, and finally wisdom. As we approached each window, the Provost reverently quoted the scriptural verse which was going to be inscribed under the stained glass.

I joined in the Provost's spirit of reverence, and again felt what a privilege it had been to have some part in the construction of such a wonderful Christian monumert. Some fitting words, with which to end, are inscribed on a tablet placed on the west wall of the ruins in 1941:— 'The latter glory of this house shall be greater than the former saith the Lord of hosts, and in this place will I give peace.' (Haggai 2:9)

The Consecration Service took place on 25 May, 1962, in the presence of Her Majesty Queen Elizabeth the Second. Sir John himself was in poor health, but determined to attend. Despite the fears of his medical advisers, he stood up to the service, saying afterwards to Ken Jerrard, 'I did not collapse: the Mayor of Coventry did! But he was sitting behind the Queen and could not hold her chair, as I could hold on to the chair in front of me!' There was a rather touching sequel. Some time after his return, Sir John discovered that his offertory was still in his pocket: in his confusion and ill health he had apparently put in his invitation to the ceremony! So the Cathedral authorities, rather late, received an apologetic note, and a belated offering.

The Company made an excellent film as a record of the building of the cathedral, ending movingly with the consecration. One who was present at the film's first showing in the cinema at the Lower Regent Street offices recalled, after Sir John's death, 'the inexpressible joy' on his face as the lights came up after the viewing.

CHAPTER 15

Matured Harvest

I N THE NEW Year Honours List of 1959, John Laing received a knighthood. He was seventy-nine; many have been honoured at a much earlier age for a smaller achievement. He responded with pleasure, seeing in it a 'recognition of the splendid work of the gallant team with which I have had the pleasure of associating for so many years'.[1]

The Company was now at the top of its own industry, and a name to be conjured with among the largest industrial enterprises of the land. Its financial structure and organisation were second to none, and were comfortably to carry a fourfold increase in business, in real terms, over the next twenty years. In an industry traditionally fragmented, and uneasy with large-scale growth, his Company had outpaced all but a very few rivals. Yet, to a great extent, it had preserved the remarkable team spirit—almost a family atmosphere—that was Laing's own creation. In the early sixties, well over 1,500 employees were shareholders in the Company, and the annual general meetings were (and still are) great Company events, reunions of old companions, at which today there will be several hundred persons present, virtually all. Company employees or past employees, at which it is now a tradition to present the valuable long-service gifts awarded after twenty-five years' service with the Company and on retirement. It is a memorable experience to be present on such an occasion, as a long list of employees receive their awards, directors rubbing shoulders in the file with men from the sites and shop floor, to receive identical gifts. The home of a Laing man of long service can frequently be identified by the handsome clock on the mantelpiece (from a famous London maker), and, if his service before retirement had been extra long, by a distinctive silver rose-bowl or other prominent piece.

These were years of fulfilment. Sir John Laing was present in September 1959, at the completion of a contract that marked a new and important development of the Company's activities, in a field where it was to become a national leader, and that derived directly from the wartime airfield experience. This was for the construction of Britain's first major motorway (only the short length of the Preston bypass was earlier): the first section of over fifty miles of the M1 from south of Dunstable to near Rugby. The contract had been completed within its nineteen-month schedule, despite an atrocious winter. The winning of the contract in January 1958, by his Company had given him great personal pleasure: ten years later he recalled, clearly, his concern with technical aspects of the construction, and a senior government official remembered after his death how he had impressed a not easily impressible Minister, by the simplicity of the grace he said at a Motorway buffet. In 1959 he also saw the retirement of some notable old colleagues and friends: W. M. Johnson and Andrew Anderson (both directors, and Johnson a vice-chairman) retired in June, and his redoubtable secretary, Miss Byrnell, in October. Four years before, William Sirey's successor, R. H. Woolliams, had (like Sirey) died in harness, as a director of the Company.

The nineteen-sixties were the golden autumn of his life. The Laing family had been gifted by a father-and-son succession that had taken the undertaking forward in each generation; James had taken it from country village to the local city; the first John had made it a respected local organisation; and now John William Laing had taken it through the major expansion barriers to national status, winning personal recognition, in his knighthood, as a national figure. He was able to see his two gifted sons take it from that point, through the critical transformation to a fully corporate and internationally known organism, and in the process to see his own early ambition fulfilled.* Sir Kirby Laing, his older son, had for his part become a leader of the industry, president of the National Federation of Building Trades Employers for 1965 and again in 1967, chairman of the National Joint Council for the Building Industry from 1968 to 1974, and of the Institution of Civil Engineers for 1973 to 1974. He was knighted in 1968. (Richard Crossman, when Minister of Housing, on one occasion in 1966 had been violently irritated by a statement from the Builders' Federation, and issued a furious challenge to the N.F.B.T.E. President to debate the issue on television. Alas, he was not up to date. Kirby Laing had just

---

*See page 70. 'Wimpeys are the biggest by a considerable margin but if you take general contracting, yes, we are.' (Sir Maurice Laing in *The Times*, 19 September, 1977.)

completed his term of office, and Crossman found himself due to debate with an opponent he considered much less worth his mettle! Crossman, who was no Aneurin Bevan, confided his disappointment to his diary).[2] Sir Maurice Laing became a director of the Bank of England, first president of the Confederation of British Industry in 1965–6 (he remains a council member), president of the British Employers' Confederation in 1964, and the Federation of Civil Engineering Contractors 1977, member of the National Economic Development Council from 1962 to 1966, and visiting fellow of Nuffield College, Oxford 1965 to 1970, with numerous other nationally important appointments. He, too, was knighted, in 1965. It was a remarkable record, with father and both sons knighted by the same monarch within a decade.

Sir John saw the Company expand, with modern technology, under his sons' leadership, into great road and other engineering programmes, overseas as well as at home; into nuclear energy construction, and into the development of engineering for natural gas and the North Sea oil programme. Its activities extended into Spain, the Middle East and the U.S.A. and Canada. As the men who had spent their lives under his direction retired, he saw them enter into the benefit of the pension schemes that he had pioneered: in 1976 there were already nine hundred pensioners on the books of the revised and up-dated pension fund.

Past his eightieth birthday, he was for the first time in his life learning the constraints of failing health. In May 1960 he wrote to a friend:

Since my return from Bournemouth in February, my health does not seem to be improving very much. I have had to cancel our holiday in Switzerland; and the doctor said I must give up the thought of our Scottish tour . . .

I have really been having the time of my life these last two months! I get up quite late; my secretary comes up for an hour or so's dictation in the mornings; in the afternoons, after a short rest, we usually go out for a car ride; and retire to bed fairly early. I have been to only two meetings at Woodcroft. Apart from having one or two people in occasionally for a cup of tea or coffee, I am taking things very quietly. I cannot say that I have made much progress during the last month or so; when I act sensibly I generally respond quickly and get a little better; but if I do the opposite it puts me back again! For instance, the other day we had two visitors and both were dealing with very interesting subjects, but the next day I felt a little worse. I have no pain; am sleeping better, on the whole, than is usual; the scenery from Fair Holme window looks lovely; and Beatrice is looking after me so well. Altogether, I am having a very lazy time, and quite enjoying it!

His mind was as alert and explorative as ever. In December 1961, he read of early plans to adopt decimal coinage (eventually adopted in 1971), and was urging full metrication of industry: 'it would reduce the time spent by our surveyors by about 25 per cent if we used the metric system. It is absolutely absurd, the way we have to work in yards, feet and inches.' Yet the old traditional methods and techniques were equally important to him. Some months earlier he had seen a thatcher at work, and dictated a detailed note on this ancient roofing craft, for the interest of his executives. He was watching technical change, alert to pick up references from others and to learn from others – a trait he never lost. A missionary from Pakistan, visiting him later in the sixties to discuss Christian work there, remembers how Sir John took him over to his desk, and proudly produced technical drawings of a radical new building technique, explaining the details with enthusiastic familiarity. In matters of staff welfare, too, he was sensitive that his Company should be in line with the developing practices of others. He urged that all new entrants – despite the great growth of the Company – should have some early personal introduction to executives at the highest possible level 'so that they feel at home with the whole firm; not just with their departmental manager'; possibly by this time he did not quite realise how difficult of achievement this ideal had become.

Through the whole of this decade, Lady Laing was beside him. They celebrated their golden wedding in 1960, their diamond anniversary in 1970, and her eightieth birthday was in 1965. Quietly, she supported and backed him with a wise understanding and judgment. 'Bea and I complementary virtues – fill book,' he confided to his diary, in some rather rambling notes in 1967. They had made a compact before their marriage that they would never let the sun go down on a disagreement between them, and through the long years their relationship had matured to one of deep loving understanding. She had shared and supported him in his modest home life, and had added her full share of personal generosity. A director of one of the companies remembers them visiting the staff restaurant at Mill Hill on New Year's Eve, 31 December, 1971, when he was ninety-two, and playfully chaffing him and his two colleagues. A few months later, in June 1972, not long before her eighty-seventh birthday, Beatrice Laing died quietly at their home; his sons found it a little difficult at first to make him realise that she had gone, and another relative remembers him standing, looking long into the grave, after her burial. The years that followed were to be a long waiting for the reunion beyond the grave in which his confidence never faltered.

They had together set their face throughout their married life against personal ostentation or extravagance. 'Everyone should have a house just big enough to serve its purpose, as to have more than that causes such a lot of work', he had written to a friend in 1962, and, indeed, they had acted on that advice several years previously when they had built themselves a modest new house beside the larger Fair Holme, and moved into it. A friend who visited them at Fair Holme while the new house (also to be named Fair Holme) was being built, had asked if it was for the gardener! On his eightieth birthday some admirers inside the business presented him with a golden bowl. He received it with dignity and gratitude; what the donors were not permitted to learn was that the bowl was later quietly renounced. On another occasion he declined a Rolls-Royce car that his family wished to present to him: he preferred to stay with the Rover that in later life he always used. (A friend who used a Rolls regularly remembers how he was quietly reproved for it: although he also remembers taking Sir John to an engagement in it, and on the journey back, John Laing turning to him and saying with his quiet humour, 'I think this car even runs a little better than my Rover.') Yet the little piece of human contrariness was present in him even in this, and the Rover proudly bore the registration JWL 1. The quiet man with his unostentatious living standards was also the same business man who had the flair for public relations that had brought the Company so dramatically to the public during the housing boom of the thirties, and had carefully chosen a unique shade of yellow for the now familiar 'LAING' house colour.

The roots of the inner harmony that enabled him to resolve such contradictions in his personality appear in a letter that he had written to his son, Maurice, at the end of July 1951.[3] Bevan, with whom he had established a friendly relationship, had resigned from the Government in April: the October general election that was to return Churchill's Conservative party to power still lay in the future. He was ill at ease with contemporary events, and radical changes in the organisation and structure of his own business were in progress (the flotation as a public company was little more than a year ahead).

31 July, 1951

Dear Maurice,

On Sunday morning I woke early to begin to practise what you want me to do—to consider objectively what is the result on this country of socialist finance, which is summed up in the limitation of dividends.

As I have often explained, paying tax was a pleasure up to a certain date, but when Dalton introduced his budget I saw that taxes were not simply the means of revenue for the country, but they were part of a policy to change our country to a completely socialised state. Since then it has been my desire to pay as little tax as is legitimate. It has altered my whole outlook towards tax paying.

I consider also that the present Government's housing policy is part of the same general policy; they are trying to exterminate the house owner, because he is a reliable, forthright, free-thinking individual, and to substitute a tenant race who will always be subservient to the State, and that in carrying out this policy they do not mind how much it costs the country. The fact that a large number of houses can be built without subsidy is nothing to them, and the fact that by liquidating private enterprise they will reduce the output of the nation and will reduce its finance is nothing to them, so long as they can carry out their purpose.

So that it hardly needs you to remind me to think of these things. My policy is to try and not think too much of them, but to bear them in mind. And that was one of the great reasons why I wanted to alter the financial structure of the Property Company. We have held that Company in abeyance for so many years, but now when they are in such a financial position that they could develop, I wanted to do so. However, it is no good just looking back.

I spent from an early hour on Sunday morning with these pleasant thoughts stirring my mind, and then realised it was getting me nowhere, and so I turned to the Book of Psalms, and among others read the 24th psalm. While there are some things in the psalm that are not readily understood, the whole trend of the psalm is a lovely thought, summarised in the first and second verses. Then we get another series of delightful thoughts in verses 3 to 6. I cannot help but feel confident that the psalmist, while he has been writing a good deal of his own experience up to this point, now by divine inspiration, moves to a future scene, the scene of the triumph of Christ and righteousness.

This changed my thoughts. We have not suffered at all, and the policy of limitation of dividends is a restriction which the Government is now imposing, but it is only what we were willingly practising, and decided to practise for another year or two; and the only objection we can have is that the Government are compelling us to do this instead of allowing it to be voluntary, and that does alter the feeling a little. One has some satisfaction in doing it voluntarily.

Then we have to remember that while the financial rewards we get from business are trivial compared with what we contribute to the State, both in service and in contribution to the national exchequer, yet we have a very enjoyable life that is full of interest, and we have happy homes, reasonably good food and a nice motor car, so that we have nothing to complain about.

At this stage I slipped downstairs and got out good old Spurgeon's commentary on the psalms and looked up the 24th; it was very pleasant and comforting to read his comments, and also the comments of godly men which he quotes, after his own, on pages 428 to 438.

It is much more soothing to think of these things than to think unduly about the folly of our present Governors. At the same time always doing our best to substitute a sensible Government if we can, and try and save old England from the catastrophe to which, in our judgment, she seems to be heading.

This letter seems to be a strange mixture of worldly thoughts and spiritual thoughts, and perhaps that mixture in lives is not unreasonable. We have our part to play in the world, although we are men, like Abraham, who 'look for a city whose builder and maker is God, eternal in the heavens', and while empires rise and fall the truths enunciated in the Old Testament, but pronounced most clearly by our Lord Jesus, stand eternally true.

With much love,
Father.

As the autumn years passed, and the tide of business anxieties and responsibilities receded, the reality of his inner life was exposed. When a strong man's faculties are reduced by age, and the power that was formerly his to exercise slips from his hands into those of others, his inner essence becomes (sometimes pitifully) apparent. The harsh test of ageing was to be applied to John Laing through long years.

In relation to the business which he had so largely created, he was at rest. Retaining his interest to the end, he showed no sign of anxiety for it, but only pleasure at the thousands of lives it had nurtured and influenced. Its future was in hands he trusted, and the future actions of governments and politics were beyond his control. In December 1972, he sent his Christmas greetings through *Team Spirit*:

> I am very pleased at this time of year to be given the opportunity of sending greetings to all staff, at home and abroad. It is wonderful to see the business prospering. I can take no credit for this, except that in the early days we established the character of the Company. Today, as in my day, that same character continues.
>
> I am glad to see the spirit of integrity is just as strong as ever.
>
> I am really enjoying my life these days. The walks, the drives, the beautiful countryside, and my visits to the office, make life as full as ever, and, of course, I have no responsibilities. That is a wonderful feeling.
>
> At my age, 93, people don't expect very much of you and that gives you a lovely sense of freedom.
>
> When I enter the Laing office I still find the same atmosphere that I used to find in the old days.
>
> So may I close by saying to every member of the company and to their families, a very happy Christmas and an exciting and fulfilling New Year.

His charitable giving raised issues that ran even more deeply. His main Trust, to him, was 'very holy . . . something between God and man. It had its beginning in gratitude to God and I hope it will ever remain a token of gratitude to our Lord'.[4] As early as 1940 he had been giving away £20,000 a year, many times the modest income he retained for himself, and with the post-war growth of the Company both that giving and the endowment with which he had provided his trusts had grown beyond recognition. The responsible control of such substantial charitable funds, when he would no longer be able to allocate their income, was something that troubled him deeply, particularly the quality and characters of the men who would be responsible

213

for their administration. Careful arrangements were made, during the sixties, for the future, but his notebooks show that they were for years a matter of deep heart-searchings, and sometimes events could cause him considerable personal distress. 'The spirit of the Trust should over-rule anything that is sectarian,'[5] he recorded. A fellow trustee remembers him, after the completion of one trust meeting, when the control of administration of very large funds had been renounced to others, standing up quietly. 'I do not want anything to get abroad about what I have done today: I know you will respect my confidences.'

During all these years he was maintaining his personal contact with his church life. A 'Counties' evangelist in whom he took a great deal of interest remembers him coming to a village tent not long after his knighthood, and talking simply to a group of children about the investiture; he drew direct lessons from his coat of arms, which displayed an open book and a bridge under the crest, a knightly arm holding a lighted lantern; and he spoke of how he had knelt on one knee before the Queen–but would kneel on both knees before his God. Late into the nineteen-sixties he was still actively running his men's group at Woodcroft Hall, and when health permitted he was to be found regularly at the services there, until his final weakness confined him to his home

In January 1974, he wrote to a close friend:

You wrote just prior to the 24th September and I did appreciate your kind thought for me on my 94th birthday. Your scripture reference to the peace of God and the God of peace was most appropriate. The order of Philippians 4:6 and 7 is
No over anxiety
Prayer for everything
With thanksgiving
The Peace of God assured.
I am glad to say I am wonderfully well. The various members of the family are most kind and attentive.

Later that year he was discussing with interest the friend's travels in America, but his strength was beginning to fail. His chief delight was in the visits of friends who could share his own spiritual understanding. Late in 1976, he fell and broke a hip: an operation was successful and, remarkably, he rallied. His sons wrote:

He is truly remarkable in every way. We could not help but be

214

impressed by the fact that when he was moved, although he must have been in a considerable degree of pain, he did not complain but only winced. He is obviously even more confused than usual, but his inner peace is revealed in his appearance which we think you could describe as being angelic!

He returned home, devotedly cared for by some remarkable nurses. When visiting him, it was now possible to obtain little response, unless the visitor read from the Bible and prayed with him, when his face would light up unforgettably. A year or two before this, he had been visited by his old friend and fellow-elder, F. M. Hudson, after a time of ill-health. 'I keep knocking on the door of heaven,' he had said with a smile, 'but Peter says, "Go away John, we are not ready for you yet."' His time came at last, on 11 January, 1978, in his ninety-ninth year. He was buried from his loved Woodcroft Evangelical Church on 16 January, and F. M. Hudson, in his address, singled out five great qualities from the initials of his name: his loyalty, his authority, his industry, his naïvety (or artless simplicity) and his generosity. It was the very month of the fiftieth anniversary of the church he had built and helped to found.

Some years before Sir John Laing died, his advisers had reckoned that his personal estate would consist of little more than his house and insurances. In April 1978, after his death, his net estate was published at £371. The man who had handled millions had given them all away.

To summarise adequately John Laing's influence and character, we need a perspective that is wider than is yet available to us. One of the remarkable aspects of his story is that he was not gifted with an obviously powerful physical presence—unless it was his ready and winning smile. A reporter who met him in 1948, at the height of his activity, described him as 'this quiet, medium-sized, gentle-voiced man looking many years younger than his age (partly thanks to a happy sanguine disposition and partly thanks to a smile of genuine kindliness)'. But the appearance hid an iron will. 'I don't think in his life he ever met anyone who said "no" to him,' said one executive who had spent his life in the Company. 'He had that way with him.' A friend who understood the religious depths within him writes:

> Few would have suspected that behind his quiet and mild exterior was a man of incredible will-power and indomitable courage. Without a taint of pride, he himself was aware that he possessed to an uncommon degree the inner resources necessary for the carrying through to completion of any task, however difficult. It was this sense of innate self-reliance that enabled him to undertake and complete tasks demanding superhuman strength. But he never forgot or omitted to acknowledge the Giver of every gift. His deep conviction of reality of the unseen only enhanced his qualities as a citizen of this world, for he was a man who bestrode two worlds.

The description comes from his later life, but it allows us to guess at other sides of his character, and the earlier struggle between the ruthlessness of his industrial environment and the 'external reference point' which was embedded within his religious beliefs. The permanent interest of Sir John Laing's character is that it was the religious ideals which triumphed, and that those ideals led, not to a heartless and inhuman pursuit of profit for its own sake, but to a true humanism, rooted in religious conviction. One of the most eminent of his Company's heads, who carried some of the intensest pressure of the Second World War years and their sequel, found that his flexibility in his personal relation-ships outside his business life was countered by an inflexibility in business management, although he was always in pursuit of quality. He felt that in the business environment the transition from being a man of charitable action to being a charitable man was not an easy one for John Laing to make. Certainly, that failure has been characteristic of many businessmen from a similar religious background, and this observer was probably the acutest judge of all his business intimates. Yet, after talking to so many who knew him and worked under him, it is difficult to feel that the judgment does John Laing complete justice.

For his religious beliefs also were shaped by his understanding of men as human beings as much as by doctrine; a happy and refreshing trait. If this understanding was sometimes less apparent in his dealings with executives, it became far plainer in his concern for the rank-and-file workers. 'There are very few of us who have not spent many hours in rain, mud, frost and snow, often drenched to the skin, but I do not know any life that could

216

be more satisfying,' he wrote in his introduction to *Team Work*, and that identification with the man on the site was a powerful stimulant to the loyalty he won from men of all grades. Visiting sites, he would make a point of seeking out the old employees he knew; one director remembers him visiting with his wife an airfield under construction at Grantham and deliberately tracking down the oldest employee to introduce him to her. The same director tells also how, after the last war, Jimmy Kelso, the old bricklayer from Carlisle,* was sitting during a tea break, reading a newspaper. There was a picture of some building strikers at a London contract (not one of Laing's) with their banners, one of which read 'Laing has a million, we want a tanner.'† Kelso growled, 'The governor is worth his bloody million more than those ———— their tanner.' 'They had no god but the old man,' added the director. Such loyalty can only be won from men who are respected and treated as men.

The one element of his character which has recurred time and again in talking to acquaintances – employees, personal friends, charitable administrators – is simplicity; F. M. Hudson's 'naïvety'. It appeared in so many forms: in the way in which he went straight to the heart of a problem; in directness of speech and (where necessary) of rebuke; in hatred of humbug; in his delight in natural beauty. 'Sir John is interested in the simple things of life,' writes an employee who knew him in his last years. 'He loves the view from Fair Holme, watching the birds in the garden, and constantly admires the beautiful oak tree. He loves nature and his enquiring mind and zest for life has made him such an interesting person.'

This very simplicity seems to have denied him any profound interest in the more abstract aesthetic interests, in literature or music. But in visual matters his sense of beauty was acute (and he took a firm, if idiosyncratic, interest in his Company's exercises in art sponsorship).

But its supreme product was tranquillity:[4]

I remember Ainsworth speaking on a psalm when I was little more than a youth [he wrote in 1963], and he said that the word 'fret' could be translated 'fray out'. How silly it is that we so often – as I so often – allow ourselves to 'fray out', spoiling what might have been a very happy hour in the very worst

*See page 61.
†The old sixpenny piece (2½p).

way. What a contrast it is to 'rest in the Lord and wait patiently for Him'. 'Rest' we associated with the word 'restore'. 'Trust' too is a lovely word and a partner to 'rest'. I am sure you are not as bad in the habit of 'fraying out' as I am!

His simplicity led too to an inability to bear a grudge, and a habit (sometimes disconcerting) of dismissing an unpleasant incident from his mind. He did not harbour resentment. One might speculate as to the extent this contributed to his excellent health and his longevity. 'He never had a pain, never had a headache,' said another friend. 'He told me this and could not understand other people having them.' To some of his friends, his simplicity became a surprising humility, despite his forcefulness in business. Asked on one occasion what he considered the greatest Christian virtues, he replied after careful thought, 'Grace and gratitude'. There is small wonder that it is said that, on his arriving at a Government committee during the war, one member remarked, 'Here comes Laing–happy as usual'; to which another is said to have replied 'And he *is* happy.'

Sir John Laing needs no other memorial than his own achievements; one may suspect that he would wish to earn no more than the epitaph that the writer of Acts gave to another great leader of men: 'After he had served his own generation by the will of God, he fell on sleep.' But he would quietly remind us that, beyond the sleep, he looked forward to a glad awakening

Notes

CHAPTER 1

1 Based on the evidence of the Town Clerk of Carlisle before the House of Commons, 19 April, 1904, in relation to the Carlisle Corporation Bill, 1904 (this gives 1893 as the largest year, with 352 houses built, and over 200 in each year from 1897–1900 inclusive. 3,736 houses were built in Carlisle from 1881–1903 inclusive).
2 In a speech at Bristol in 1951 (*Team Spirit*, April 1951).
3 Quoted Godfrey Harrison *Life and Belief in the Experience of John W. Laing* (Hodder and Stoughton, 1954), p.26.
4 Quoted in obituary notice in *Cumberland News*, 31 January, 1942 (the story derives from Sir John Laing himself).
5 From unpublished reminiscences to K. G. Jerrard, 24 January, 1968.
6 *ibid.*
7 At interview, 23 May, 1977.

CHAPTER 2

1 In the monthly newsletter of Hebron Hall, Carlisle, January 1969.
2 Olive Moore in *Scope* magazine, June 1948.
3 *Team Spirit*, May 1949, p.5.
4 Quoted Godfrey Harrison, *op. cit.*, p.46.
5 *This I Believe* (North of England Evangelical Trust, c.1960), p.17.
6 *ibid.*

CHAPTER 3

1 Quoted Olive Moore, *op. cit.*, from figures provided by the Company.
2 *op. cit.*, p.44.
3 Quoted Olive Moore, *op. cit.*
4 From unpublished reminiscences of 19 April, 1964.
5 *Team Spirit*, September 1949, p.4. (The article is anonymous.)
6 *Team Spirit*, September 1948.
7 *Team Spirit*, December 1952.
8 Recorded by Godfrey Harrison, *op. cit.*, p.58.
9 From reminiscences written for a Mill Hill parish magazine *Focus*, November 1960.
10 From unpublished reminiscences to K. G. Jerrard, 24 January, 1968.
11 R. H. Tawney *Religion and the Rise of Capitalism*, 1922 (John Murray 1964 reprint, p.127 quoting from *Winthrop's Journal, History of New England 1630–49*).

CHAPTER 4

[1] From *This is Your Life* (reminiscences of friends, presented to J. W. Laing, 25 April, 1958).
[2] In the monthly newsletter of Hebron Hall, Carlisle, January 1969.
[3] *This is Your Life*.
[4] *ibid*.
[5] Quoted in Godfrey Harrison, *op. cit.,* p.64.
[6] *Team Spirit*, June 1949, p.7.
[7] Unpublished reminiscences to K. G. Jerrard, 24 January, 1968.
[8] Molly Lefebure, *Cumberland Heritage* (Victor Gollancz, 1970), p.28

CHAPTER 5

[1] In *Team Spirit*, December 1974.
[2] see p.36.
[3] A. Lakeman, *Concrete Cottages, Bungalows and Garages* (Concrete Publications 2nd. edn., 1924), p.36.
[4] The early Easiform specification is taken from the preliminary report of the Inter-Departmental Committee on House Construction (the Burt Committee) of 1943 (*Post-War Building Studies* No. 1, H.M.S.O. 1944).
[5] Lakeman, *op. cit.,* pp.39–41.
[6] A. A. Jackson, *Semi-Detached London* (Allen and Unwin, 1973), pp.91ff.

CHAPTER 6

[1] The 1920 rates are from the reminiscences of John Hindmoor, who joined the Laing office staff in Carlisle in that year. The 1924 rate is that for 31 December, 1924 in *Statistical Abstract for the United Kingdom 1913 and 1923–1936* (H.M.S.O., 1938), p.156.
[2] *Statistical Abstract* (*op. cit*), pp.150 and 136.
[3] *ibid.,* pp.142f.
[4] *Team Spirit*, November 1946, p.1. (From his message in the first issue.)
[5] Max Weber *The Protestant Ethic and the Spirit of Capitalism, 1904–5*, trans. Talcott Parsons (Allen and Unwin, 2nd. edn. 1976), p.166.
[6] *ibid.,* p.179 (quoting Sir William Petty).
[7] *ibid.,* pp.176f.
[8] R. H. Tawney, *op. cit.,* pp.146f.
[9] C. M. Kohan *Works and Buildings* in U.K. Civil History of the Second World War series (H.M.S.O. and Longmans Green, 1952), p.440
[10] Olive Moore, *op. cit.*
[11] A. A. Jackson, *op. cit.,* p.93.
[12] *Team Spirit*, February 1948, p.7.

CHAPTER 7

[1] Desmond Young, *Member for Mexico*, a biography of Weetman Pearson, first Lord Cowdray (Cassell, 1966), p.233.
[2] Details from a press cutting of 9 October, 1923 in possession of John Laing & Son Ltd. (source not noted).
[3] *Statistical Abstract, op. cit.,* p.49 and A. A. Jackson (*op. cit.*), table p.100.
[4] A. A. Jackson, *op. cit.,* pp.71ff.

[5] Unpublished reminiscences of 19 April, 1964.
[6] Quoted Olive Moore, *op. cit.*
[7] *Housing in Britain* (Central Office of Information Reference Pamphlet 41, H.M.S.O., 1975), p.8.
[8] Unpublished reminiscences of 19 April, 1964.
[9] Unpublished reminiscences of 26 April, 1966.
[10] A. A. Jackson, *op. cit.*, p.195 (referring to an article by John Laing on 'Guarantee Mortgages' in *House Building 1934–36*, 1934).
[11] Sir Basil Spence *Phoenix at Coventry* (Bles, 1962), p.95.
[12] Anecdote from Margaret Spence, Personnel Manager of Carrs of Carlisle.

CHAPTER 8

[1] Oliver R. Barclay *Whatever Happened to the Jesus Lane Lot?* (Inter-Varsity Press, 1977), p.106.

CHAPTER 9

[1] *Team Spirit*, May 1952.
[2] Statistics from the special brochure issued by the Company for the opening, 31 May, 1934, pp.3, 39.
[3] Unpublished reminiscences of 31 May, 1963.
[4] *Annual Abstracts of Statistics* (Central Statistical Office).
[5] A. A. Jackson, *op. cit.*, pp.153ff.

CHAPTER 10

[1] According to Dr. W. J. Martin, who quotes Clarence Perry *Housing for the Machine Age*.
[2] From a letter of 27 April, 1967.
[3] William Ashworth, *Contracts and Finance* in 'UK Civil History of the Second World War' series (H.M.S.O. and Longmans Green, 1953), p.67.
[4] C. M. Kohan, *op. cit.*, p.282.
[5] *ibid.*, ch. XIII (pp.279ff).
[6] *ibid.*, and also the Company's own publication *Serving a Nation at War*, pp.68ff.
[7] *Statistical Digest of the War* in 'UK Civil History of the Second World War' series (H.M.S.O. and Longmans Green, 1951), p.195.
[8] C. M. Kohan, *op. cit.*, p.282 (over £200 million as cost of wartime airfields excluding buildings), and note 7 above.

CHAPTER 11

[1] *Housing in Britain* (*op. cit.*), p.1.
[2] Published as *Post War Building Studies* No. 1 by H.M.S.O., 1944.
[3] Statistics from C. M. Kohan, *op. cit.*, pp.222ff., and more detailed files in the Public Record Office.
[4] *Team Spirit*, April 1947.
[5] *ibid.*, August 1947, p.5.
[6] Quoted Michael Foot *Aneurin Bevan 1945–1960* (Davis-Poynter, 1973), p.22.
[7] *ibid.*, p.78.
[8] *Team Spirit*, November 1946.

[9] *ibid.*, July 1949.
[10] *ibid.*, December 1947.

CHAPTER 12

[1] *Team Spirit*, February 1952.

CHAPTER 13

[1] H. H. Rowdon *London Bible College, the First Twenty-Five Years* (Henry E. Walter, 1968), p.19.
[2] From a letter of 17 March, 1959.
[3] From a letter of 10 March, 1958.
[4] 'Films and their Influence' in the 75th anniversary publication of Counties Evangelistic Work, *Yesterday Today* (1974).
[5] *Team Spirit*, May 1953, p.4.
[6] Sir Basil Spence, *op. cit.*, p.95.
[7] A personal note prepared privately as the basis of a published account.

CHAPTER 14

[1] *Team Spirit*, February 1959, p.1.
[2] Richard Crossman *The Diaries of a Cabinet Minister. Vol. I. Minister of Housing 1964–66* 1976), p.548
[3] From undated personal notes, c.1960.
[4] *ibid.*
[5] From a letter of 18 November, 1963.

Acknowledgments

MY FIRST PLEASURE in detailing the sources on which this biography is based is to thank Sir Kirby and Sir Maurice Laing for their constant kindness and help, both in providing access to personal papers in the keeping of the Company, and also for their own reminiscences of their father. Other relatives to whom I am grateful for assistance include Mrs. Ella Armstrong, Mr. and Mrs. E. Farrell, Mr. J. I. Hetherington, Messrs. Stanley and Ronald Laing, Dr. Margaret Marsh, Mrs. Isobel Thompson, Miss Irene Turrall and Dr. Arthur W. Wood.

Sir John Laing left comparatively few personal papers, but I have had the advantage of recollections and information from well over one hundred persons, some in writing, but a great number in meetings extending over a period of two years. Nearly half of these have been with former and present executives and employees of the Laing organisation, of all grades, and it has been a particular pleasure to meet and talk to so many grand men and women. The memory of those talks will remain a permanent delight, and the spirit of them was a tribute to the atmosphere created by Sir John himself, which this biography, I fear, reflects all too inadequately.

Many of those who contributed most (especially from the societies in which Sir John took so much interest) asked me not to give prominence to themselves; it is difficult to honour this request if any names at all are to be mentioned, and perhaps therefore it is fairest to content myself with a general expression of gratitude to all those who helped me so generously in my researches. A few names, however, must be listed, and I wish especially to thank Mr. Andrew Anderson, for so long Secretary and Director of John Laing and Son Ltd.; Mr. Wallace Haughan C.B.E., Director and former Head of the Canadian operations; Mr. Nigel Redfern, Carlisle Regional Director; and especially Mr. K. G. Jerrard, whose unrivalled knowledge of the Company and family history has been put generously at my disposal, and who has followed every stage of the production of the biography with close interest, and without whom the task (if possible at all) would have been infinitely more difficult. I would also mention two friends of Sir John who helped me greatly but who are sadly no longer here to read this note: the late Stanley Graham of Carlisle and the late W. T. Stunt of Bath.

Apart from records and documents in the possession of the Company, I have been grateful for access to papers in the Cumbria County Archives at Carlisle and Dalton-in-Furness, in the Public Record Office at Kew, and for information from Carlisle Grammar School by courtesy of the Headmaster and from the Revd Arthur Penn, Vicar of Brampton. Mr. J. P. Templeton of Carlisle gave me access to his excellent collection of historical photographs, and the Companies Registry provided information on the early constitution of the Company.

Other written sources drawn upon include:

(i) Material on personal and Company history
Godfrey Harrison: *Life and Belief in the Experience of John W. Laing C.B.E.* (London, Hodder and Stoughton, 1954).
K. G. Jerrard: *Historical Information on the Laing Family (1730–1875),* unpublished, prepared for John Laing and Son Ltd., 1972.
This is Your Life: script of a programme presented to J. W. Laing at Woodcroft Evangelical Free Church, 25 April, 1958.
Teamwork The centenary history of John Laing and Son Ltd. Published by the Company, 1950.
Serving a Nation at War. The Second World War history of John Laing and Son Ltd. Published by the Company, 1946.
Team Spirit. Monthly house magazine of John Laing and Son Ltd (First issue, November 1946).
Sir Kirby Laing, script of commissioned profile article on the Laing Group for *Building Construction* (Chicago, 1968).
Sir Kirby Laing, *The Growth and Organisation of John Laing and Son Ltd.* Address at University of Birmingham Department of Extra-Mural Studies, 8 December, 1960.
Sir Maurice Laing, *The Managerial Problems of Rapid Expansion.* Address at the Administrative Staff College, 7 July, 1959.
Sir Maurice Laing, *John Laing and Son Ltd.* Address at *Financial Times* and *Investors' Chronicle* Investment Seminar, 24 January, 1974.
Olive Moore, *John W. Laing.* 'Man of the Month' profile 75 in *Scope* Magazine, June 1948.
Obituary of Mr. and Mrs. John Laing, Carlisle, in June 1924 issue of *The Believers' Pathway* (Pickering and Inglis, Glasgow).

Britannic House
(British Petroleum Company HQ)

The company today:
Sir Kirby Laing (*left*);
Sir Maurice Laing (*right*)

Sir John and Lady Laing
at the investiture, 1959

Signing of the contract for the
building of Coventry Cathedral,
13 December 1956 (p. 202)

Sir John W. Laing, biographical notes published in *This I Believe* (North of England Evangelical Trust – apparently in 1960s).

E. H. Broadbent, unpublished diary containing account of visit to Russia with J. W. Laing, 1935.

(ii) The Carlisle Background

T. F. Bulmer, *History, Topography and Directory of East Cumberland* (Manchester, Bulmer, 1884).

James P. Templeton, *Carlisle – a Photographic Recollection* (Clapham, Yorks, Dalesman Books, 1976).

James S. Adam, *A Fell Fine Baker*, the story of United Biscuits (London, Hutchinson Benham, 1974).

The Story of Carr's Biscuits. Published by Carr's Biscuits. Undated.

J. C. Middleton, *Through Two Half-Centuries 1850–1950*, centenary history of the Cumberland Building Society. (Carlisle, Cumberland Building Society, 1950).

A Brief Sketch of the Aspatria, Silloth and District Water Undertaking (published by the Undertaking, 1913).

Old minute book of the Carlisle Brethren Congregation, 1874 to 1883.

Trust documents relating to certain Brethren halls in Carlisle.

Annual Reports of the Cumberland and Westmorland Gospel Tent Work 1912–61.

George Winter, *With Tent and Caravan*, the story of thirty-seven years evangelising in north-west England (Penrith, Reeds, 1950).

(iii) Further material on the religious background

F. R. Coad, *A History of the Brethren Movement* (Exeter, Paternoster, 2nd. edn., 1976).

David J. Beattie, *Brethren, the Story of a Great Recovery* (Kilmarnock, Ritchie, 1940).

W. T. Stunt and others, *Turning the World Upside Down*, a history of Brethren Missionary work connected with *Echoes of Service* (Eastbourne, Upperton Press, 1972).

F. D. Coggan, *Christ and the Colleges*, a history of the Inter-Varsity Fellowship of Evangelical Unions (London, Inter-Varsity Fellowship, 1934).

Oliver R. Barclay, *Whatever Happened to the Jesus Lane Lot?*, a history of the Cambridge Inter-Collegiate Christian Union (London, Inter-Varsity Press, 1977).

Brochures of the International Conference of Evangelical Students, Cambridge, 27 June to 3 July, 1939.

H. H. Rowdon, *London Bible College – the First Twenty-Five Years* (Worthing, Walter, 1968).

Yesterday, Today, 75th anniversary publication of Counties Evangelistic Work, 1974.

(iv) General background material

OFFICIAL SOURCES

Statistical Abstract for the United Kingdom 1913 and 1923–36 (H.M.S.O., 1930).

Annual Abstract of Statistics No. 84 (1935–46) (C.S.O., 1947).

Housing in Britain, Central Office of Information Reference Pamphlet No. 41 (H.M.S.O., 1975).

Trends in Population, Housing and Occupancy Rates 1861–1961 (H.M.S.O., 1971).

Report on Training for the Building Industry (H.M.S.O., 1942).

Report of the Inter-Departmental Committee on House Construction (Post-War Building Studies No. 1) (H.M.S.O., 1944).

The Cabinet Office to 1945 (Public Record Office Handbook No. 17) (H.M.S.O., 1975).

The Second World War – A Guide to Documents in the Public Record Office (H.M.S.O, 1972).

U.K. Civil History of the Second World War (H.M.S.O. and Longmans Green).

Vol. *Works and Buildings,* C. M. Kohan, 1952.

Vol. *Contracts and Finance,* Wm. Ashworth, 1953.

Vol. *Statistical Digest of the War,* 1951.

History of the Ministry of Munitions, Vol. 5 – Wages and Welfare.

GENERAL

Britain's Industrial Future, the report of the Liberal Industrial Enquiry of 1928 (London, Benn, 2nd imp. 1977).

Richard Crossman, *The Diaries of a Cabinet Minister, Vol. I, Minister of Housing 1964–66* (London, Hamish Hamilton and Jonathan Cape, 1976).

Michael Foot, *Aneurin Bevan 1945–1960* (London, Davis-Poynter, 1973).

Alan A. Jackson, *Semi-Detached London,* Suburban Development, Life and Transport 1900–1939 (London, George Allen and Unwin, 1973).

Albert Lakeman, *Concrete Cottages, Bungalows and Garages* (London, Concrete Publications, 2nd. edn., 1924).

Laing, John W., *Modern Methods of House Construction,* paper read

ACKNOWLEDGMENTS

to the General Meeting of the Chartered Surveyors' Institution, 3 December, 1945.

Sir Maurice Laing, with J. R. Fisher and E. U. Broadbent, *The Application of the Lessons Learnt in Airfield Construction to the Construction of Concrete Roads* (a post-war technical paper).

Sir Maurice Laing, *The Shape of the Industry*, speech to the Institute of Building's annual conference, 23 November, 1976.

J. Lester, 'A Short History of the Institute' in the *Journal of the Institute of Quantity Surveyors*, Jan.–Apr. 1968.

Sir Basil Spence, *Phoenix at Coventry*, the Building of a Cathedral (London, Bles, 1962).

R. H. Tawney, *Religion and the Rise of Capitalism* (London 1922, reptd. John Murray, 1964).

Max Weber, *The Protestant Ethic and the Spirit of Capitalism* (1904, Engl. trans. Talcott Parsons 1930, reptd. London, George Allen and Unwin, 1976).

Desmond Young: *Member for Mexico*, a biography of Weetman Pearson, first Viscount Cowdray (London, Cassell, 1966).

Index